A Fire to Light Our Tongues

Texas Writers on Spirituality

ELIZABETH JOAN DELL *and*
DONNA WALKER-NIXON, *Editors*

With RACHEL CRAWFORD, *Poetry Editor*

FORT WORTH, TEXAS

LIBRARY OF CONGRESS CATALOGING-IN-PUBLICATION DATA

Names: Dell, Elizabeth J., 1957- editor. | Walker-Nixon, Donna, editor.
Title: A fire to light our tongues : Texas writers on spirituality / Elizabeth J. Dell, Donna Walker-Nixon, editors.
Description: Fort Worth, Texas : TCU Press, [2022] | Summary: "A Fire to Light Our Tongues: Texas Writers on Spirituality brings together the works of writers in Texas. The title is taken, with permission, from Naomi Shihab Nye's introduction to Salting the Ocean: 100 Poems by Young Poets, where she states the role of poetry serves as "a fire to light our tongues." This view describes the role that creative writers, encountering the challenges of this past decade, face as they grapple with shifting views of spirituality. While the project started before COVID-19, given the current worldwide pandemic, a book of creative work responding to writers' spirituality could not be more timely. This anthology offers readers creative works by Texas writers as they wrestle with evolving systems of belief or nonbelief"— Provided by publisher.
Identifiers: LCCN 2021048318 (print) | LCCN 2021048319 (ebook) | ISBN 9780875658056 (paperback) | ISBN 9780875658117 (ebook)
Subjects: LCSH: American literature—Texas—21st century. | Spirituality— Literary collections. | LCGFT: Literature.
Classification: LCC PS571.T4 F57 2022 (print) | LCC PS571.T4 (ebook) | DDC 810.8/038204—dc23/eng/20220211
LC record available at https://lccn.loc.gov/2021048318
LC ebook record available at https://lccn.loc.gov/2021048319

On the cover: Sunset over the mountains in Brewster County, Texas, south of Alpine. Carol M. Highsmith, photographer. Courtesy Library of Congress, 29989

The editors wish to thank those who generously gave to the Indiegogo fund for *A Fire to Light Our Tongues*.

TCU Box 298300
Fort Worth, Texas 76129
To order books: 1.800.826.8911

Design by Julie Rushing

Dedicated to

Daddy, for his strength and determination
Mrs. Joiner, George and Tim, Joe O'Connell
Drue Porter-Parker, for her support and advice

—DONNA WALKER-NIXON

Joan Wilson Dell

—ELIZABETH J. DELL

Left to right:
Donna Walker-Nixon, Elizabeth J. Dell, Drue Porter-Parker

Donna Walker-Nixon (1953-2021) passed away before she could see this anthology completed. In many ways, *A Fire to Light Our Tongues* represents who Donna was: a true Texan, raised near Stephenville, whose stories affirm her rootedness in people and place; a writer's writer, who passionately pursued her projects, seeking truth through storytelling; and a mentor, editor, and friend to many fellow writers, nurturing with her selfless will, genuine and kind heart, wry good humor, and uncanny vision that brought others' words together—which she has done one last time in this work.

"My heart in hiding
Stirred for a bird,—the achieve of, the mastery of the thing!"
—"The Windhover," Gerard Manley Hopkins

CONTENTS

KNOWN AND UNKNOWN

TRUTH AND BEAUTY

JOY AND GRATITUDE

INTRODUCTION

On Christmas day, the sign outside Real Life Bible Church in a quiet, manicured Temple, Texas, suburb read: "The trouble is you think you still have time."

The procrastinator inside me wrestled with those words for days. I knew death was the great unknown, the cliff awaiting our free-willed leap (or our largest protests). That of which we do not speak. Years ago I was tapped to join a group of writers and visual artists who would spend scattered hours over a few months at a residential hospice interacting with the dying, their families, and those hired to care for them all. I claim only small epiphanies from the experience:

- The kind will become kinder near the end.
- Few really care about sports or politics.
- There will be unfinished business.

The fortyish man was shirtless, gripping a small blue bucket at which he aimed blasts of vomit. His back was overtaken by tattooed wings ready for flight. He turned to me in anger and asked if I was a cop.

My wife's ninety-year-old grandmother was on the old-school telephone when we arrived at her house. Next to her rested an ancient black-and-white cat, J. J., his mouth agape in death, his eyes glowing with fear.

A hospice nurse told me the eyes of the man who took me for a police officer revealed the same in his final moments as wings flapped and he scraped desperate fingers through the dirt of life. The leap out of this world was forced upon him.

We're used to those pithy church signs with "Jesus had two dads and he turned out fine" or "We are not Dairy Queen, but we make great Sundays." This church sign was different. I Googled the words and first found the "time" passage attributed to the Buddha. A second search revealed it came from Jack Kornfield, a Buddhist writer. I dug slightly deeper and learned Kornfield was paraphrasing a line by Yaqui shaman Don Juan in Carlos Castaneda's book *Journey to Ixtlan.*

This jumble of cultures and belief systems is apt when discussing *A Fire to Light Our Tongues*, a book written for/by a mix of Texas believers/nonbelievers of many faiths. Originally conceived by coeditor Donna Walker-Nixon, this anthology of short fiction, poetry, and creative nonfiction challenges the reader to question, seek, and wonder—to allow, as Naomi Shihab Nye's line suggests, "a fire to light our tongues." The answers offered here aren't simple. If there are to be answers at all. Christian Wiman writes: "What does faith mean, finally, at this late date? I often feel it means no more than, and no less than, faith in life—in the ongoingness of it, the indestructibility, some atom-by-atom intelligence that is and isn't us, some day-by-day and death-by-death persistence insisting on a more-than-human hope, some tender and terrible energy that is, for those with the eyes to see it, love."

Kevin Prufer reminds us from his mother's deathbed in his poem "In This Way" that, particularly with the advent of COVID-19, change is the only certainty, and we're all doing the best we can.

It's also very much about "Mister Death," as poet Charles Taylor writes of the creature lurking, "the great white blob out in life's ocean . . . that smells his upcoming meals miles away." Mister Death is messy and as unavoidable as the second law of thermodynamics—the entropy of the universe is increasing exponentially, and there is little we can do to stop it. So stop making your bed.

Disorder is the rule. Searching for a sense of order is at once futile and vital. Writers and other humans attempt it every day. The first rule of good writing? Synthesis. Weaving seemingly disparate ideas together to form something new. That's what you will read in this book when Nan Cuba tells us the Nahua believed "each person's life goal was to maintain balance upon the slippery earth," and "religion can be called way-seeking rather than truth-seeking."

Coeditor Elizabeth Dell conceived the notion of organizing this book in complementary and opposing themes (again, fighting the entropy in search of meaning!): belief and doubt, good and evil, love and hope, known and unknown, truth and beauty, joy and gratitude. It works well to lead the reader down different paths to Robert Okaji's "world so incomplete even sound hides its face," to Diana López's notion that if you "ditch the concept of an afterlife, you have nothing but love to blame for your kindness," to Tarfia Faizullah's Qur'an quote, "And the intoxication of death will bring the truth; that is what you are trying to avoid."

Grief, regret, and love dominate in the excellent short stories and essay contained here. Mary Helen Specht's "The Pilot" offers us a parent facing the loss of both his child and his own life. In Brian Van Reet's story "The Window," a soldier exploring the Big Bend before returning to war admits to a stranger that he is a killer. Owen Egerton's seriously funny "The Martyrs of Mountain Peak" takes us to a religious summer camp where counsellors agree to die so campers will find Jesus.

Mother Nature is the culprit in a series of Al Haley poems about the devasting 1997 Jarrell tornado and how inconsequential the material world is when "a diamond ring of a 30-year marriage is spit out like a watermelon seed." Octavio Quintanilla writes of a different storm that leaves victims watching as "someone's socks speed down the street, into the gutter."

The young remain immortal until death touches them. The Rick Bass story "Pagans" tells of three teens, none churchgoers, who "had found a lazy place, a sweet place, to hang out, in the eddy between childhood and whatever came next." They spend their days exploring waterways outside of Houston that have been poisoned by refineries and abandoned with nightmarish, otherworldly metal cranes.

Shame. Miracles. Fear. The afterlife as a reward, as a dessert. All are present and accounted for here. In Robert Flynn's "Guns and Hard Candy" a girl is afraid to believe she is getting her Christmas wish.

Can a quippy saying outside a Texas church lead to enlightenment? Can we find the meaning of life in the words of a group of Texas writers striving to fend off entropy? Yes. No. Maybe. That's up to you, the reader, to decide. Enjoy the journey.

—JOE O'CONNELL

Pandemic Time

In the summer of 2020, as the number of COVID-19 cases rose in the United States, the editors of this volume asked contributors for appropriate work for this section. Jill Alexander Essbaum gave permission for the section title, "Pandemic Time."

JULIA GUEZ

The New Cartography

This is about borage and compline, anything to still the mind.

This is about money, the lack and the brine. It will be epic

To forth a family (hence the boat full of postage, rum, citrus and

Eiderdown for an eventual pillow). Never mind the reed and sedge,

I have a compass and corkscrew, two blankets to keep us warm.

This is not entirely nautical. A lot depends on wind and water, though.

This is also about blood-work, the pageantry of robe and coin,

How we faculty the ocean, rereading the *Odyssey* alongside *What*

To Expect When You're Expecting, but we're not expecting.

This is about travel then. This is about translation.

LIAUNDRA GRACE

Treasures Within the Temple

I am in conversation with this house,
sharing stories stored in craft boxes
as I move from room to room.

With subtle offers of assurance,
conclusions are not drawn.
Even this house, itself, is flawed.

The caulking along the tub has gaps.
Its pure white tone fades with each bath.
What am I to make of air

that neglects the bedrooms and prefers
to cool more accommodating spaces
meant for gathering and laughing?

The other night I spoke to the light above
the kitchen sink, said there had to be more
to life than mothering and masks.

This house with its backward door locks
as confusing as a child's mind.
Regardless of time spent together, I know

I remember which way to turn, yet forget
to trust that I remember, and somehow
still end up turning in the wrong direction.

What does this say about me—housed up
by windows and roof for days? I've lost track
of counting, purposely. Who's counting?

My hands wash, hold, prepare, balance, and fold.
At times, these hands feel bar-weight heavy.
They console, but do not find time to give

back to the body that make them relevant.
My father, the preacher, texts again
and the office window mimics my reaction.

I take heed of the mixed sky.
This bewitched house creaks above the last stair,
says the heavens are both blue and obscure.

Bibles and virgins fill this house.
I find new nicks every day, though I've been
here since touching was declared toxic.

Twelve crosses, neatly tucked away in the guest
closet, wait to be hung while the carpet absorbs
prayers the hard wood is unable to embrace.

These days, I save my consecrations for bed.
Position does not postpone promise.
One of the many gifts of this house.

NAOMI SHIHAB NYE

The Road Between San Antonio and Comstock, Texas

I think of it as a bloodline, clean thread stretching west,
the mind emptying so gently as it ranged farther from billboards,
chains, farther from access roads, exits, deeper into sky,
that road is why I love this state, despite politics, pronouncements,
the boy called Cody in Comstock who wrote me,
a year after I visited his class,
Basically poetry changed everything,
it made me see where I was,
could you please come back and stay forever?
Finding his letter again thirty years later,
looking him up to learn he died young, a cowboy hat over his downturned face,
I want to say *Your roads are still stretching outwards,*
the fields you walked through,
we are here soaking in the mystery of time,
trapped in our little houses, scared of a virus,
feeling connected through the spaces, all of these new ways,
and I remember you.

OCTAVIO QUINTANILLA

[Through plaster walls I hear the wailing]

Through plaster walls I hear the wailing
Of my neighbor in pain.
She casts her screams like fishing nets
Over the night's undertow.
I want to say a prayer,
But the words clog
At the root of my tongue.
Dios te salve, Maria . . .
I imagine someone is with her,
Taking her hand,
Soaking her forehead
With a wet towel.
Maybe her daughter,
Or her son,
Anyone brave enough to nudge
Her lips with drops of water.
I imagine someone enters my room
And keeps me from falling off the bed.
But someone is always falling.
Our first grief is what sets our house on fire.
By this light, we travel
Across the wire of the night.

ROBIN BRADFORD

Memos from Afar

you only die once the billboard for cremation
services promises, but the Buddhists
I am driving around are busy talking
so I can't invite debate

the turmoil is invisible, the famous
cartoonist said about her process—
mine is to throw the dog a ball
then put on lush vibe and get down to it

the universal consciousness in me
bows to the same in you my chiro says
when I go in with a stiff neck and sinus
drainage and my pain quiets down

the last message is simple: blankets everywhere
in the grass and over bushes, against a late
hard freeze—what if in broad daylight we tucked
each other in like this?

*

historical importance.
A virus in the population
among, let's face it,
people I love
emerges to a vastly different result.

In this way, the germ of memory is not an actual
germ.
In this way, the nurses
who might, for instance, tend to you
will adjust their masks
before they enter
your room.
"How are we doing today?"
they'll ask, though they know
you are dying.

*

"Doing the best we can," I'm thinking,
here in the past,
looking out my window
onto the dark street.

JULIA GUEZ

Still Life When All Our Symptoms Seem to Have Symptoms of Their Own

the dark is very dark

on the night-side of things,
long is very long.

My heart is feathered

fire, smallest
flying flag,

wings are sad,

sad, singing
not at all slow.

My heart

closes
in on itself not

unlike a peony

whose own process of
becoming has been

set back until

the open-handed
flower is tight and green

like a fist, poor thing is

thrumming in this
invisible glass case

which is also a frame

where the most
contagious are taken

to be alone

there all together,
praying the same prayer—

JILL ALEXANDER ESSBAUM

House. Church.

> *Give my greetings to the brothers and sisters in Laodicea, and to Nympha and the church in her house. Colossians 4:15*

Sunday, May 17, 2020. The church has been closed for ten weeks. Services stream live on Facebook and the bulletin can be found on the church's website. Worship lasts less than an hour, Afterwards we are invited to stay for a virtual hospitality gathering via Zoom. We greet, drink coffee, see into each other's homes. These are friends I've known for years, Decades, even. There's so much to say. There's nothing left to say.

*

I've been up since 4:30 a.m. I can't pin my restlessness on the pandemic, though. My sleep has always been fragile.

*

Today's gospel is from the fourteenth chapter of John: *I will not leave you orphaned; I am coming to you. In a little while the world will no longer see me, but you will see me; because I live, you also will live*, The words read dry and vacant. Chaff without wheat,

*

My husband is a Buddhist. He keeps a small altar in the living room on which sits a white ceramic statue of Quan Yin—the female Buddha, mother of compassion and mercy—and a photograph of his father, who died in 2015. My husband offers them apples and tangerines, boxes of candy and fancy cookies, sparkling water and beer. Twice daily he prays at this shrine. A prayer upon leaving for work, a prayer upon returning, Now he works from home. He prays when he rises, then prays again before he comes to bed. Lauds and compline, *Please. Thank you.*

*

Last week the body of a homeless man was found outside the church. He was tucked into an alcove and curled into himself, not easily seen. And who would have seen him? *The church has been closed for ten weeks*, Did he die of the virus? We don't know. His name was Gary.

*

I, too, keep an altar, Atop a red drawer pushed against the wall of my office rests an old family bible, a Lutheran hymnal, *The Picture Story of the Life of Jesus* (a children's book my grandmother gave me forty-five years ago), candles, prayer cards, saint medals, and a pocket-sized New Testament I picked up at a resale shop. A boy named Ryan signed the inside cover, On the last page, scratched in pencil, he wrote: *Trust the Lord w/all your heart & don't depend on your own understanding.*

*

There are 31,102 verses in the Bible.

As of this morning, the US Covid-19 death toll is 94,729.

If you wanted to, you could assign three names to each verse—names of the dead—and still have names left over, If you wanted to.

*

The pastor invites us to interact with the service by posting comments:
Hi.
Good morning, church family! Sound is good.
Great to hear the organ!
(heart emoji)
I miss your faces.
Thanks be to God!
Amen.
Hallelulia!
Amen.
Amen.

*

I have an antique picture of Christ crowned with thorns that belonged to my mother, Pressed beneath the glass and arranged around Jesus' neck is a garland of desiccated edelweiss, I remove the frame, Under a burgundy-colored mat are the words *Herzlichen Glückwunsch*, It's a German birthday card dated 1890.

*

In the beginning God created the heavens and the earth. (*Wilson. Sally. Nita.*)

*

A brief digression on the nature of time.

Christians speak of *khronos* and *kairos*, Khronos is sequential time. Clocks and calendars. Datebooks. Stopwatches. It is measurable, longitudinal, Moments are points on a line. They chase each other and cannot be stopped. For, just as a moment occurs it is gone and replaced by another moment, which evaporates at the instant of its occurrence as well.

Kairos, by contrast, is God's time. Appointed time, The season of *in due season*. It has neither end nor beginning, It is unpossessable and existential, the boundless circumstance of eternity which belongs all and only to the unfathomable, uncreated mystery we call God.

I don't understand it. But I'm not to depend on my own understanding.

*

I ask a friend what he thinks of online worship. He says it's better than nothing but that sometimes the sound's for shit, He says he wants to hug people and that he misses communion, I miss communion too. Is it possible to virtually consecrate the wine and the bread? What if I set them close to the screen? What if I set them *really* close? Lutherans have no solid theology of broadcast worship. But all things are possible with God.

*

Even though I walk through the darkest valley, I fear no evil; for you are with me; your rod and your staff—they comfort me. (*Marylou. Tadashi. Sister Georgianna.*)

*

I propose a third version of time: *pandemic time*, Pandemic time is a wily, ill-bred creature with few precise markers, Days come and go as impositions, *Is it Wednesday or Saturday? Noon or 6 am?* It doesn't matter; I haven't changed clothes in a week. Light and dark have lost meaning, But I find a curious consolation in the ticking by of aimless minutes. I rest when I'm tired. I work when I'm not, Pandemic time blesses the insomniac.

*

Jesus wept. (*Annie. Leilani. Jonathon.*)

*

My mind wanders during the service. I text my friend Wendy. I text my friends Julie and Emily, both of whom are also watching the service. These are say-nothing texts, inconsequential hellos that could have waited, I send them anyway. I get up to stretch, to go to the bathroom, to refill my coffee mug. I file my nails and wonder what to cook for lunch. We pray the prayers of the people. *Hear us, O Lord*, I remember there are Brussels sprouts in the refrigerator and search for ways to keep them crispy as they roast, *Your mercy is great*,

*

I ask my husband what he says to his father, to the Buddha.

"I say '*hi*.'"

*

A correction: it's the building that's been closed for ten weeks.

The church is always open,

Contraries

In *The Marriage of Heaven and Hell*, William Blake explains the contrary nature of God as seen in the progression of all creation, a movement that is impossible without contraries. In *Songs of Innocence* and *Songs of Experience*, Blake explores contradictions in human nature that he connects to religion. Blake pits contraries against each other to show man's journey from a state of innocence to one of experience, where he ultimately regains innocence. Blake shows the progress of man's nature, with both innocence and experience portraying vital aspects of human development. The nonduality of experience that Romantic poets once explored is represented in the works of Texas writers as they grapple with issues of faith and doubt. Writers may accept the Christian tradition, other monotheistic traditions, or faiths outside those often considered traditional. Some writers may conclude there is no God. Arranging this book around contraries and complementaries offers a way into nondualistic thinking.

Belief and Doubt

CHRISTIAN WIMAN

Tender Interior

In my early twenties I found myself reduced to living in a twenty-five-foot trailer in a tiny, dying town in far west Texas. There was a certain, unresonant symmetry to the experience, as I had lived in the trailer as an infant, along with my older brother and our almost-infant parents. By the time of this second residence, the trailer was in my grandmother's backyard, where my great-grandmother had lived for thirty years until her death in 1990. My grandmother's sister—Aunt Sissy, to me—a gentle, whiskery woman with failing health and an obvious but undiagnosed lifelong mental deficiency, also lived in the "big house," which was a small house with six shadowy rooms, a million immaculate nooks, and museum stillnesses. I read and wrote all day, then sat with my grandmother and aunt in the evenings to pass the time.

Or to recover the time. After college and knocking about in various countries, after falling away from my childhood faith and transferring that entire searching intensity onto literature, it seemed to me that, though I was home again, I would never be able to *be* at home again. It's an old story, as is the lost world and wisdom the prodigal discovers beyond his own ambitions and self-assurance. I began asking questions about my family's past out of politeness and boredom. I ended up arranging my days, my thoughts, and my work around the world that emerged from those conversations: the mythic migration from South Carolina to Texas during the dust bowl; the years spent sharecropping; my grandmother's many miscarriages; my aunt's thirty years of waitressing at a cowboy café just off the interstate. God was almost instinctive in them, so woven into the textures of their lives that even their daily chores, accompanied by hymns hummed under their breaths, had an air of easy devotion. I looked down on that unanguished faith at the time, but now, after living with my own vertiginous intensities for all these years, that quiet constancy is a disposition to which I aspire.

Not that there wasn't, in the end, anguish for them. Sissy died with my grandmother and me leaning over her hospital bed, as we had done for days and nights since she had suffered a heart attack. She was not conscious during that time, but just before the end, when my grandmother and I were leaning over her inert and unresponsive body to tell her that we were there, that we loved her, that God was there and loved her (I didn't say this), she rose up, took each one of us in her trembling arms ("Praise the Lord," said the nurse in awe), and then, without a word or even any clear indication that she was conscious, let us go. Later that day she died.

My grandmother was destroyed. Not by grief—she'd had too much of this in her life to be undone by this point—but by the strain of taking care of Sissy during the last year of her life, and then the intense ten days or so when Sissy was hospitalized. My grandmother's own heart began aching ominously just as Sissy's finally stopped, and though my grandmother had yet a month of modern medicine to endure, she never made it out of the hospital. And so it was that I found myself, just weeks after Sissy's last improbable act, leaning over another hospital bed trying to understand another dying woman's desperate gestures. I asked my grandmother if she was cold, and she shook her head no. I asked if she was thirsty, and she shook her head no. Finally I asked—I did not want to—if she was scared, and her eyes widened even farther and she began to shake terribly as she nodded yes and tried to form words around her breathing tube: yes, yes, yes. I suppose I don't know definitively whether she was afraid of dying or of further pain—she had been through so much by that time—but all my instincts argue for the former. I could see a pure spiritual terror in her eyes. I can see it now.

The last words of Gerard Manley Hopkins, a poet and priest who died of typhoid at the age of forty-five, are striking: "I am so happy. I am so happy. I loved my life." How desperately we, the living, want to believe in this possibility: that death could be filled with promise, that the pain of leaving and separation could be, if not a foretaste of joy, then at least not meaningless. Forget religion. Even atheists want to die well, or want those they love to die well, which has to mean more than simply a quiet resignation to complete annihilation. That is merely a polite nihilism. No, to die well, even for the religious, is to accept not only our own terror and sadness but the terrible holes we leave in the lives of others; at the same time, to die well, even for the atheist, is to believe that there is some way of dying *into* life rather than simply away from it, some form of survival that love makes possible. I don't mean by survival merely persisting in the memory of others. I mean something deeper and more durable. If quantum entanglement is true, if related particles react in similar or opposite ways even when separated by tremendous distances, then it is obvious that the whole world is alive and communicating in ways we do not fully understand. And we are part of that life, part of that communication—even as, maybe even *especially* as, our atoms begin the long dispersal we call death.

Hopkins's last words are striking to me not only because it's rare and heartening to witness someone expressing joy at an occasion for grief. No, it's the last sentence that gets me—*I loved my life*. Hopkins was a religious person; he believed in an afterlife. But he seems to have experienced something more complicated than the typical (and, I feel, pernicious) religious sentiment of being happy to be "going to a better place"; the last sentence seems offered as an explanation for the first two: he is happy at the moment of death because he loved his life. On the face of it, this makes no sense: if he loved his life so much, how could he be happy that it was ending so early? The answer, I think, lies in that dynamic of life and death that I've just described, that capacity of dying into the life that one has loved rather than falling irrevocably away from it.

As it happens, I have been close to death myself lately. The cancer I have lived with for seven years has of late become aggressive, and in the past year I have in many nights lain awake in hospital beds and wondered what last gesture or insight I might manage or be granted, have felt despair rising like a palpable and impenetrable liquid in my room. Though I have not yet known that knife edge of time—and timelessness—that Hopkins and my Aunt Sissy and my grandmother all knew, I have been close enough, and deranged by pain enough, to conclude that one is not always responsible for one's last acts, nor are they always worth interpretation. Sissy seemed to reach out of the shell of herself for one last loving touch of life. My grandmother shook as if the scream she couldn't release ricocheted around inside of her. I treasure the memory of Sissy, flinch from that image of my grandmother. Yet I don't feel that one died well and the other badly, that one received the grace that the other either denied or was refused. Hopkins's last words are about life, all of life, and its ultimate relation to death. That they occurred at the last moment of his own life makes them more poignant and powerful, but that he had the wherewithal to speak them is chance.

What does faith mean, finally, at this late date? I often feel that it means no more than, and no less than, faith in life—in the ongoingness of it, the indestructibility, some atom-by-atom intelligence that is and isn't us, some day-by-day and death-by-death persistence insisting on a more-than-human hope, some tender and terrible energy that is, for those with the eyes to see it, love. My grandmother, who was in the world too utterly to be "conscious" of it, whose spirit poured and pours over the cracked land of her family like a saving rain, exemplified this energy, and I feel that to be faithful *to her*, faithful to this person that I loved as much as I have ever loved anyone, then I must believe in the scope and momentum of her life, not the awful and anomalous instant of her death. In truth, it is not difficult at all. Nor is the other belief—or instinct, really—that occurs simultaneously: that her every tear was wiped away, that God looked her out of pain, that in the blink of an eye the world opened its tenderest interiors, and let her in.

ROBERT OKAJI

Even Sound Hides Its Face

Today's sky leaks gray.
The atmosphere surrounding it rolls on.

Placing my thumb over the hole, I listen.
A few windows open, a door.
Wind enters, exits.

This tune is no tune
but a loose-fitting shirt
in a dream of sequence and cold rain.

Perhaps it is God.

Perhaps it is creek water soothing stones
or air collapsing around the finch's vacated space.

Perhaps it is nothing.

A world so incomplete even sound hides its face.

ULF KIRCHDORFER

Beginning to Shape

Yesterday your hands performed the ritual of praying,
though I have long thought the blades of the windmill
turning in silence when I sit on horseback are as close

as I can get to whatever spirit can comfort, the reflection
of my thoughts as if I could ever see myself in the whirl
of those blades, even when they have come to a standstill.

Too many thoughts about squeaking and the need to grease,
like days gone by when large ranches had a man to lube
them all, as if efficient use of the wind was a call greater

than hard church pews, and then I remember my brother
mucking the stalls on his small farm outside of Willow City,
the lap lane of 50 meters two Broadway producers had put in

before he went there to find peace, goats breaking into the
henhouse he was so proud of having built, beginning to shape
real things, after a life of corporations and flying the Concord

as if that brought him and others closer to God, the dreadful
sight of hundreds of computers in a pen of business-shirted men
mostly, the notion of a corral not revealed to any of them,
not even as some died with their expensive shoes on, selling short.

CHARLES MCGREGOR

Jesus Likes to Hang Out on the San Juan Water Tower

Jesus pokes his cruddy Birkenstock sandals
through the white railing—he has risen
above Highway 281 crossing the sun-weathered dashboards.

I know water tower Jesus isn't the only one—
Krishna let the lepers keep their skin too.

Where have all the miracles gone?

My mind's fat fingers can only paint Jesus

on photocopied coloring pages; Sunday School was the opportunity
to give the shapes definition. I want to evolve beyond the Crayola deity
and feel Our Lady of San Juan's golden robe dissolve melting my spine

into a prostrate position—I'll know that my eyes will either open to an ornate
belief
in the power of San Juan's basilica, or I'll pull myself up by the jagged whites
of the Valley's creamy stars assured that space travel means eternal life.

Instead, I take refuge in the fallacies

of the fundamentalists.

But maybe the spiritual gifts are enhanced
like an ear that knows to cringe at a flat C?

Without a belief in doubt, there is no hope of developing a truth
beyond the coloring pages. As a believer, I go too far
East on 281—I face the setting sun on South Padre Island

worried about my soul.

OCTAVIO QUINTANILLA

Grace, 1982

Funny how no one in your house
truly believes in God,

but early Sunday morning you kneel
before a priest and a gigantic wooden cross.

The unintelligible sermon reaches you
with lonesome words:
Antichrist. Armageddon. Heresy.

How hard it is not to think of milk,
not to look at women's backsides,

peek at their bosoms, half-asleep
underneath black fabric.

Satan. Idolatry. Salvation.
Hands in pockets after the final blessing,
you kick a rock all the way home.

NAOMI SHIHAB NYE

Texas, Out Driving

The Solid Rock Church of Kerrville
has moved to another location.
It says so on the sign
under the name—Solid Rock.

Also the entire town of Comfort
appears to be for sale.
This does not feel comforting at all.

How many times we drove these curves,
pale fence posts, bent cedars . . .
but nothing needs us here.
No sentence we said, thought, forgot,
took root in the ditch around the bend.
I always want to stop at historic markers,
see what happened long before, but
the pull of motion keeps a car going,
passing by till next time,
which soon won't come,
though everything we know
says *slow.*

DIANA LÓPEZ

El Cuarto de los Milagros

Last spring, my mother and I drove past the Chapman and King Ranches in South Texas, past Raymondville, past the palm trees that line 77 before the turnoff to 83. I was writing a novel inspired by the tradition of *promesas*, promises to God, and I wanted to send my editor pictures of *el cuarto de los milagros*, the miracle room, where the faithful leave offerings—crutches, splints, braids, wedding veils, dog tags, Purple Hearts, trophies, baby shoes, toys, roses, wreaths, photos, hundreds of photos, and letters voicing gratitude and pleas, *ayúdame, por favor.*

I first made this trip after Grandpa Lupe's stroke. I was in the fourth grade when my family jumped into the Suburban and drove to this shrine for La Virgen de San Juan del Valle. Mom bought candles at the gift shop and, for me, a St. Christopher medallion that pretended to be gold.

I don't remember a church, only a room with rows of cafeteria chairs upholstered in red vinyl and a man clasping a rosary as he walked on his knees. His pants were already torn at the kneecaps, and a smear of blood trailed him the way slime trails a snail. What inspired him to wound himself this way? I didn't understand, but how I tried, how I spent years trying.

"Pray for your grandpa," Mom instructed. "Tell God you'll do something special if He helps."

I made the sign of the cross and silently said, "Dear God, if you help Grandpa, I'll do something special." It sounded like a bribe to me, but what did I know? Besides, why would God help us, even if I promised the most difficult task in exchange? After all, He was the guy in charge of the galaxies, the wars, the hurricanes brewing in the Gulf. He had so much on His mind already, and here I was, asking Him to fix Grandpa.

I must have seemed worried because Mom said, "God hears you," and she put her hand on my shoulder to reassure me.

That's when Dad stepped in with a story about an uncle who had polio—how this uncle promised to let his hair grow for three years if God cured him and how the uncle's hair got long—all during the forties when men weren't supposed to have long hair—so he was kicked out of school for the scandal but he endured, and in return, God cured him.

"It was a miracle," Dad said.

The history of the church we visited, the Shrine of La Virgen de San Juan del Valle, goes back to Jalisco, Mexico. In 1542, a priest brought the statue of La Virgen to the town now known as San Juan de los Lagos. She's indio with brown skin and dark, long hair. She wears a globe for a crown and a cape adorned with gold roses and shaped like a slice of blue pie. She stands on the crescent moon where she's been patiently listening to the pleas from the sick and lonely for nearly five hundred years. She first listened, the legend goes, to a peasant family whose daughter was ill, and she interceded on their behalf, begging God to heal the girl. He did, and from that moment, people have whispered to her their *promesas*.

In 1949, Father Joseph Azpaizu brought a replica of the statue to the border town of San Juan for the people of Texas who couldn't travel to Mexico. The site became a favorite destination for a pilgrimage, and soon, thousands of people journeyed there each year. Then on October 23, 1970, a suicidal pilot crashed his plane into the jam-packed church. The plane burst into flames, burning the entire building, but a steel beam kept it from falling onto the parishioners. Over one hundred people and the statue of La Virgen escaped. Only the pilot died. It was, by all accounts, a miracle. After all, the pilot did not intend to die alone, and even if he did, he certainly didn't have the mathematical genius required to crash his plane at the right angle, the right speed, the right spot on that steel beam.

When my parents told the story, I saw the arms of fire lashing out like the arms of the Mexican boogeyman, El Cucuy, for that was how I had imagined him. My parents said, "Everything burned down, everything but the statue." So then I imagined La Virgen quaking in fear but protected by a flame-retardant bubble, a gift from God. Then, the aftermath—priests, nuns, and firemen poking through the rubble, crying perhaps, but eventually finding her, La Virgen, totally unscathed, not even sooty. I trusted this story until Belinda, a girl on my seventh-grade basketball team, died in a fire after her father's cigarette ignited the couch. Her house burned down with Belinda and her sister trapped inside, no flame-retardant bubble for them. For this, I was told that God had His plan.

And His plan was to leave Grandpa alone, for he remained half-paralyzed and speechless. And the St. Christopher medallion that I treasured turned green. (Later, much later, perhaps I was in college, I learned that no magic protected La Virgen de San Juan on that October day when the pilot crashed his plane. A priest, Father Patricio Dominguez, had grabbed the little statue before he ran out of the church.)

*

For the longest time, I prayed out of fear. Even when I thanked God, I did so to avoid the repercussions owed an ungrateful heart. I became obsessively thankful. At first for things I could not choose like my parents and the beauty of the moonrise over the Corpus Christi bay—even, vainly, for my hazel eyes. Then, for things I *could* choose like my school grades and friends.

At times, I resented the "Our Fathers" and "Hail Marys" of the rosary because I couldn't daydream while reciting them. So I tried talking to God, the way I talked to friends. But imagine a brown teenage girl in corduroys and Converse talking to an old bearded white man in a robe. He wasn't my type, and neither was Jesus with his turn-the-other-cheek philosophy. They seemed so lofty, while I worried about silly things.

So then I tried *not* praying. "Don't pray," I dared myself, over and over again, and the most amazing thing did not happen—*no se lo tragó la tierra*.

I recently read a book by Nadine Gordimer, *The House Gun*, where a character defined prayer as a "heightened form of intelligent concentration." When his wife asked him to justify the word, "intelligent," he said that "there exists the possibility of a bug-eyed concentration on something trivial, which does not imply intelligence in the religious and philosophical sense." What an interesting passage for me who had abandoned prayer precisely because it made me feel "bug-eyed." I'd kneel in church and lose focus. I'd glance at my watch or shift my weight because my knees hurt. I'd anticipate lunch or brainstorm an assignment. I'd look around and wonder what everyone else was whispering. Were they petitioning God? Were they thanking Him? Were they pondering the great mysteries of life? I didn't think so. For most, prayer is *not* intelligent concentration. Or, it's not *regularly* intelligent, though I'm sure many have had moments of insight. But when I looked at all those kneeling people, I saw bug-eyes.

A few years ago, my parents were formally inducted into the Dominican Laity Society. The ceremony involved the vestment of habits. How strange to see my mother dressed as a nun and my father as a monk. In preparation, my mother asked me to help her prepare a speech about a Bible passage with the refrain, "His love endures." "I like how it sounds," she admitted, "but maybe you can help me with the word 'endures.'" I told her it means "to last," and she smiled since she understood that concept. Then, I explained how it's more than lasting, how it means to overcome. "A tree," I said in my teacher voice, "which has sufficient light and water, does not endure even if it lives a thousand years, but another tree, after drought, winds, and insects, does. Maybe the two are the same age but only one has had to prove its worth. It is, in a sense, a truer tree. And a love that endures is a truer love."

My mother smiled again, this time proudly, and she said, "You see, *mija*? You know how to talk."

I enjoyed discussing the Bible with her—at the kitchen table while sipping tea—and as a work of literature. I admit enjoying the poetry of the "Hail Mary" and the "Act of Contrition." I recite them sometimes just as I recite Shakespeare's "Sonnet 116" and Frost's "The Pasture," two poems which say everything I need to know about love. I recite Emily Dickinson too, because, like her, I prefer a "bobolink for a chorister." If prayer is how you find answers and peace, how you tap into the cosmic life-force, then I pray—by walking, by writing, by making love, by attending to this here and this now.

Prayer is appreciating sounds, for example, like the white-noise of household machines—like the cardinal's morning hymn, so robust and celebratory—the wailing of dogs that comes long before the ambulance sirens hurting their ears—how the dog wails reminds me that beyond the creatures and machines I hear are sounds too low or high for me—sounds even in the silence—waves of sound bombarding me, relentlessly.

People say we need the afterlife, that it keeps us good. How frequently we throw the promise of heaven like a dog biscuit and the threat of hell like a clenched fist. So the afterlife keeps us "in line," right? Obedient? That's the argument. But there's a difference between obedience and goodness because, if you ditch the concept of an afterlife, you have nothing but love to blame for your kindness. You must rely on a higher form of morality, one that doesn't base its decisions on eternal bliss or pain or any kind of consequence.

I've reassigned the word "god," no longer a noun but an adjective. The closest synonym is "sublime" though "god," for me, is earthier. It describes the refreshment of iced water on a hot day, the renewal of a good night's sleep, and the reassurance of an embrace. It describes the moments I recall my insignificance and corporality as when I stand at the Gulf of Mexico, looking "neither out far nor in deep," the soft sand swallowing my feet and in that act saying, "*you* are the sand, shaped by waves, pitted by mollusks, etched by sandpipers and crabs." How well I understand Edna Pontellier at those moments, her willing submission to the sea.

I do have faith—that my husband will comfort me when I'm worried, that my brother will reply when I call, that my parents will forgive when I apologize, that my friends will answer when I knock. And that is the only kind of faith I need.

So when I go to church, I find myself thinking like an anthropologist. I study the rituals, the bell that rings when the priest holds up the host, reminding me that once he stood behind a screen and this bell let the congregants know that they could glimpse the body of Christ if they looked up at that moment. I think about the mnemonic devices in the "Apostle's Creed," the repetition of "we believe . . . we believe . . . we acknowledge." I think about the symbolism of the vestments, the green or purple or gold, and of candle-bearing altar boys (and now girls) flanking the priest to "light the word" as he reads the gospel.

And, pretending to be an anthropologist, I returned to the shrine of La Virgen de San Juan del Valle this past spring, my mother with me because this place is such an integral part of my family's history, as we have come for Grandpa, for Grandma, for Aunt Gloria, for Aunt Beatrice, for my brother who was in the navy during Desert Storm, for my niece who was born premature, for my father who had quadruple bypass surgery. My mother accepted my camera. She knew I was writing a book, that I wanted pictures. She wanted them, too, though for different reasons. I photographed the fountain that lies between the gift shop and church. I photographed the small mosaic of La Virgen above the spout where Aunt Gracie once leaned to sprinkle holy water upon her breast. I photographed the bottle brush trees and grassy lawn. I photographed a man kneeling before the offertory candles. And I readied myself to photograph the miracle room as I imagined my editor's fascination, for she lives in New York where some think Texas is a different country. Is there a place, I wondered, as interesting as this? As pagan with the little pewter arms and legs that people leave there? I could not wait to take my photographs, and I secretly hoped for something sensational like a mayonnaise jar full of teeth. But then I walked in, and the room was empty. For the first time, it was empty! No miracles for me. "But, of course," my logical mind quickly said. This was Friday before Palm Sunday. Hundreds were expected. The room had to be emptied before they arrived. It was a simple matter of making space.

Still, I could not measure my disappointment, and then, I could not measure my shame. For I did not go to make a *promesa*. I do not bribe God anymore. I am an observer, a scientist, when I visit a church. Yet I know that if my mother heard my heart's true intent, she'd say, "You see? This is proof. God *hears* you. He is not make-believe. Our *cositas* are not for a museum! And you should think twice before writing an essay that says so."

MARY HELEN SPECHT

The Pilot

In that moment—after straightening out for the downwind leg of the traffic pattern and before lowering the gear and extending the flaps—Bill realized that what he should have said to the Kid was this: it's a lot like flying. Everyone thinks it's so goddamn amazing the first couple times they do it. Old ladies about shit their pants. Some folks even confuse the lights of towns with the stars in the sky. But after you've been up in the air every week for practically your entire life, there's little magic in it anymore. Hour after hour spent balancing on bones of your body the despair of another ordinary day.

Yes, that was what he should have said, thought Bill as the moist, brain-colored clouds dropped away to reveal the jungle shivering in the wind. He should've told the Kid the truth: he wouldn't be missing much in not growing old. Not really.

Bill heard his passenger rap knuckles against the cockpit's snug entryway. Felt hat, chops, an expensive watch: they sure knew how to dress the part, thought Bill as he gave the man a nod to show he was listening. For over twenty years Bill had been flying private planes for an oil company based out of Houston; he never bothered to remember individual names but called them all "boss" and thought of them all as Cowboy. This one was new and younger than Bill, looked to be about forty, lean-bodied but with a bloated, jowly face. When they'd taken off that morning, he'd winked once at Bill and promptly fallen asleep with his hat perched atop his face.

Ugly ain't it?—asked the Cowboy above the roar of the engine, pointing out the front windshield.

The jungle? I seen uglier.

No, our pipeline. Looks like a hose of shit.—They could see a section of it down below stretching alongside the two-lane highway that connected the "airport" to the town. Running parallel, the wide Rio Aguarico looked oddly bedazzled in the glare of noonday sun. Bill compensated for the drag of the flaps by pushing the yoke forward.

Shit worth its weight in gold, Bill said, not for the first time. Banking the plane for the final approach, he pressed the radio to his mouth: Lago Agrio traffic, Cessna Citation CJ1, turning base to final, runway 36.

And that gold's how come the Big Boys can get me out to this cesspool—the Cowboy slapped his leg as he said this.

Bill flared the airplane; he completed each action without thought. This trip was the first time he'd left the Kid since the accident, but Bill still felt his presence, could still sense the process of his body, hundreds of miles away, disintegrating like a video stuck in fast forward. With a lurch and jerk, the nose leveled, and the main landing gear punched into the runway.

What'll you do here while I'm off wrangling these motherfuckers in meetings all day?—asked the Cowboy, unbuckling his seatbelt.

Prob'ly a little piranha fishing in the river like usual, said Bill. In truth, Bill had only attempted to piranha fish once and caught nothing. Most times he just walked or watched TV if the satellite was working at the hotel; he preferred pastimes without concrete objectives, although he didn't know why that was so.

Well, Pilot, what I wanted to tell ya's this: I plan on jumping in the bottle tonight, and I want a native English speaker along, if you know what I mean. Speak Spanish?

A little, yeah.

Well, maybe if I did too I wouldn't be such a racist asshole, huh?—asked the Cowboy, standing and moving toward the hatch, looking out the corner of his eye as if daring Bill to agree.—I can tell that bothers you a little, and I think that's real nice. I like you, Pilot.

Bill, as usual, said nothing.

*

While they waited for the company car to pick them up for the hotel, Bill called the Kid from a public telephone in the hangar office. At Methodist, the Kid had a private room but not a private extension, so Bill had to connect through the nurses' station, and the woman on the other end of the line always sounded—something about the upward inflection—like she were in the middle of telling a dirty joke. This made Bill feel aroused and uncomfortable at the same time.

—How goeth Mercury, the mighty God of Flight?—asked the Kid right off. The fact he guessed it was Bill calling must have meant the other calls, from hysterical dorm mates and young women with tragic crushes, had tapered off.

Not bad, Kiddo. Not bad, said Bill. His son was no longer really a kid but at that particularly modern age where he thought of himself as an adult but still lacked any practical skills on how to live a life.

So, pay attention, old man, I been thinking, said the Kid, his voice rushed and deep, salesman-like. This was his favorite persona: The Performing Kid.—I been reading, actually. About ecological cemeteries. I want to go all-natural, back into the earth from which I came. Imperious Caesar, dead and turned to clay, might stop a hole to keep the wind at bay.

Jesus Christ, thought Bill.—What are you talking about exactly?

The Kid described the research he'd been doing on something called natural death, supposedly a big movement in Britain he said was gaining popularity in the States. The cemeteries were parks: no gravestones; all bodies, free of chemical embalming fluid, were wrapped in nothing but a shroud and buried in graves dug with hand shovels by the funeral attendees.

Do we have to talk about this now?—asked Bill, feeling his voice a thin string slipping up his throat, a tiny thread pulled taut. Why couldn't he let the elephant in the room be an elephant for once? The Kid was obsessed: his last moments on Earth spent studying the feeding behavior of vultures, the memoirs of morgue employees, the three hammer strokes of fate in Mahler's Sixth Symphony. And poems: Youth flickers out like wind-blown flame. The Kid needed a heart donor within the next few weeks, and the likelihood of that happening was not good.

No, no, we don't have to talk about this now. We don't have to talk at all. Why don't we just put this entire conversation off until after I'm dead?—cried the Kid, the range of his moods these days stretched to melodramatic limits, desperate playfulness rising into brittle anger abating into defeat, and Bill felt tossed about, unexpected turbulence he had nevertheless begun to expect. And everywhere he looked, as if it existed inside an invisible fluid surrounding Bill's being, was the ghost image of his son as a small boy, long dark hair and dark eyes sunk deep—other children looked milky and washed out in comparison—and how he'd been shy and accepting, pleased and yet unsurprised by any gifts Bill brought home from his trips, the kind of child you could take anywhere and he would just sit and watch with an expression that seemed to say, yes, this is the world. Everything as it should be.

He told the Kid to put aside his notes on the cemetery, that they'd look them over together when Bill got back to Houston.

Come home, the Kid said. Defeat. The Glass Kid.

I'll be back late tomorrow.

Yes. Good. Alex brought more video games. That'll keep me distracted today. One of them looks almost fun.

*

The Cowboy shook Bill when the company car pulled onto the property of the hotel. Bill opened his eyes reluctantly.

I'll call your room when I'm ready, he said. Don't start to town without me now.

There was little chance of that. Lago Agrio was perhaps the most depressing oil town Bill traveled to for his job. In all his years as a pilot, Bill had found most places in Latin America to be more modern and beautiful than he'd expected, but Lago Agrio was an embodiment of the worst possible visions of the Third World. Sewage ran black down the streets, trash surrounded the ankles of street whores dressed in threadbare t-shirts and plastic jellies, the faces of residents ravaged by malaria and whiskey and desperation. Bill had told his son that this trip was an emergency, that he'd had no choice. But really Bill asked for the assignment. He'd felt his mind rubbing up against a breaking point; he had to get away from the hospital for a day or two but not to some place nice. It wouldn't be fair. Lago Agrio was as close to fair as he could get. Life hardly worth living here. However, the hotel, a shelter from the realities of the town, had been built for oil honchos and the smattering of adventure tourists who left from Lago Agrio for weeklong jungle trips down the river. It was built on several acres of manicured wilderness—toucans, jungle hogs, and howler monkeys displayed their exoticism in large cages covered by the stunning plant called King Red. There was even a swimming pool, in all likelihood the only one for hundreds of miles in any direction.

As Bill groggily collected his standard-issue roller suitcase from the trunk and walked toward the Miami-style reception area, stretching his limbs in anticipation of a nap, he decided that what he should have said to the Kid was this: life is just the dream you wake up from to something better. That would have sounded nice, he thought. Even if it wasn't true.

*

The clock read two-thirty when Bill woke. He'd missed lunch. Struggling to focus on the room, pastel colors and curtains like doilies, Bill ran through possible options for the empty afternoon. He could call the Kid again, but knew he wasn't up to it. He could go for a swim. Take a shower. Masturbate. He could read the book he'd brought, a gift from the Kid, an anecdotal account of birds in famous literature. The Kid was a thoughtful yet calculating gift giver; he always found things that vaguely pertained to Bill's interests but could also potentially improve upon them, maybe even improve upon Bill himself. Bill was a birder in his spare time but the passive type who preferred watching at the backyard feeder to seeking out the new and unusual. Bill had solitary and simple habits: turkey hunting, gliding, collecting international newspapers.

On the ranch outside Wink, Texas, where Bill grew up, there hadn't been anyone his age for miles, and his brothers were all older and worked as ranch hands. His father told Bill once, after he'd complained of being left behind from an Oklahoma cattle run: Loneliness gives you time to become more interesting. Bill had shrugged away such sentiments—in fact, he saved his money for flying lessons and left for the big city the day he turned eighteen—but, as things of this nature tend to do, his father's words came back to Bill at age twenty-nine after his wife took off and left him alone in a small house in a suburb called Sugarland with a ten-month-old baby boy. He quit his job with Continental and took the position with the oil company because it required fewer overnights away from his son, who slept on the pull-out couch of their retired next-door neighbors the once or twice a month when he was assigned South American trips. Bill wasn't sure if loneliness had made him more interesting, but it may have done so for his son, who would mark passages in books and take notes on baseball games to tell Bill about when he got home. Bill had on occasion attempted to give advice or breach fatherly topics like sex or financial responsibilities, but he and the Kid only seemed to really connect when discussing the small and the concrete: how to fix a cabinet, cook pigs-in-a-blanket, distinguish World War II fighter planes. When Bill was asked whether or not he and his son were close, he really couldn't say. Yes and no.

Bill was hungry. He called the front desk to see if the cafe had food left over from lunch. Quinoa soup will be fine, he said. He'd learned not to speak Spanish to the hotel staff; it offended them for some reason he couldn't understand, as if it were an accusation of gross incompetence.

A few minutes later, spooning the soup, made with a barley-like grain mixed with corn and squash, into his mouth, Bill turned on the television to the sound of crackling, the satellite reception bugging in and out, in and out. He stood up, his tall, meaty frame towering over the set, and flipped through channels, but the only one coming in clearly was a religious station showing Catholic priests or brothers of some sort leaning over hospital beds speaking in Latin and making the sign of the cross. He flipped it off in disgust.

Growing up on the ranch, they'd been an implicitly religious family, something that was understood but never discussed further than the prayer before Thanksgiving dinner. But Bill had never felt the presence of God. He told one of his brothers after their mother's wake, *I've searched everywhere, Neddo—in the sky and to the corners of the Earth—if something was really out there, don't you think I'd have sensed it?* Which was why he found it so difficult to relate to the other parents of those killed or injured in the accident, to listen to their platitudes, in private gatherings and in the media. They still thanked God for the beautiful world he created and for all the love and support they had been shown during these difficult times, blah, blah, blah. The memorial being erected at the University was almost as upsetting: letters chiseled in remembrance, as if those kids had died for something worth dying for, as if they'd sacrificed for a cause greater than the ridiculous collapse of a forty-foot-tall bonfire during its construction *primarily due to a containment failure in the first stack of 5,000 logs*, which were to be lit the next day as part of a tradition during what was essentially a pep rally before the football game against their state rival. That autumn the leaves never changed color, rains stripping them from the branches just as they'd begun to loosen their grip for the long goodbye.

*

The moment the company car pulled away, Bill and the Cowboy became the center of a small churning mass: two loud whores shaking their breasts, a beggar pulling at their sleeves, children with sticks and skinny, scabby dogs. All looking for scraps of one kind or another, thought Bill. The sun was beginning to set, casting a wicked flush onto everything, and the heat was so pervasive he could feel it in the beating muscles of his heart. The whole place stank.

It was a familiar story the world over: a town built to facilitate the greed of the civilized world, drawing in members from the surrounding indigenous population with promises of a livelihood to replace the one being swallowed by the march of progress, and then spitting them back up again into, well, into *this*, thought Bill, as he and the Cowboy silently made their way down the road, past market stalls selling plastic watches and knockoff baseball caps, to the only bar with a sign: El Delfin Roso. The Pink Dolphin. Supposedly, the lakes and rivers of the nearby jungle were home to a freshwater species of dolphin, a pink dolphin. But nobody had seen one in years.

Dark. Smoky. Full of slow-moving men. Bill and the Cowboy sat on stools at a plastic table in a corner at the back. There was no bar in the traditional sense, but a man crouched behind a small counter with unmarked liquor on a shelf behind him and a cooler full of beer at his feet. Bill doubted this was what the Cowboy had had in mind for a night out, and part of him hoped they would leave soon, back to the secure monotony of the hotel. The other part of him wanted anything but to be alone.

Order us each two glasses of something brown, said the Cowboy, his voice soft and drawly.—Here's the situation, Pilot. Right about now, my soon-to-be-ex-wife is moving my shit out of the enormous, ugly house I paid for, and then she'll fuck her creepy pharmacist in our king-size bed on the sheets she always claimed were white but sure looked yellow to me. I, on the other hand, am getting drunk. Your job is to make sure we get back in one piece. Gratitude in return.

Bill had long since accepted this kind of thing as part of the job. As far as pilot gigs go, flying for an oil company is cushy and lucrative, and you don't have to worry about being transferred out of Houston. The downside is that you have to keep assholes like this happy without entirely losing your self-respect. Bill nodded stoically and went up to the counter, turning back around immediately after placing the order so the Ecuadorian would have to bring the glasses over on a tray.

How long you worked in the business? asked Bill.

The Cowboy raised his eyebrows as if to say *what a fucking bore* and then downed his first drink and began to sip on the second. There was something genteel and graceful about the man's movements despite his barking edge; he had a habit of stroking his freckled cheekbone with the inside of his wrist.

Know how most folks want their kid to turn out like 'em? he asked, finally. Well, it's funny cause mine did, and I can't hardly stand him.—He said his son was something of a high school football star, a whole teenage cult building up around him.—His mother gives him anything he wants, and he expects me to do the same. Hell, he expects us to worship his ass. Be tickled pink basking in the glow of his athletic talent. And, god, you just can't talk to him. Nothing but game chatter can get through that meatheaded skull. The Cowboy stopped for a moment. Truth be told, and I know it's a cliché, I'm not opposed to starting over. Doing a better job the second time around, you know? Just ain't sure I got the energy left. He laughed and shook his head. They sipped their drinks in awkward silence.

My son's a nerd, said Bill.—The Cowboy was looking down vacantly at the table, but he fluttered his hand as if to say, continue.—Always real curious. A reader but not of novels or comics or stuff like that; he likes to read *about* things, 'bout astronomy and psychology and wars. He talks about things like how human consciousness is just an evolutionary trick of natural selection, that we'll fight harder to survive if we think we're unique and worthy.

The kid's got theories.

Yeah.—Bill could feel the liquor beginning to flush his face.—But the weird thing is my son's never chosen friends like himself. He works his way into the shitkicker crowds, the tough guys. He becomes kind of like their mascot.

Why you think that is?

Maybe he likes to show off, be the smart fish in a dumb pond. Maybe he fancies himself on a mission to improve them somehow. Where he went to college, the other students called him The Professor.

So what's he do now?

Bill thought it strange the Cowboy didn't know; he'd assumed his son had been hardcore gossip fodder throughout the company. Taking some time off from school, Bill said, as the Cowboy motioned toward the counter for more drinks. And Bill thought about how his lovely son was dying while the Cowboy's boy would go on. And he thought about growing up here, in Lago Agrio, where your baseline existence was to be barefoot in sewage as a child and elbow deep in oil spillage once grown. Some politically correct experts might say that it was wrong to judge, that they might be as happy as anybody else on this broken planet, but, looking around the room, Bill didn't buy that. Not really. And as he ordered another round, Bill decided that what he should have told the Kid was this: in some ways it's actually better if the end really is the end. Oblivion is a more attractive option than being reborn to most places, most lives.

The door to the bar suddenly swung open, and in streamed light and a furor of voices. A group of young men pushed inside. The one in front, who appeared to be the leader of sorts, tough and sneering, was surprisingly well-dressed; he wore pinstriped pants, a tight button-down covered with elaborate embroidery of roses the size of fists, and a black fedora. There was something unmistakably feral about him as he circled the room. Like a pimp. The counter man immediately brought over drinks to the new group, and the eerie silence was overturned by whooping and cackling.

Someone thinks he's the cat's pajamas, said Bill, and the Cowboy barely grunted. He was turning out to be a sullen drunk. And boring. He talked about his whore-of-a-wife and about a young woman attorney he'd recently met at Marfareles and about how much money his accountant had screwed him out of. Bill eventually lifted his index finger to halt the flow of monologue and stood up. He had to piss. On his way to the bathroom, he noticed a flash of silver coming out of the pants of a young man in a black t-shirt standing protectively to one side of the fedora-wearing Catman, who was speaking intensely to a group of older men. Guns didn't usually scare Bill—in Texas they weren't a signifier of death but a mere argument to power, a tool of sport—however, here, in a faraway corner of the world where the rules and prerogatives were shrouded in mystery, the sight unsettled him, sharpened his sense of awareness that had been dulling from drink.

When he walked out of the bathroom/cleaning closet a few minutes later, the Cowboy was no longer at the table. Bill scanned the room and saw his boss standing in front of the counter talking to the Catman, whose face was expressionless, arms crossed. What the fuck was going on? More men had entered the bar and were moving back and forth, partially obstructing Bill's view of the exchange. The Cowboy seemed to be attempting to explain something, gesticulating grandly, pointing at his torso. Then he was taking out his wallet, handing the Catman a wad of cash, at least two twenties and maybe a third bill underneath. Was his boss being mugged? Making a drug deal? Should he do something? But then the Catman began to unsnap his rose embroidered shirt, slowly, eyes trained on the Cowboy, eventually revealing an immaculate wife-beater and arms with muscle definition but not the kind that comes from working out in a gym.

The Cowboy hung the shirt in the crook of his elbow, and reached out the other arm to try and shake the man's hand as one does after the completion of a mutually beneficial transaction. The young man just gave the Cowboy a half smile and walked back toward his friends at a table by the door. It was surreal. A surreal thing to do, buy a shirt off somebody's back, thought Bill, as the Cowboy returned to their table. It's a sharp shirt—the Cowboy kept saying—you gotta admit it's a sharp shirt.

Yeah, replied Bill.—It's sharp all right.—They both took another drink. Bill looked around the bar, at the squalor and dirt and cheap plastic, at the mean, tired old men and the mean, anxious young men, at the shredded posters hanging from the walls and the milky homemade liquor served in jars. And then Bill looked at the shirt embroidered in roses and realized something: in all this ugliness, the Cowboy still managed to find and take away the one beautiful thing. Bill began laughing hysterically, uncontrollably, from the muscles of his flabby abdomen that no longer responded to a daily dose of morning sit-ups like it used to.—Just doesn't seem like your style is all, said Bill. Soon, the Cowboy was laughing too, guffawing like a cartoon character.—Yeah, well, I'm a new man. Take notice.

Ladies and gents, this man here has been reborn into embroidered roses.

From now on, I wear my roses on my chest! Like the truth.

A man of strength *and* beauty!

From caterpillar to butterfly, I am remade.

And the Cowboy slipped off his own starched, white button-down and pulled on the new top, which fit okay although it was tight across the chest and armpits. They ordered more rounds and made toasts to the new shirt, the new man, and just kept on toasting, round after round, to quarterback Roger Staubach and Mercury the god of flight, to blowjobs and pink dolphins, to their first love and their first fuck, they toasted and toasted—everything but their sons—for what seemed like hours, until they were both drenched in sweat and ready to face the night. Arms slapping at the doorway for support as they slipped out of the now empty bar, Bill mumbling something about the sawdust on the floor at Arky Blue's Silver Dollar back when he'd been single and young with his whole life ahead of him, they lifted their heads to a sky filled with stars and nothing else.

*

The two men walked down the dark, muddy road—it had rained while they'd been inside—and one or two dim streetlamps flickered in the distance. They walked along as if walking along this road in this town was the most natural thing in the world. As if it were something they did every night. As if they were entirely alone.

When the group of Ecuadorians slipped out of a side street and stopped in front of them, Bill's first reaction was mild curiosity, an assumption of benign intentions such as a desire to help lost Americans find late-night food and a cab ride back to a hotel. When he saw the Catman in his fedora draw a knife and his buddy a gun, Bill's second thought was this: *He didn't buy that motherfucking shirt. He rented it.*

Holy mother of God. What do you want? . . . Tell us what you want, and I'm sure we can work somethin' out fellas. . . . Just tell us. Anything. . . . What do you want, goddamn it?

And Bill thought about telling the Cowboy to shut the fuck up cause they don't even speak English, but he didn't. He just stood there. Unafraid and uninvolved. The Ecuadorians were also silent and motionless until the Cowboy finally stuttered out and stopped talking. Bill watched the Cowboy. The Cowboy watched the Catman, who pointed definitively at his shirt. The Cowboy unsnapped the front, his hands slow and trembling, until the third Ecuadorian finished the job by grabbing him at the collar and shaking him violently until he basically fell out of the shirt and onto the ground. Catman's boot pressed into the Cowboy's back, and he slashed the man's naked tricep with his knife, drawing a line of blood.

The man with the gun shoved Bill onto his hands and knees, mud splattering up onto his face, his elbow coming down hard next to the Cowboy's as his wallet was wrenched from his back pocket.

Voy a matar*te*. Y voy a matar*te*.

The Cowboy looked over at Bill, and from his expression it was clear no translation was needed. Not that Bill would have offered one. Crouched there on the ground like a dog, he felt one emotion: anger. Anger toward the Cowboy, not for getting him killed, but for enticing him into that desperate revelry back at the bar and for being the one beside him at his death. He thought about the Kid, who at that moment would be suspended over his hospital bed, the blue afghan Bill had brought from home crumpled up at the foot, falling in and out of painful sleep, taking in a shallow breath and letting it back out. And Bill wasn't sure if he was more upset about the waste of the Kid's life or of his own; they suddenly felt like the same thing. But waste wasn't the right word because what would unwasted life look like? In a sense, all life was wasted because all life ended. Bill had no desire to come to terms with death because there was no justification encompassing enough to account for the unfairness of it all, the fact that life itself could be so hard only to end with the final, humiliating punishment of extinction.

Ten years ago, when Bill received the news his ex-wife had died in a car crash of some sort, he hadn't said anything to his son because it seemed unnecessary—she had been dead to them for a long time already. Except that wasn't exactly true, because the Kid radiated her image with his dark skin and coffee-colored eyes, her Colombian heritage dominating Bill's Irish one. It was as if, no matter how hard you might try, your genes wouldn't allow you to completely abandon your progeny. Bill had felt comfort in that.

And moments later, after a commotion further down the street—another gang or maybe police, Bill never found out for sure—caused the Catman and his friends to flee suddenly, what Bill felt, bent over amongst the trash and muck in a dark corner of the jungle, was not gratitude or a newfound appreciation for life, for the color of the moon or the feel of wind against his skin, or even a desire to live better, fuller, more meaningfully. What he felt was subtle and faint. It was like standing in the middle of the river between a warm and cold current. Relief and disappointment. Relief that it wouldn't happen today. Disappointment that it wouldn't happen to him first.

*

The next afternoon, Bill flew home, stopping in Panama City to refuel. As he looked out at the sky and the clouds—enormous, stretching in every direction—there was absolutely nothing Bill wanted to tell his son. No words of false comfort or explanation. He just wanted to be with him. He wanted to be with him right then.

As they made their descent to 1000 AGL over the tendril-like sandbanks of the gulf coast, Bill could just barely make out a flock of seagulls down below. They are flying together, he thought. I am flying alone.

TARFIA FAIZULLAH

Kafir 1

It's been twenty years since my sister died in the car accident. For twenty years I've been telling slightly different versions of her death and the aftermath. None of them are true. All of them are true.

Kufrul-'Inaad is disbelief out of stubbornness. This applies to someone who knows the truth and admits to knowing the truth, and knows it with his or her tongue, but refuses to accept it and refrains from making a declaration.

One night during college at a party in someone's dark dorm room, someone decided it would be fun to make a drinking game out of how many things in common we had with our siblings. The lava lamp in the corner made our faces seem like the topographies of far-away planets. "What about you, Tarfia?" he asked.

"Throw into hell every obstinate disbeliever," Allah says. "Why are you so stubborn?" everyone in my life who has ever loved me has asked. "Why is it so hard for you to back down?"

"I don't have any siblings," I said, thrumming the amber neck of the beer bottle with my fingers.

A few verses earlier, in 50:19 of the Qur'an, Allah says to the disbeliever, "And the intoxication of death will bring the truth; that is what you were trying to avoid."

"She's not dead," I said when my parents came to visit me in the hospital a few days after my sister had gone into cardiac arrest. My arm was in a sling, freshly plastered hours after surgery that was meant to correct the damage done to my shoulder during the car accident. My mother's face was a map of bruises. I couldn't look directly at any of the new countries of her ruptured skin. "She can't be."

How can death simultaneously intoxicate and bring truth? If the very cells that allow us to experience intoxication stop functioning, how do our brains process, allow, or deny truth? That is to say, truth is like memory in that it is not so much a set of discrete memories as much as it is a set of processes by which we encode, store, and retrieve information.

"It's just me and my sister," I say to the lipsticked and rouged woman ringing up the bottle of perfume I'm buying for my mother at the makeup counter at Dillard's. It is strange how easy it is to not continue with *but she hasn't been alive for twenty years.* "I'm about five years older," I say, and she lights up. "That's the age difference between me and my sister!" she says, and I smile and sign my name on the credit card slip with a flourish.

In many ways, *kufr* is synonymous with *atheism*, which is the rejection of a belief in the existence of deity. But is it still disbelief if you are rejecting belief in someone or something that no longer exists?

"I'm here," my lover says, shaking me awake from another nightmare. When I turn my face into his warm chest, I am aware of my own self as vibrantly cellular. "I'm here," I said every week for a year after my sister died to the tan and buff receptionist at the physical therapy facility where I had to retrain the nerves in my arm to remember that they, too, existed.

TARFIA FAIZULLAH

Kafir 2

The Arabic word for disbeliever is *kafir*. It can also be translated as infidel. The term refers to one who rejects God in Islam. The word *kafir* is the active participle of the root *k-f-r*, to cover. As a pre-Islamic term, it described farmers burying seeds in the ground, covering them with soil while planting. Thus, *kafir* implies that a disbeliever is a person who hides or covers.

My father was driving the car. It was summertime. My sister and I were thrown out of the car. She had an instant brain aneurysm. We had been in Houston, vacationing. I landed in a fire ant bed. We prayed in the hotel room, orienting ourselves toward the direction of the Kabah. I had argued with her about who would lie down on the long dusty blue seat of the 1984 Suburban and who would lie on the floor beneath it. I had won the seat. Neither one of us wore seatbelts. My father crawled over to me where the bones of my right arm were twisted above me. It was dusk. "I think Tangia is dead," he said. I don't know where my mother was. My sister was seven years old. A stranger brought ice to place beneath my back to discourage the ants away. This is what I know of the accident and its immediate aftermath. This is all I know.

I finished reading the entire Qur'an from cover to cover by the time I was seven years old. My parents threw a party to celebrate the *khatam* and invited the entire Islamic community of west Texas. My mother made milky rice pudding flavored with rosewater. There is a picture of me and my father sitting on the old blue couch in what we called the family room: I'm wearing a blue and red *salwaar kameez*, and my father is wearing a white panjabi and crocheted skullcap. He has his arm around me. Both of us are grinning. I was both pleased and embarrassed to have accomplished something monumental, something worth his pride. Then and now, I could read Arabic script flawlessly without knowing the meaning of a single word.

Kafir, and its plural *kafirun*, is directly used 134 times in the Qur'an. Its verbal noun *kufr* is used 37 times, and the verbal cognates of *kafir* are used about 250 times. These numbers, just like what I know of the car accident in which my sister died, are facts. They don't describe the look in my mother's eyes when she sees girls who are approximately seven years old. They don't describe how the word *kafir* does not change meaning over the course of the Qur'an, but rather accumulates in meaning over time. They don't describe my father needing two back surgeries because he has to work himself to distraction in his garden. Facts and numbers don't describe the manifestation of *Kufrul-Inkaar*, for example, which is disbelief out of denial, practiced by someone who denies with both heart and tongue. "I think Tangia is dead," my father had said. "No," I replied. "She's not."

ANGÉLIQUE JAMAIL

Magdalen

Always with a book or two, a human skull—
The trappings of a hermit.

Penitence by the light of a forlorn candle,
Eyes pleading upward, or

Waiting with her reflection in a mirror,
Eyes turned inward on her assumed sins.

Robes, folds of clothing, enshroud the transgression
And grief of her body, or

Slough off from her shoulders, from her hips,
Part at her chest while she weeps.

Some or another holy man decided from his removed
Perch centuries later she must have been a prostitute.

Painted woman, sainted woman among many, another
Silenced and spoken-for creature in the multitudes,

Forgive us for projecting every man's sin and every Eve's
Shame upon your figure, for consigning you to the grotesque.

You've fallen into the museum's menagerie of masochism,
Of Christianity's groveling obsession with the Divine.

They heaved *villainous*, *demon-possessed*, and eventually *whore*—
Witch is the only epithet still in the arsenal.

Oh virtuous, maligned lunatic, drying Jesus's feet
With your luxurious, perfumed hair—and how He wept

Oh Mary, Mary, Mary, Mary
Like the untarnishable Virgin, Mary like

My old maiden aunt with a rosary hung from her bedpost,
Mary like my great-grandmother reminding me,

Only whores wear lipstick, Mary like
The verve that dies in *every good, righteous girl.*

Good and Evil

CHAITALI SEN

When I Heard the Learn'd Astronomer

I could have retired after a period in which the biology department of our College of Natural Sciences split into two. I had served as the department secretary for thirty years and had already submitted my retirement papers, but I decided to stay on another year. The head of the newly formed Department of Ecology and Evolutionary Biology, Dr. Joseph Fernandes, was instantly likable and cheerfully intelligent. He was quite young and had spent the last five years abroad at Stockholm University. He seemed happy to have escaped the monotonous chill of Scandinavia. Those first few weeks, I often observed him standing by his open window, enjoying the warm, bright days.

On his desk, he kept a picture of his wife, standing in front of a stone wall with a handful of tulips. A liveliness in the photograph caught my attention every time I passed it. I wondered when she would come prancing through the offices to introduce herself. In all my years as a department secretary, the wives always did this, refusing to be forgotten, even at times getting involved in controversies that had nothing to do with them. But his wife, whom he called Kitty, did not come and announce herself, and I soon learned that nothing in this small, fledgling department would happen as expected.

Early one morning, at the end of August, Dr. Fernandes stood by my desk instead of going directly to his office. He was holding a newspaper. "I need your help," he declared.

He had already made a habit of saying this to me.

"Did you happen to see this editorial in the paper?" He put the newspaper on my desk and pointed to the article in question. It was authored by a Dr. Robert Smith of the Society for Science and Ethics. Dr. Fernandes asked if I'd heard of him.

"I haven't," I said truthfully. I never had much interest in reading the newspaper.

He waved his hand over the paper. "He completely mischaracterizes the scientific process. He equates the teaching of evolution with religious dogma."

I nodded, trying to understand his mood, which I could only describe as a kind of calm panic.

"Everything he presents as the truth is actually an inverse of the truth. I was reading it to Kitty this morning and, suddenly, some things about this place started to make sense. The behavior of the students, for example, and some of the faculty, for that matter."

"I see. Would you like some coffee, Dr. Fernandes?"

I was relieved that he said yes. I went to fetch the coffee and expected to take it to him in his office, but he had pulled up a chair to my desk and was frowning over the newspaper again.

When I sat back down, he continued to tell me about the myriad falsehoods in Dr. Smith's editorial, most notably his claim that a legitimate minority of scientists was raising doubts about the age of the earth.

"But is all this really new?" I interjected. Here I felt the advantage of my age. I told Dr. Fernandes that in my thirty years with the department, evolution was one of those topics that had no shortage of detractors.

My word choice concerned him. "Detractors?"

"Yes, you know, a student from a devout family might write a letter of complaint."

"Is that why the department broke up, because of detractors?"

There I hesitated, fearing I had misspoken. I certainly didn't have the expertise to explain why the department had split. From what I understood, Dr. Elam, who was the dean of the College of Natural Sciences, wanted the biological disciplines to have more of a professional emphasis, to prepare the students for careers in medicine and such. The split into two departments was meant to be a compromise, with the larger Biological and Biomedical Sciences absorbing most of the faculty, and our smaller department emphasizing foundational theory and investigative process.

Dr. Fernandes confessed to me that he hadn't asked many questions when he was interviewing for this position.

"I don't know how much they would have told you anyway," I said. "I believe some of the conflict was personal."

I was present at some of the meetings to take notes, and had read and filed some of the correspondence, but when he asked me if they had discussed evolution, religion, pedagogy, truth, reality—in other words, if they had mirrored the criticisms in the editorial—I simply couldn't answer. Ultimately, the decision was made behind closed doors and came as a surprise to everyone. I don't know what department secretaries were like in Sweden, but his inflated view of my role was somewhat amusing.

"There is a pull toward agnosticism among the students that worries me," Dr. Fernandes continued. "A weak foundation in scientific thinking and, in my opinion, a fair amount of intellectual laziness."

That felt a little unkind. After all, he hadn't been with us very long.

"Perhaps there is a more rigorous style of education in Sweden," I offered.

He sat back with his coffee, silent for a moment. The halls began to thrum with activity, students going to classes and departments opening their doors. One of our new faculty arrived and commented on the editorial as well, saying he had noticed it but thought it was laughable and poorly written. After a brief exchange with him that left Dr. Fernandes unimpressed, he asked, "Why is this argument in the paper? Why such a call to ignorance now? There's nothing timely about it that I can see."

"It does seem rather academic for the general public," I said.

He nodded. "Something is happening here. Something is happening." He kept repeating it, convincing himself. I couldn't have known what he meant. I might have thought he was overreacting.

He asked me to schedule a department meeting. Then he went into his office and stayed there for several hours, refusing any calls. Around midmorning, he came to me with some roughly handwritten paragraphs and asked me to type them. It was a rebuttal to Smith's editorial, giving short shrift to his philosophical argument, which he called "an empty and bold attempt to deny reality." He said that apparently, these days, any fool could claim that black was white and up was down and call himself a doctor. I wondered if we ought to get approval from the college, as he was speaking on behalf of our department, but it wasn't my place to get involved in that. He had the right to publish whatever he wanted. He was defending the discipline, which was ultimately good for everyone. While I worked on getting his letter to the newspaper, Dr. Fernandes found out more about Robert Smith and his organization. These findings disturbed him even more. Hovering over my desk again, he said Smith was dangerously influential, with grand political ambitions, and this would be a disaster not only for science but for all of modern society.

The letter appeared the next day, and to my surprise, it caused an immediate controversy. I don't know that there was really an order to the incidents. It felt more like the whole ceiling coming down than a series of leaks. Maybe it began with the phones ringing. I took the first angry call as some sort of prank or wrong number. But they kept coming, threats of punishment so incommensurate with the supposed offense that many of us would gather around and laugh in disbelief. After a while, we had to screen the calls and turn over the tapes from our answering machines to the campus police. The letters were easier to sort through. I recruited a student to help me catalogue them, but she began to have nightmares and had to stop.

Instead of coming to our defense, the college reprimanded Dr. Fernandes for publishing the letter without approval. He and I were both called in to Dr. Elam's office. For a few terrible years I had served Dr. Elam when he headed the biology department. How he made it to the dean's office was a mystery to me, but I was glad to be rid of him. He complained that Dr. Fernandes had not gone through the proper channels. He said these were not the passions they had hired him for.

I was outraged. "I take full responsibility for this," I said.

"Yes, you should have known better," Dr. Elam agreed.

"It doesn't matter," Dr. Fernandes said. "Even if she had advised me to take the proper channels, I wouldn't have complied."

This was maddening to Dr. Elam. His little mouth puckered and he had nothing to say.

The following week, six students, two boys and four girls, stormed our office to confront Dr. Fernandes. I tried to get them to identify themselves, but they would only say that they were concerned members of the campus community. They wanted to ask Dr. Fernandes some questions about his editorial. Hearing the commotion, Dr. Fernandes came out of his office and offered to speak with them in the conference room, where there was more space and they could talk freely.

They refused to move, beginning their interrogation on the spot. One of the boys, with an intensely serious face and a silly haircut, claimed that everything Dr. Fernandes had said about religion could also apply to science. "In fact, isn't science just another belief system?" he asked.

Dr. Fernandes answered the question without hesitation, not that he had much choice. "Science is a process for investigating reality, based on evidence."

I wondered if he should have just hidden in his office. Everything he said prompted a new question, and it seemed we would never get rid of them. They asked him to define reality and he said, "Reality is everything that exists in the material world." What about the spiritual world, they wanted to know, and he said that wasn't the realm of science, unless it materialized as part of the natural and physical world, in which case the evidence would be evaluated scientifically. His answers were starting to frustrate them. They asked him why he insisted on lying to students and he said, laughing, "I'm not the one lying to you."

This they took as the highest order of insult. They all started shouting at once, and the escalating scene attracted a larger crowd, until there was no more space in the office. Soon, the small group of protesters was surrounded by students and faculty who had spilled out from the classrooms and offices on our floor. I could see the situation getting out of hand, and called security to come and help clear the office, before someone got hurt. Perhaps it made things worse. The disrupters were forcefully taken out, and later used their removal as a reason to claim persecution.

During a relatively quiet moment afterward, Dr. Fernandes tried to apologize to me. I didn't allow him to continue. It wasn't only that I felt loyal to him. I could easily be disloyal if that was what I deeply felt, but in this public and volatile situation, I felt only pride. It would not have occurred to me to temper or discourage him. I sent him away brusquely, and after that it was always to be taken for granted that I was on his side.

*

In the midst of all this, he had been guarded about his wife, Kitty. I didn't meet her but by chance one morning in September, at the farmer's market. Every Saturday, I arrived before dawn to watch the pastel sunrise mist the aisles while the vendors set up their stalls. At the market, I was part of this constant motion of light and sound and people and bounty and voices, experiencing all the layers of life, all of its richness, through all my senses. I was happy there.

I recognized her around midmorning, standing by the flower stall with a handkerchief to her nose. She loved flowers, obviously, but perhaps her constitution did not allow her to enjoy them. She turned away, sneezing repeatedly, and when she was finished, she straightened her posture with a slightly panicked expression. Her dark eyes shimmered with tears. She wiped them dry as she walked down the aisle, away from the flowers. I wanted her to see me, to recognize me in return, but of course she had no reason to know what I looked like.

I caught up with her at one of the pastry stalls and touched her arm to get her attention. She turned around, and before I finished introducing myself, she grabbed my hand and cried, "It's you. I know who you are."

I blushed, wondering how she could have identified me so quickly. I knew her face well from the photograph on his desk. I couldn't quite believe I was seeing her now in the flesh, and my disbelief caused me to cackle. Kitty smiled. "I want you to come for dinner one day. I keep telling Joseph to bring me your number but he forgets."

"He's dealing with so many important matters," I said, but I didn't think she had understood our situation. I was sure Dr. Fernandes was not eager to change the nature of our relationship.

She let go of my hand and reached into her bag. "I don't have a pen," she said. As she searched she seemed suddenly distracted. Her hand moved protectively to her belly, and I noticed then, with her dress pressed against her abdomen, that she was pregnant. I was just as distracted by her gesture, by her slender fingers and her nails trimmed all the way down to the fingertips.

"Are you all right?" I asked.

"I can't find a pen," she said, recovering. "Would you write your number down for me?"

I rummaged in my purse for a pen and the notepad where I made my shopping list. I wrote down my phone number, ripped off the paper, and gave it to her.

"I know how well you look after my husband," she said, "I hope you're happy with him."

"I feel very lucky to work with him. I say so all the time."

I don't know if she heard me. Whereas she'd looked bright and energetic at the beginning of our interaction, now she seemed exhausted and empty. "I should let you go," I said.

She again said she would have me over for dinner, and I said I would wait eagerly for her invitation. I watched her weave through the crowd and disappear.

On Monday, it was Dr. Fernandes who first mentioned my encounter with his wife. "You saw Kitty at the market," he said.

"Yes, by the flower stand."

"I thought it was pastries."

"Yes, it was the pastries. And you're . . . she's pregnant?" I asked.

He smiled a little. "Yes, I guess she's showing a bit."

"What good news."

With some hesitation, he told me that she had been pregnant before. I knew they had no children, but still, it took me a moment to understand what he was trying to tell me. By the time it dawned on me, I was embarrassed and didn't know how to react. I stumbled and said, "I'll keep her in my prayers." It sounded entirely false. I was not an avid atheist, like him, but I hadn't prayed in years.

"How did she look to you?" he asked.

"I'm sorry?"

Then he was the one who appeared embarrassed. He put his hand up and said, "Never mind."

*

The students who had been removed from our office circulated a petition demanding an apology from Dr. Fernandes. They gathered a hundred signatures and delivered the petition to Dr. Elam's office. Naturally, Dr. Fernandes refused to issue an apology, and the college decided to hold a community meeting about the controversy, a misstep on their part. Dr. Fernandes had managed to galvanize some support among the students and faculty, and the group that had invaded our office that day was largely outnumbered. The meeting only highlighted the absurdity of the situation. When Dr. Fernandes was invited to speak, he said, "A powerful group of religious ideologues is convincing our young people that there is no provable reality, that reality is a matter of opinion. Surely, our college would want to dispute that notion." One of the agitators tried to heckle him during the speech, but was quickly silenced by the audience. One thing was clear. Dr. Fernandes could not be easily deterred.

Yet, despite being in the minority, the agitators didn't give up. They kept circulating their petitions and making their case. They began disrupting classes, staging demonstrations, and putting flyers up around the campus. They didn't come back into our office, but they did often gather in the lobby, where their amplified voices made them sound much more numerous than they were. Most troubling was that their numbers did grow, not by many, but enough to make us wonder if there wasn't a silent majority of them. The students on our side were not as passionate.

Even Dr. Fernandes seemed worn down by the constant activity, but he had other problems. Only a few weeks after I saw Kitty at the market, he called me from the hospital to tell me that she had lost the baby and that he would be out for a few days. He gave me explicit directions about whom to inform, and said they didn't want any visitors. I spent some time ordering flowers and almost had them delivered, until I remembered her sneezing by the flower stall at the market. I canceled the order and chose a simple card instead, which I circulated within our department and mailed to their home.

When he returned, he was no different than before. I saw people hesitating, wondering if they should offer their condolences, but he managed to discourage us without saying a word. There was no time to mourn anyway. Keeping our department alive was a consuming battle, and after a while, Kitty and her lost pregnancy were all but forgotten, though I thought about her often. Every time I saw her picture in his office, I felt unsatisfied. I wanted to inquire about her, or send her a note. It seemed wrong to treat her loss with so much austerity, but the opportunity to bring it up didn't present itself.

*

Eventually, some of the disruption fell away, or else we got used to a certain level of conflict and moved on. By November, we were beginning to function more smoothly. Midterm exams were given, grades were entered, and everyone—the students, professors, administrators, and staff—settled into their roles.

Dr. Fernandes was invited to give a talk at an important conference and would be away for two days. He told me Kitty would not be going with him. He asked if she could call on me. She had been wanting to invite me ever since she'd met me at the market. He thought this would be a good time.

She called me Saturday morning and invited me over for lunch. Before I left, I took a pill for palpitations. I don't socialize easily and worried that I wouldn't say the right things. The medicine stops my thoughts from racing, makes me better able to listen and respond in situations that would otherwise turn me mute. Indeed, I was very calm as I walked among the willows and cherry trees to the faculty apartments, sensing the whole world to be this tranquil. The leaves fluttered against a chalky gray sky. I carried a bottle of wine as a gift.

I had been to the faculty apartments often over the years, to make deliveries and occasionally help set up a luncheon or cocktail reception. They were lovely old dusty apartments. To me the halls smelled like sweet pipe tobacco. Outside of Dr. Fernandes's apartment, on the third floor, there was a tall cathedral window looking out to the university clock tower. I paused by the window, thinking of the first time I saw this campus when I was twenty years old. I had thought if I could make a home here, my luck would be unsurpassed.

Kitty opened the door before I had a chance to knock. I turned awkwardly, holding the wine bottle up in the air. She took it from me and invited me into the living room, treating me as if I were a frequent guest in her home. She looked much healthier than I expected. The only possible indications of her grief were her black dress and black cardigan.

She set the wine bottle on the coffee table. Mismatched furniture, arranged around a worn Persian rug, cluttered the living room. The walls were lined with overfilled bookshelves. In a corner nook, two leather armchairs flanked an antique end table. I imagined a couple growing old in those chairs, reading side by side when there is nothing left to talk about. It was a sharp contrast to my apartment, which was spare and sunlit, with golden walls and three large, square rooms. I could easily account for the few things I owned. I never had people over.

I accompanied her to the kitchen, where something was simmering on the stove and a pan of dough balls sat readied to go in the oven. We talked about nothing of consequence until the air was thick with the sweet smell of butter rolls. She filled two bowls with a thick beef stew and sat us down at a small table by a window that looked out to the courtyard. I broke open a warm roll and let a bite of it melt on my tongue. I rarely have more than a cup of soup for lunch, but in front of Kitty I could not seem to stop eating. She ate slowly and seized an opportunity to talk more openly.

"I wanted to thank you for the card you sent. People sent me chocolates and stuffed toys. Does that seem strange to you? What would I want with a stuffed toy? Why would I eat a chocolate after losing my baby?"

I dropped my spoon and drank some water, thankful that I hadn't sent her a stuffed toy or chocolates. "How are you now?" I asked.

Her left hand was strangling her napkin. I reached for another roll.

"My uterus is misshapen. The baby . . ." she paused and corrected herself, "the fetus can't get enough oxygen. It suffocates in my womb. My womb is a death chamber. That's what the nurse said to me."

I doubted a nurse would say such a thing. Those had to be Kitty's words.

"She was right," Kitty said. "I had to accept that she was right. It kept happening, always at twenty weeks. I thought it was Sweden, the cold, the water, the doctors. Joseph didn't want to come home, but I was unbearable."

I had not expected her to be so frank. This spilling-forth of her marital conflicts put me in an awkward position.

"I thought it would be different here, but it isn't. I was born this way. My body's no good for having babies."

These difficult thoughts tumbled out of her one after the other, as if she had no control over their release. "I'm so sorry," I said.

"I wanted to have my uterus cut out. I mean, what's the point of keeping it? But they would only tie my tubes."

"It's less invasive," I said.

"See, Joseph was going to have a vasectomy when we were in Sweden. But I kept thinking, what if he could still be a father, with someone else? A Swedish woman! Men can become fathers at any age."

I took a deep breath. "I'm sure he wouldn't want that."

She nudged her bowl, still half filled with stew, away from her. "I've made you uncomfortable. Joseph says I should let people get to know me before I start talking about his balls."

I coughed into my napkin, and when I was finished I could not help laughing, and Kitty also began to laugh, to quake with laughter, at one point covering her face. I was moved by the motion of her hands, a swift caress of her cheeks as her laughter subsided and she revealed herself again, her eyes still bright and playful. I saw her as a husband might see her, an incarnation of pure joy.

After lunch, we went back into the living room, where she eyed the bottle of wine on the coffee table. She picked it up and studied the label. "I forgot all about this," she said. She went back into the kitchen and returned with two crystal glasses and a corkscrew. She knelt down, freed the cork, and poured wine into our glasses. There was an ashtray on the coffee table. I took out my cigarette case.

"You don't mind?" I asked.

"Of course not," she said.

She watched me light my cigarette.

"Joseph tells me you're not married."

"It's true. I've never been married."

"May I ask why?"

"I missed the opportunity, I suppose." I didn't feel like telling her that I'd had a chance once, when I first came to work at the college. He was a doctoral student and would have been a good husband, kind and devoted, but hard as I tried I could not love him. After some time, he went away, and that was for the best.

"I wanted to buy you a gift," Kitty said. "But Joseph couldn't tell me what you would have liked."

"A gift? Why?"

"To thank you. For standing by him. It all sounds very difficult and I couldn't help him. I couldn't listen."

I shook my head. "You are both very hard on yourselves."

She smiled. "He admires you. He said maybe in another life, you would have been a scientist yourself."

"Oh, good God, no. He's wrong about that."

"But someone in your own right."

I thought this was strange. "I am someone in my own right, Kitty. So are you."

She demurred, but I could see she wasn't convinced.

"Tell me what you would like to do with your life now," I said. "Before you were married, what did you want for yourself?"

"I wanted to be a mother."

"What else? There must have been something else."

She didn't take long to think. "No. There was nothing. I wanted to be a dancer once, but I wasn't any good."

I gave up, realizing she had not invited me here to advise her.

"What about you?" she asked. "I don't believe it was your dream to become a department secretary." This didn't offend me. I was pleased to see this spark in her.

"All I ever wanted was to be able to stand on my own two feet. But for a while, I studied painting."

Kitty was shocked. "Why did you stop?"

I didn't have a satisfactory answer. Over time, I might have become good enough to call myself a painter, but I didn't like being so hungry. "It was expensive. I didn't want the struggle."

She looked disappointed. I took out another cigarette. "May I have one of those?" she asked.

I passed her my pack and lit her cigarette for her. She was tentative, but this was not her first time smoking. She stood up, walking back and forth with the cigarette between her fingers as if she were trying out another identity. All I could see now was a dancer. She stopped in front of a gold-framed mirror on the wall next to the sofa where I was sitting. She watched herself inhale, and then she parted her lips, letting the long ribbons of smoke unfurl and drift away. For the first time in many years, I had a desire to paint.

We kept on drinking and smoking. She told me she'd grown up in a strict Catholic household, one of six siblings. She was terrified all her life of hellfire and purgatory, but she had loved being part of a large family. Eloping with Joseph had been her one great rebellion. For her it was like coming out of a dark cellar into the sunlight. No one had ever told her the truth before. When he asked her to marry him, she said she wanted to have many children, and he said he had nothing against children. She was happy to remember this. Her cheeks were flushed and she became animated. Suddenly, she glided to one of the bookshelves and grabbed an old book. I didn't know what she was up to until she stood in front of the coffee table and asked me if I knew Walt Whitman.

I swallowed some dread. "'Oh Captain, My Captain'?"

She laughed. "No, this one. It will remind you of Joseph." She read the title, "When I Heard the Learn'd Astronomer," and recited the poem in a clear voice.

When I heard the learn'd astronomer;
When the proofs, the figures, were ranged in columns before me;
When I was shown the charts and the diagrams, to add, divide, and measure them;
When I, sitting, heard the astronomer, where he
lectured with much applause in the lecture-room,
How soon, unaccountable, I became tired and sick;
Till rising and gliding out, I wander'd off by myself,
In the mystical moist night-air, and from time to time,
Look'd up in perfect silence at the stars.

I couldn't remember the last time I'd listened to a poem. At first, I gathered the poet could not understand the astronomer's lecture and walked out, but in spite of that, or because of it, he was able to look in amazement at the stars in the night sky. I would have liked to hear the poem again. I didn't understand the use of the word *unaccountable*, and I don't think he actually said he didn't understand the lecture, but that he felt sick and tired, so perhaps he did comprehend it, more than he wanted to, and his body repelled it, rejected knowledge in favor of awe, insisting on an incomprehensible universe.

After she read the poem, Kitty didn't look up from the book. Just as quickly as her mood had lifted, it fell again. I told her that I enjoyed the poem, that it did remind me, in a way, of Dr. Fernandes, but she kept holding the book, staring into it.

"It's not that I can't be something else. But I wanted to give birth. I wanted to be a part of the wonder."

My heart broke for her, even if I didn't understand this compulsion. "You already are, Kitty." She herself couldn't see that her vitality, even in this state, was breathtaking.

She tried to smile. "You're very kind."

I prepared to leave. It was late in the afternoon, and Joseph would be back in a few hours. She walked me to the door and we said good-bye, but she held on to my hand. She took a deep breath and said, quietly, "Joseph doesn't tell me how he feels. He only tells me what he thinks." This, I could see, was what she had been waiting all afternoon to tell me. I was grateful that she'd found her courage.

"Maybe he doesn't have the words, Kitty."

She nodded, and kissed me on the cheek. It had been a long time since I'd felt anyone's lips press into my skin, but somehow it was familiar enough. I wanted to return the gesture somehow, but all I could do was smile and take my leave.

*

On Monday, Dr. Fernandes thanked me for spending time with Kitty. He himself looked exhausted, beleaguered by the battles of his private and professional life. I didn't want to be thanked for spending time with Kitty, any more than I wanted him to apologize for writing his editorial. On that day, after he went into his office and closed the door, I remember feeling a profound sadness that made my skin hurt. There was no relief from it, all the more so because I didn't know what had caused it.

Then Kitty appeared without warning, only a few days later. She slipped into the department while I was typing and appeared at my desk without a sound, like a ghost. I looked up, startled. She looked sick and disheveled, and was clutching some kind of parcel in her hand, tightly. I went to her right away, and when I was in front of her she fell forward into my arms and wept like a small child. Dr. Fernandes was in a meeting. I couldn't phone him and console her at the same time, but I didn't want anyone else to see her like this. I guided her into her husband's office and sat her in a chair. I knelt down and tried to get her to look at me, but she kept dropping her head. Tears from her eyes fell onto the parcel on her lap. "What happened, Kitty?"

I could see her struggling to speak. A few words came out in gasps, nothing I could understand. I took the parcel away, a thick brown envelope that bulged at the bottom, addressed to their home. There was no return address. I unwrapped her hand from my wrist. "I'll only be a minute, Kitty," and as quickly as I could I ran to my desk and called the conference room. I told Dr. Fernandes to come back, that it was urgent, and hung up the phone. I dropped the parcel and went to get a glass of water for Kitty.

I returned to her and held the glass of water to her lips, cradling the back of her head while she drank. She was exhausted, but she cried again when she saw him at the door. I stepped away and let him come. He encapsulated her, swallowed her up in his arms and allowed her, for as long as she wanted it, to disappear. I didn't realize, until that moment, that I'd never seen them together.

It was nearly the end of the work day. I left them alone and emptied the contents of the parcel onto my desk. There were at least twenty items inside, handwritten and typed letters, pamphlets, and one glossy, professionally bound booklet with a picture of a pregnant woman on the cover. It was called *Understanding Fertility*, but it was all about the three levels of "barrenness"—inability to conceive, miscarriage, and stillbirth—and their causes. Miscarriages, for example, could be caused by heresy and demonic possession, from which a woman who is given to unholiness turns her womb into a death chamber.

Someone had carefully curated this package, included psalm cards and brochures and a stack of letters, all of which were signed by people who saw no crime in sharing God's love with a grieving woman. Kitty had opened all of the letters, had read about her body, soul, and marriage, about her sins and those of her husband. The price of the cure was surrender. It must have sounded easy after a while.

The sun went down and the office fell dark. I turned on the desk lamp and waited for Dr. Fernandes to come out and tell me to go home. I began to hear Kitty's muffled voice through the wall, and his, less frequently. As they talked, I started thinking about the things no one knew about me anymore. I was an orphan, but it wasn't that I'd never known love. I loved very fiercely, and for that I was punished in every way imaginable. Perhaps I had not turned out like my caretakers, as I vowed not to, but still, sometimes, I think they did win.

I don't know how long it was before he opened and closed his door softly. He came to my desk and stared at the remnants scattered across it. He had aged over the past few months. The lines on his face had hardened, but now, as he watched me gather up the materials and place them back in the envelope, he looked young again, unconfident, confounded. He wasn't capable of understanding this. He asked me what they wanted. I looked up at him, and as gently as I could, I said, "They want to save her."

I put the envelope in my drawer. I would make copies and hand them to someone when it mattered. Dr. Fernandes never would ask to see it. Even he had limits to what he wanted to know, and I thought foolishly that it wasn't necessary for him to understand, that I could understand it for him, and Kitty could understand it, but we didn't need to impart our understanding to him. I know now that was a mistake.

We sat together, mostly in silence. Kitty had fallen asleep as they talked. He wanted her to rest a little longer before he took her home.

After a while, he told me what Kitty had said. It wasn't the package that upset her. She said she had been fine when she left the apartment. She was coming to show it to him, and find out what he wanted to do about it.

I thought something must have happened to her on the way. Maybe she was being followed, or saw one of the flyers that had been posted around campus a few weeks back. But it was nothing like that. He explained that as she got closer, she thought about turning back and couldn't decide. She stood outside the building for a long time, and this was when she became distraught. When something that should have been easy, showing her husband a violation of their private matters, became difficult.

He rubbed tears from his eyes. "When Kitty lost the baby," he said, "it was a relief to be here. To have this fight. Even if Kitty was alone. Even if she had nothing. I thought it would hurt her more if she knew how much I wanted our children to be born."

I reached across and took his hand. "You won't leave her alone again," I said. I would make sure of it. It was important to me that they not lose each other. I told him how I'd loved a girl like Kitty once. I lost her, and I never recovered.

*

There were months after that, in which I loved and looked after them as well as I could, but still they left me. Joseph gave talks about a war brewing, a war of ideas that we couldn't afford to lose. He said it was science, not myth, that could best serve our need for revelation. He worked that part out with Kitty. She wanted him to inspire people, not frighten them. I remember hoping it would never go beyond a war of ideas. We weren't ready for anything else.

The night my telephone rang, I was half-awake, peripherally aware of the physical world, but I knew something terrible had happened. I thought if I didn't answer it, if it stopped ringing, then reality too would recede into the darkness. But it didn't stop ringing. As soon as Dr. Elam started talking, I understood that I was alone again. He told me that Joseph was dead, that his car had blown up on the street where they lived. He had left Kitty out of the story, but of course she was with him in the car, and was also gone.

I was taken to the office, where Dr. Elam had a list of tasks for me. I walked away from him. He followed me and watched from the doorway as I took the photograph of Kitty and slipped it into my bag. I closed my eyes, but there was nothing, no memories or thoughts or voices. Only silence. Only stillness. I could have stayed there forever, but Dr. Elam demanded my attention. He had already decided to shut our department down, hoping it would stop the barbarians at the gate. It would not.

I opened my eyes, and in the shock of light I turned to him and said, "I'm ready."

AL HALEY

Five Snapshots of Jarrell, Texas, May 27, 1997

1 - Safe Place

They are a Baptist family.
Dad a blue-suited deacon.
Mom helps with the youth
group. Their three girls
wearing purity rings
and their quiet beauty
on this day when school's out,
all of five work down
at the family hardware store.

Intuition. Air electric,
leaden by late afternoon
when the alarm sounds.
One of them (the father?)
scrawls a sign and leaves it
swinging on the door.

GONE HOME.
TORNADO.

Bins of nails, rolls
of wallpaper.
Step ladders,
coiled garden hoses.

Brackets, fasteners,
and shiny toasters.

Expecting any minute
they'll be back.

2 - Double Creek Estates Subdivision, 5 p.m. CDT

You can walk across the acreage
where the houses stood one hour ago,
each fronted by a brick-brown
summer lawn.

You can imagine them going up
in that great swirled funnel.
Or you can review video taken
by a camera glued to someone's eye
that ten seconds in begins shaking
itself into obscurity.

For now let us sit down and write
an incomprehensible caption:

No wood, no walls, no tiles,
no doors, no windows.
No furniture, no appliances,
no toys, no pets.

No people.

You look at 12 slab foundations,
and imagine a grandmother in the kitchen
scraping off dinner plates over the trash can.

With a paper towel she wipes them clean.
She sighs. Then she plunges her arms
up to elbows in the sink full of suds.

3 - Landing

Day drains into night as the girls run
and hunker in the beige bathtub.
Howling, 200 mph wind blur.
Baptized in sound, grit, and F5 debris.
They feel the moment of lift-off but cannot
see, hear, live because already they are
bereft of breath, moved on to another world.

"Look!" One of them thrusts out a finger.
Parents, neighbors, friends stroll below
in fresh mown hay. Cows chew cuds,
edge up to a clear tank. Horse tails switch,
sheep are white puffs in green inverted sky.

Down,
down,
down,
thump.

Shaking like leaves at the end of a limb,
they climb out, holding hands,
blinking away the dust of what was.

Back at the scene. A trio of copper pipes
pokes through scoured concrete.

4 - Theodicy

Sky twists and whips and swallows. Of zero consequence
dollars in the bank or your résumé or one's gentle or evil nature,
and you can't find a piece of paper to change how you're wheat
bending in the field, and if the lord of the harvest swinging
the golden scythe sneezes, the blade droops, it is done.
Who fashions the vile black funnel? Who throws Job's cattle
into the sky and drops them with hailstones another lifetime away?
What being allows the tilting back of walls, the ripping
of roofs, the flinging aside of photos and treasured memories?
Who is watching when a diamond ring of a 30-year marriage is spit
out like a watermelon seed beneath the shady oaks in the park?

You have questions, but no answers, just 27 bodies, young, old,
in-between, for your community to stand over, weep and pray,
commit tomorrow to the relentlessly unsentimental Texas clay.

5 - Services

On Sunday voices will rise
heavenward, carrying the best
of them, which they dutifully
affirm, is preordained to be
taken from this world
and joined to the unseen,
the place of the eternal note,
the one their tongues, quaking
throats never quite reach.

Afterwards sober, black garbed,
watch them file out. The flowers alongside the five caskets were so lovely.
Many sent from around the nation.
Pinks, yellows, whites, and blues
intended to garnish dry hearts.

Of course, it is cliché this last
thing they'll choose to do. Looking
up at blue sky devoid of even
a wisp 72 hours after the devil
dropped down to claim his due.

Then the ride home, no talking,
only silent acceptance of facts
bearing down upon God's country
where roads run painfully straight.
Narrow blacktop, fields blurring
past. Soon the road will become
dirt, lead to driveway, porch step.

A door with a curtained window
in it. Entrance awaiting the key,
thin piece of metal that has been
designed to always master the lock.

OCTAVIO QUINTANILLA

God's Hands

God has tiny hands.
He feeds hummingbirds, feeds gnats.

No, God has gigantic hands.
He feeds dictators, feeds egomaniacs.

I'm not really sure about the size
of God's hands.

I've only heard stories.

One day, after work, I saw Him.
He was in the sun descending, leaving us.
It was this descent that almost made me tear up.

Then I felt silly for thinking the sun closing shop
for the day had anything to do with God.

I looked for it the next day, and there it was,
the sun descending, covering its face with billboards.

I didn't think it was God this time.
I saw the sun devoured by the trees.

That was all.

Which reminds me about the storm
that came a few days later,
decapitating trees,
burying our cars under branches, hail
breaking our bedroom windows.

Afterwards, neighbors huddled
on their porches to watch
someone's socks speed down
the street, into the gutter.

Someone lost their socks, I heard a woman say.

They, standing around, watching
the rain lose its breath, must also know
that God has tiny hands,
and not the big hands I thought he had.

There He goes again, squeezing the sun
between His thumb and index finger,
dropping it an inch right above
the horizon.

RICH LEVY

A Jew at the Airport

. . . he had little love left for nature. It gave nothing to a Jew.
—Bernard Malamud, *The Assistant*

A nun walks ahead of me
through the crowded terminal,

and in spite of the zig-zags of travelers
who seem to want to get somewhere
or are dreading it,

there's a Wyoming of spiritual space
around her, a DMZ of aloneness. She stops
to look at her ticket, and I can
see in her chalk smile

a hawk pasted on a white sky,
and below it, a valley scooped
out of scumbled granite.

As in most desert landscapes,
the mountains look bruised,
which begs the question,

why are biblical spaces invariably arid,
methodical, vast.

Not so my inner life, a street
of shops selling chicken, bread, sheet music,
foundation garments, Chinese food.
There's a synagogue on the corner,

and people walking yelling weeping grinning,
a baby asleep in a buggy,

an old man hobbling down
the center of the sidewalk, a boy with
a book under his arm, thinking of a girl and the plush
of her skin and the mystery of the book,

and a candy store, in which the boy
buys a rope of licorice
black as a hawk's eye.

But my nun's solitariness is clean,
paleolithic, yielding one or two artifacts,
but only through a perpetual sifting.

And then she veers to her gate,
and it's as if she's gone from the earth.

Next to me, a *Hasid's*
on his cell phone—possibly

a diamond merchant—
and I feel the weight of years and loves and things
dragging behind me and, Jew that I am,
am not unhappy about it,

while some part of me floats
down the concourse
and follows her.

RICH LEVY

Sinful

The guilty are so boring, the priests
must snooze in their confessionals

after years of people lining up to *mea culpa*
about the rotten things they've done. It's like

sorting someone's laundry—greasy collars,
shit-streaked underwear—just thinking about it

makes you tired. Of course, it would be easier
not to do rotten things, but how do you stop

the rock from breaking the window
once it's thrown? And if someone held Cain's arm,

or Cain had some self-restraint, think
of how storytellers and Sunday school teachers

would suffer. When I did something
that hurt my friend in a big public way,

in writing, with my name at the bottom,
I didn't kill her, but it felt like it,

with one humiliation heaped on another.
Then it's a dog pile of gang bangers,

and the top jerk's pate is pink with shame,
which makes him easier to pick out

of our conscience's line-up later,
when we're cooler headed. And when

we've outed our rotten selves, then
finally we have the *cojones* to admit

we shot the paper clip at that man,
stole balloons from the drug store,

broke the neighbor's basement window,
didn't stick up for a pal in the schoolyard,
lied to one girl and another about exclusivity,
or wrote the deadly lines that went too far

and pummeled a friend. Now instead of mumbling
Hail Marys, I go around being annoyingly nice

to children and colleagues and some strangers even,
holding doors and helping them to unload

their cars and listening to their stories. I try
not to react. Not this week. Not today. Not now.

STEVE WEATHERS

Witnesses

It didn't happen that way, not the way they said—not even the way I said the first times I told it. There was wheat, to be sure. But that afternoon it awoke, spoke, throbbed. There were cattle to be fed, true. And they were fed. But the black angus, their shifting anatomical patches bronzed by the declining sun, studied your eyes. Mute, the beasts sampled your soul ruminatively, sensing, Dee, that you would rise to the challenge and pass the supreme test—supremely. Whiskered heads of grain nodded.

The intimation came swiftly, contracting bowels, shriveling womb. The as-yet-inchoate message tightened into a fist, you would explain, and struck you forcibly in the abdomen. Spiritual momentum palpable, an intervention gathering, you suddenly knew: the family would soon be taken, winged away from the earth, so that you might be free to begin your itinerant ministry, wandering the world in the last apocalyptic era, witnessing to the vainly imaginative nations.

You read the landscape. *This wheat is good.* As a witness went about testifying to the secularized governments of a Christ-denying planet, it might be necessary that she flee to the wilderness for refuge, as did Elijah in days of old, and there find sustenance from God's good earth. It might well be she'd need to pluck this grain by hand, winnow it in her palms, as did our blessed Lord's disciples on one occasion, and consume it raw. So it was good, infinitely good, that there was wheat.

Keith loaded the boys in his pickup while you, solo, proceeded in your white Chevrolet. A song, maybe, upon leaving the fields? A hymn of self-renunciation, Dee? *Must Jesus Bear the Cross Alone?* Perhaps not. Grim and silent certainty, then, as you drove into the city limits, ordered at the Burger Barn, and sat at table with these walking dead. You scavenged half-heartedly among impotent fries.

In telling contrast, the marked souls consumed their last meal with the oblivious delight of death row's mentally deficient. Keith extending his elbows enthusiastically, throttling squeeze-bottle condiments; the boys begging in vain for quarters to play dangerously risqué arcade machines; Aaron drooling, his grin eliciting answering smiles from the elderly at surrounding tables—it might have been a normal evening in Tyler. But the dry hiss of bats insinuated itself. A dark mandate hovered above the café table. You scanned the walls' cheap paneling for death-writ inscriptions, for the finger bone of heaven, and, though none appeared, your still-settling conviction now grounded itself decisively, foundationally: *Be it unto me according to Thy word.* A cornerstone dropped. You steeled yourself for the catastrophic auto collision that would shortly come.

As you rumbled over the metallic cattle guard, however, there could be no mistaking the telltale headlights of Keith's farm truck sweeping the yard behind you. He and his sons had returned safely. You mouthed the Texas license plate numerals to be sure. No wreck. As the four males noisily dismounted from the cab, Keith mildly chastising one boy about his shoes, you observed them briefly, then looked heavenward. They'd not been taken. Standing beneath an ebon expanse peppered with frigid cinders of blue, you shaped muted words that may well have been delivered by benevolent angels, if such beings exist: "I was wrong." The phrase sat awkwardly on a tongue accustomed to triumphant declamation. "I guess I was wrong." How did this good confession later fail you, Dee, as you tiptoed along the smoking, fraying tightrope, the overtaxed strand stretched high above the hungry conflagration?

Maybe they weren't benevolent angels after all. It's so hard to tell. Subtle, crafty, the arch-tempter. His messengers of doubt find ways to undercut faith. They slave tirelessly to lure even consecrated lips into syllables of blankest incertitude.

The French fries you'd forced down did not rest well. Around midnight, souring dyspepsia drove you into the bathroom. But your hand drooped atop the untouched light switch, for in the translucent rectangle of the full-length window, somewhere just beyond the new blinds your good Keith had recently installed, a human figure reared monstrously, portentously. About his knees a quadruped or misshapen dwarf frolicked, a junior fiend. Nausea now forgotten, you launched into ejaculatory prayer ("O great God, our protector and shield, hurl this devil from my property lines, banish him from . . .") with unblinking eyes fixed upon the enemy. The factotum imp tried the window latch—was repulsed by the spiritual force field you'd hurriedly generated—then made for the master bedroom windows on the south side of the house. You intensified your petitions. The dark shadow of the Black Man remained an instant, dwindled to charred twigs, then vanished.

When you returned to Keith's slumbering side, all portals, thanks be to the Omnipotent, had proven secure.

Friday dawned with new mercies, one would assume, the black-bordered presentiments of the preceding day now fading, all but forgotten, essentially dismissed. There was housework to be done, for one thing, and there were the endless homeschool assignments to be enforced.

As Joshua's fragile head tilted obediently above his Bible lesson—a quiz would follow after lunch—and as Luke felt his way phonetically through his primer, Aaron, the toddler, trundled about the house, intent on his own infantile pleasures. For you, Dee, vacuuming soothed any troubling residual memories from yesterday. The rhythmic push and pull of a dead weight lulled the spirit.

"What are you doing, boy?"

Aaron had for some time, it seems, been standing behind the Franklin stove, holding and hiding some contraband.

"What you got there?"

In the wholesome buttery yellow of morning, the child lifted his forbidden prize, gripped in the puny fist of human rebellion: a miniature spear, secretly removed from his two brothers' toy chest. The toddler directed a mischievous but inquisitive look at his mother's petrified countenance.

Mammoths turn up frozen, it is said, with fresh green foodstuff still pulpy in their masticating jaws. When an Ice Age descends, it wastes no time. The tubular blood solidifies instantaneously. The eyes, frost-glazed, remain trained on the last scene, likely of summertime abundance, they innocently recorded. The heart, of course, locks down all entryways and exits. The brain seizes a final snatch of incoming data and dies throttling it.

A *sacrificial blade.*

That Friday morning the old earth with its primitive life forms perished, and you awoke to the new realm, a place of rarified atmosphere, just capable of sustaining terrestrial lungs. Staring at the unspeakable object, Dee, you found your thoughts not so much racing as resting. Here at last was the divine ordinance, served up symbolically, of course, but unquestioningly clear to the discerning: your sons must be removed from the world by your own maternal hand. Before the great end-of-time tribulation, before successive waves of God's wrath should begin lashing the frenzied nations, your children would need to be squared away, shipshape, secure in the beyond. Like Abraham of old, you'd been handed the instrument. Unlike Abraham of old, you did not readily seize the hilt.

Striding purposefully across the living room, wrenching the plastic spear from Aaron's pygmy grip, you replaced it in the toy chest. Perhaps you slammed the lid or weighted it with a book. Likely. That box, however, had now been opened, and the child proved persistent. It was only minutes before God's tiny medium returned with the toy. Once more, beneath the therapeutic drone of the vacuum, you spotted the toddler's repeated peccadillo and pounced. This time you confiscated the spear, burying the abominable item deep in a closet. Your resolve was as yet firm: *I'm not doin' that.*

The Holy Trinity permeates all things, and this encounter with the infinite was no exception. The universe is constructed of triads, we all know, so three signs would have been expected and, somehow, mandatory. The customary knock at a door, the billiard rack of male genitals, the triune blend of a dominant chord, the fruitful nuclear family, the balanced pawn shop mobile, the galloping hoof-beat of a pony—all testify to the essential pyramid from which reality is shaped. Three signs, then, would have been anticipated and, somehow, obligatory.

A bit later that Friday morning, the toddler produced a rock. The back door was often left open so that the child could enjoy the fenced perimeter behind the home; clearly he'd been excavating in open patches of dirt.

By this point, one would assume, you'd given up quibbling over alternative interpretations and refused all parley: *I'm not* doin' *that!* While the curious eyes of Aaron settled on your fear-tight features, you plucked the stone from his dusty palm. Marching out onto the patio, you flung the detestable pellet into the backyard, far over the fence. Aaron's visionary stance was uninterrupted by this pettish display. He coolly observed your return to the room, studying your stiff-necked recalcitrance. Stoning, after all, is a well-attested practice in Scripture, as familiar to you, Dee, as the Feeding of the Five Thousand. Yet you resisted. No matter. There was still time. The child drifted off, apparently leaving you to your housework. But he was, you were shortly to see, still about his Father's business.

Aaron, evolving quickly into a miniature archpriest of the Almighty, pattered back still again. He'd ranged farther this time, had ventured into the bush, maybe in pursuit of the discarded rock. Just as surely, this third sign he now bore was intended to terrify. A startled frog caged in his fist, the child stared meaningfully into your face: *You have rejected my summons a first, yea, a second time. See you do not refuse Him who calls.* The wilting creature, you mentally noted, would die if not quickly released from the boy's grip. You freed it.

Pauses would punctuate the psychiatric interview. In some of these, the placid face would undergo upheaval and crack into shifting platelets, exuding hot tears. In other pauses, the pallid countenance would look to the interviewer with indomitable naiveté, obviously soliciting empathy—indeed, anticipating agreement. And who could be so heartless as to demur? The court-appointed interrogator, off camera, would apparently nod, for the sing-song testimonial would then continue, the subjugated soul once more taking up its burden, making God's inscrutable will intelligible.

Here, then, were the conditions, toothed and unyielding as granite tablets, entailed in your incipient ministry. To be a witness—and not just any witness but one of the two, martyred and revived and translated, one of those two prophetically foretold—a woman must be free of earthly entanglements. Bearing testimony to the nations would leave no room for maternal duties. The parchment had been issued, then, but the stipulation was firm. The boys must go. Only the choice of method remained undecided.

The three options now lay nakedly before you: by blade, by stone, by hand.

Your heart rebelled, of course, scratching at the divine mandate with the fragile fingernails of sentiment. Yes, the boys would be resurrected—of that reality you entertained no misgivings. They would stand, erect and radiant and wholly restored, on that Last Day. But what would you say to Keith? Was he of sufficient spiritual maturity to accede to the necessity of the thing? He might not understand. And what of the Boatrights? Here was another snag. Would vision or voice or trance or dream be granted to inform your parents of the propriety of this act? And what of you, yourself, Dee? Would your feeble hands find adequate strength for the doing of the undoable? It seemed beyond all human capability. Beyond all *human* capability.

This is faith. You must trust. You cannot see the why. It is not for you to inquire. For you, it remains to obey.

Pensive, at last rewarding the interviewer's patient effort to elicit the precise grounds of confirmation that had removed all doubt and enabled you to act, you would recount the intrusion of the horse.

After lunch, Joshua studied silently. Luke still battled his reading assignment and accompanying vocabulary list. Aaron prowled the house, ghosting from room to room, a potential distraction to his brothers. As you sought to shepherd the bothersome toddler back to his own quarters, away from the two students, Luke's toneless iteration of practice sentences registered: "My father owns a black horse." And then on to the next: "God is love."

An undramatic juxtaposition, to be sure, but as you stood listening to the six-year-old's syllabic struggles, Aaron reappeared. He strolled softly alongside. His presence may have momentarily gone unnoticed. Finally you looked down. From the forbidden toy box the child had selected a plastic figurine. He now rose on tiptoe, straining, energetically extending the black horse for your acceptance.

Here, then, was the all-confirming capstone to the earlier signs. Scruples and doubts collapsed beneath the revelatory precision of God. As you would explain to the psychiatric interviewer, the meaning of the black horse was only too clear: death. The boys, you were now convinced, must be spared the Great Tribulation by an intervening hand. The time of the removal remained unspecified as yet, and the three options as to method remained available to your choice. But the brute necessity of the act dropped into a mental slot and settled.

How did you err so grievously—how stray so far from the exegetical mark? How is it possible, Dee, to have cultivated such chummy intimacy with the Apocalypse and yet misconstrue this sign, if, indeed, it was a sign? The book of Revelation, a grab bag of symbols, is uncharacteristically explicit in attaching meanings to the four eschatological horsemen: "And I beheld, and lo a black horse; and he that sat on him had a pair of balances in his hand." Warnings of dearth, of exorbitant commodity prices, then follow. Famine and want, not violent death, sit astride the back of the third charger.

Why, Dee, did you not attempt to starve the boys? Why not mete out their daily rations with a postage scale, slowly draining life and energy from their bodies? You have much to think of, I'm aware, and here I am badgering you with my petty requests. Still, I need to know. Was your local pastor lax in hermeneutical instruction? Or was your own reading of Scripture willfully selective, whim-driven? Help me here, Deanna LaJune. I'm on your side. Really. How did the apocalyptic writer's description of those two witnesses become the all-privileged passage for you, the sole excerpt to command interest?

The black horse, properly discerned, might have purchased precious time—if time has any value in such matters.

You watched from the patio. The lateral glow of the late-afternoon sun suffused the undisturbed tableau. You did not quite realize it, Dee, but it would be the last time in the history of the planet this domestic symmetry would be on display.

In the shop, Keith busied himself with some home-improvement project. The boys did what boys are designed to do. They loitered and asked irrelevant questions, losing the answers as soon as articulated, while working on self-devised, non-utilitarian tasks. Maybe they devised awkward, homemade gifts for the day after tomorrow, Mother's Day. After worship at Victory Assembly, the extended family would likely convene for a meal and the traditional gifting. None of that mattered at present. You watched. The boys' muscular and skeletal systems functioned flawlessly. Their hidden lungs, relaxed and rhythmic, expanded the still-hardening cartilage of the ribcages. Skin tissue stretched elastically with each languorous movement.

Through this idyllic canvas, terror hacked its ragged hole.

The baby picked up a rock and threw it at Joshua, striking him in the head. He complained loudly. Enthused, Aaron snatched up another and flung it into the open shop door at Keith. It bounced off his chest. The man scolded the child. That angry reprimand hung suspended in the fading light. Undeterred, Aaron marshaled still another stone and directed it at Luke.

Three stones. Your circulatory system congealed, no doubt. The playful paw of your once domesticated deity, till now merely toying with his prey, had suddenly evolved functional claws, for in that moment the procedural instructions had unmistakably been issued.

The precise order in which the deaths should occur had been vexing, you would admit to the psychiatrist, and some divine light now seemed to have been vouchsafed. Firstborn Joshua must not be first; that much was clear. Keith's intervention in the episode just enacted served as an explicit warning that the order was important; if Joshua were selected first, there might be a noisy struggle, alerting your husband. But the warning went further. Should Keith attempt to intervene, he too must be dispatched. That formidable interference must be avoided, therefore, if at all possible. The proper order now seemed to unroll, scroll-like, before you. Joshua, in his eighth year and the most likely to resist, must be summoned last to the site. Luke would, logically, be placed in the middle. That left Aaron in the unenviable position of going first. But, then, what did it matter so long as the blows were swift, decisive, and final?

Contemplating Aaron's vatic pantomime, less vague than ever, you once more recalled Andrea, Andrea of Houston, Blessed Andrea of Clear Lake. She, too, had been selected—that fact was indisputable—for what else would explain her systematic drowning of all five? Yates, you recalled, had been conscientiously attentive to the order, ensuring that the procedure went smoothly. Her care had been meticulous. Andrea, the first witness called, had set the efficiency standard high, granted, but the Lord's grace would be sufficient.

Ongoing arguments with the Almighty transpired the entire time, you would later testify, as jets of water thrashed the decorative shrubs Keith had placed about the border of the house. While you mindlessly attended to this vegetable life, dependent upon you for its May-through-September survival, you fought valiantly for more precious life still in your protective keeping, not yet surrendered on the altar.

Lord, I don't understand why. Why, Lord, why? To what purpose? What purpose?

No response was forthcoming. Nothing. In time, the struggle subsided. You quieted. The mechanical watering went on. A darker question, however, soon began shaping itself in consciousness, throbbing: *What rock? What rock?*

In the interview, you would explain the rationale for your having now embraced the second option, not the first or third. The psychiatrist, unregenerate, would be slow to perceive, dull of understanding, so you were to delineate the logical underpinnings. The spear, one could easily see, had been rejected twice—two times. You had restored it to the toy box and, when it was again proffered, you had decisively hidden it in a closet. This double denial constituted a firm no. The blade was disqualified, then, and no longer on the bargaining table. But stoning was another matter. You had thrust away the rock only once. It remained, therefore, a charged particle, a viable possibility.

What softened you, what soothed your antipathy to the abrasiveness of the second option, was the enormity of the third option Aaron had presented. Strangling, you would make clear to the interviewer, was the least palatable method imaginable. It seemed to have been mentioned by your Lord, almost casually, as a tactful reminder that obedience could be made still more difficult should His servant balk. He could play contractual hardball, if necessary, this God of the desert wastes.

At that instant, tugging the garden hose to a new section of the flowerbed, you stumbled on something. How long did you stare at it, Dee, unblinking? This was no mere pebble, manageable in a toddler's palm, but a hefty sample of sedimentary hardware, one of those slabs Keith had tastefully spaced across the yard as steppingstones, a weapon of respectable biblical proportions.

As the water continued to rain upon the shrubs, you stared at this once neutral object. *A stone of stumbling, a rock of offense.* Care of the plants completed, you twisted the weapon from its resting place in the entangling lawn and, back inside, secreted it beneath Aaron's crib.

*

Friday night, the Laney household eased into sleep. In not-so-distant fields surrounding the house, Keith's spring wheat grew and matured by infinitesimal degrees, drying, pale yellow, blanching to desiccated straw, as it advanced toward early-summer harvest.

That court-appointed inquisitor, in the closing segment of the interview, would ask why you had failed to seek counsel as you struggled against the fiat. He would, as always, pose the question gently yet, somehow, diabolically: Why, as you wrestled with God's will, did you not broach the matter with your helpmeet or with your local pastor? You, of course, were to sense the trap he'd laid. The compelling proof-text would be close at hand: "I thought of that verse about Mary treasuring all these things in her heart. I thought I was supposed to be like that, you know? Not tell anybody." With that you were to stop the mouth of the gainsayer.

Under the night sky, the kernels hardened and the crop edged toward finality and the Laney family slept. At 11:30, as you would specify in the deposition, you awoke. The command forcefully struck your torso, another fist to the abdomen: *It's time.*

A simple task had to be performed, so, operating by the auto-pilot mechanism that guides mothers through the chores of late-night breastfeeding and pre-dawn diaper changing, you rose and started to work.

Aaron's room first. Lifting the limp toddler from his crib, you placed him on the floor. The left side of the skull presented itself providentially, the soft, fleshy temple pulsing rhythmically. The appointed stone was, of course, in its appointed place. With the deft, decisive movement you'd used countless times in the kitchen, kneading bread dough or tenderizing steak, you raised the weight and brought it down smartly, shattering bone. Irregular, blood-laced breaths stirred the gloom of the nursery.

Months later, the courtroom audience understandably entranced, you would explain your strategy, clarifying the seemingly odd fact that all three boys were struck on the left side of the skull. Aaron, you would say, had been in the habit of seeking out a parental hand and placing it on the left side of his head, apparently to enjoy the warmth of the touch. Each time he grinned—drooled with pleasure. It was the fifteen-month-old's gesture you had spontaneously recalled and taken as procedural.

Unexpectedly, Keith peeped into the unlit bedroom.

Alerted by who knows what chthonic force, your husband, silent and groggy, peered at your stooped figure alongside the child. In the videotaped confession, you would say that you heard his step and glanced over your shoulder. No words had passed: "I just looked at him." Assuming Aaron's diaper was dirty, he turned, satisfied, and withdrew to the master bedroom. The rattle of the child's labored breathing had not reached him.

Another blow recommended itself. You considered it. The harsh, ragged wind refused to stop. But the stone had magically alchemized, transforming itself to the densest substance on the Periodic Table. You found no resources to again lift the burden: *That's all I can do, Lord. You're gonna have to do the rest.* With that silent admission, you placed a pillow over the open hole to mute the gurgling.

You next woke Luke and led him outside the house, directing him to the row of decorative steppingstones. ("I just got this feeling: *Take him outside.*") Home-schooled to honor father and mother, dazed by sleep, he complied unquestioningly, following without resistance. The night was cool—it was early May—and the boy's underclothing thin. Perhaps he shivered as you instructed him to lie on the ground in the earth's enveloping chill. He once more obeyed without qualm and, in compliance with your directive, turned his head, exposing the left temple. You selected a new weapon, ready at hand, from the evenly spaced slabs. Luke died with relative facility, but the corpse had to be dragged away so that his older brother would not see it as he approached the execution site.

Joshua awoke more easily than had Luke and soon became alert: "Mama, why are we goin' outside?" It was a fair question. "And at night?" The oddness of it all at last impinged. The child looked up expectantly. What could you say? A linguistic vacuum prevailed. No verbiage presented itself. In the precise moment of need, however, you recalled an incident from earlier that day. Joshua had suddenly arisen from his lessons and had thrust a paper into your face. "What's this?" you'd asked. "It's a test," he'd triumphantly replied, awaiting praise for the high mark his Bible quiz would receive. That incident now leapt into consciousness, providing the heaven-sent answer in your moment of desperate need: "It's a test, boy. It's a test."

On the courtroom's television monitor, you would pause reflectively, head inclined at a pietà pitch, eyes fixed warmly on some distant scene irretrievably beyond repetition, a last conversational exchange with the firstborn.

Joshua must have fought a bit after the first blow; it was likely necessary to pin his arms with your knees and continue bludgeoning him. His tongue bore contusions, the forensic specialist would say, from having called for help. How many blows were administered is, of course, academic. The outcome was assured. When the body ceased to writhe, you placed the damp stone atop his vacant chest, and the Holy Scriptures echoed in your new swept-and-clean emptiness. These two witnesses, you recalled having read, will command earthquakes. They will summon the stones to fall upon the inhabitants of the earth, and it shall be done as they have said. Gazing down at the lifeless boy, you realized afresh that the Bible is deeply, forever true.

*

The world mutated—how could it have remained unchanged—but in what way? Did the sky metamorphose from a black vacuum to a rich, royal mantle of purple? Did the stars, scattered chips of windshield on asphalt, all at once become patterned astral gems, each individually mounted by a master jeweler's hand? Perhaps the reverse?

"Call 911," your familiar now counseled. You retrieved the cell phone from your car and dutifully dialed the number.

Killed my boys. 13674 Arizona Drive. Chicago brick—it's not a color; it's all different colors. No, no dogs. There's cars out in the front yard. A white Chevy and a pickup truck. Me? I'm outside—no weapons, no—back behind the pond.

The boys? A couple are out around the fence line. One's in the house; I believe he's still alive. No, you'll have to find them by yourself. I can't go back.

Listening to a recording of that ensuing conversation, your journalistic account of the killings complementing the dry professionalism of the emergency operator, one would encounter the borderland where shadows meld: "I did wrong by Aaron."

Still grappling to the last with God's maddening tendency to rely on prophetic playacting and ventriloquism, you had patiently worked your way to absolute lucidity. You could now perceive what the symbolic communiqués had intended all along. Aaron had *thrown* the rocks. He, himself, had not been struck by a rock. Aaron, then, was to have remained untouched, unharmed.

"I did wrong by Aaron."

Confirmation was to come. Aaron would survive, blind and debilitated, but alive.

*

Meteorologists claim to possess data for all lightning strikes on a given day. Each of these individual cloud-to-ground events, we are assured, has inscribed itself on a plotted radar chart. On the graph for any given twenty-four-hour period, luminous pixels mark all points of contact between the kingdom of heaven and this terrestrial vale of tears.

It is perhaps needful to consult the meteorological records of May 9 and 10, from dusk till the following dawn, for you would maintain, Dee, that lightning scarred the empty vault overhead immediately after the task was complete. There is no reason to doubt your report, I suppose, though you did not explicitly say the bolt touched terra firma. And the interpretation you were to impose on this phenomenon might also be disputed. You took it as yet another sign, an assurance from the throne that all had been accomplished as decreed.

That may be. But some of us have scanned the sky in vain, Dee, glimpsing random discharges yet never receiving that flash of affirmation. Still, I admit, that may be.

LESLIE JILL PATTERSON

On *Forgiving*

> adj., (of a thing) easy or safe to deal with: *If you'd like to look a couple of pounds lighter, black is a forgiving color.*

By the time I met Tyrone, I'd studied all of the affidavits and memos his defense team had gathered from several Texas Youth Commission workers, who warned that Tyrone was capital-T Trouble strolling down the street. None of them had seen him in over a decade, nor could they remember his name or any particular offenses he'd committed while in custody, but when they saw his photograph, they recalled his flimflam smile, the kind that made you forget his explosive temper seconds before he swung a fist. Which might have been a sparring tactic he'd honed back in the day, when he was five and his uncles taught him to "dogfight," pitting him against other kindergarteners in a makeshift ring in their living room and casting bets on the outcome. He was a quick and certain study: all these years later, he'd beaten three of his "baby mamas" as well as the one wife he truly loved. Days before the homicide, Tyrone's most recent girlfriend filed charges with the police, accusing him of beating her with a box-fan until she'd fallen unconscious. Twice. I knew he'd killed two adults—while three children and one infant howled in terror as he fired the gun, again and again, until it ran out of bullets. The infant was his. Prison officials at county lock-up where he'd been housed ever since thought him so dangerous they wrote him up when they found a "weapon" in his cell: a single staple, which he had used to slit his wrists. The judge overseeing his case summed up everyone's impression: he set Tyrone's bail at $1,000,000.

When the guards brought Tyrone into the private client/attorney room at Randall County Jail, he wore orange prison garb but wasn't shackled at the belly and the ankles as other defendants had been. His eyes, wide and brown and wary, overwhelmed his narrow face and undercut his notorious smile, which he flashed right away. As his defense team introduced a couple of student attorneys and me, he nodded at each of us, polite but dismissive. He wasn't sure we were anyone he needed to impress. I'd heard he would put on a show—all hood slang and profanity, a rooster cocking the walk. Certainly, his orange pants were slung so low on his hips, I thought they would slide to the floor, and he had a way of zigzagging his chin and jacking up one shoulder that seemed pretty street to me, white woman that I was. Despite his swagger, though, and my expectations of a "killer" physique, Tyrone was rawboned—knobby elbows and lean as a starving coyote. Striking, in a fierce sort of way.

*

His family and friends swore Tyrone's sense of humor could spike a funeral into a New Year's bash, and sure enough, to my surprise, he could crack a joke. When he found out I was divorced, he said, "You need him bounced? I got people. I can make some phone calls." We fell quiet, stunned. One of our team's mitigators, Rob, involuntarily looked overhead for a recording device. Our client couldn't afford to land in the newspaper again for another in-house infraction—this time, attempted murder for hire. Max, the team's attorney, looked at me and swiped a hand across his throat: *let's garrote this conversation.* But then Tyrone's face cracked open, all teeth, and he said, "I'm kidding, man. White people, you so serious." Then he proceeded to run down a list of vocabulary words we used that he found hilarious—we had to stop appreciating him all the time, for one thing. What kind of hokum word was that: *'preciate.* "Bullshit," he said. "Stop talking like damn honky psychiatrists." I'm saying, he had us unstitched pretty quick.

Halfway into the meeting, though, Tyrone quashed the comedy routine and sobered up. He turned to Max, the type of defense attorney known at the courthouse as a "gunslinger" because you don't want to square off with him in front of a jury. Recently, Max had represented Calvin Solomon—a man who pled guilty to the shooting deaths of a family he didn't know: a man, his pregnant wife, her teenage daughter, even their dog. A ringer for the needle if ever there was one. But Calvin skirted death row because Max's efforts led a jury to settle on Life Without Parole instead, an outcome unheard of in Texas if a capital charge goes to trial. Sitting next to Tyrone, Max looked like a mafia mechanic. Two considerable gold rings lent his hands a Vito Corleone respectability, and he weighed a solid 250 pounds. I'd seen him break in two, one after the other, a stash of ballpoint pens made from recycled cardboard, simply by gripping them to write. He wasn't the type you looked at and thought: *sensitive.* Or: *Let's talk.*

To Max, Tyrone said, "You read the Bible?"

Max showed no expression. His empty face suggested he might need to admit something I'd seen a character confess in a Steve Yarbrough short story: *There are lots of books in this world I haven't read, and among them is one called the Bible.* But I knew Max was a devout Catholic. He'd shown me his church when we drove around town one afternoon. I figured he'd cracked a Bible at least once.

Tyrone asked him again. "You read the Bible?"

Max couldn't or didn't know how to react. He stared at his client. Maybe he was trying to calculate where this discussion was headed; maybe he thought the question was a con. Honestly, it seemed pretty suspicious to me. I'd had my fill of men sidling up to religion for my benefit. When my ex-husband found out I'd lost the ability to have children, he'd said, "See, even God knows you shouldn't be a mother." When I'd answered, "You don't believe in God," he'd said, not missing a beat, "Yeah, but you do."

"I read the Bible," I finally offered, though I rarely owned up to my spiritual beliefs since they hadn't served me so well. Too, in Texas, for the most part, if you're a Christian, you're also a lot of other things I didn't want people assuming about me. Republican, for one. Both a Muslim-hater and, by bogus association, an Obama-hater. Sometimes in Texas, there's a triple-digit heat to Christianity which makes it unlikely that devout churchgoers, the kind who brag about their convictions, can chill the Old Testament wrath and show compassion toward people who haven't earned it.

Apparently, that attitude is catching. See what I just did in that previous paragraph? I myself cast Tyrone as the type of person who didn't deserve understanding. *People who haven't earned it*: I was talking about him and the other defendants the team represented, right?

Tyrone sized me up, nodded. "Ah'ight," he said, "you know what I'm conversating then."

I shook my head. "No. What are we talking about?"

He leaned forward in his chair and clasped his hands in front of him, as if they were shackled, and pumped them in the air. "The Bible say we got to honor our parents. It don't say if they nice to you or deserve it."

Everyone in the room stiffened. By that point, we knew that Tyrone's mother, when she paid attention to him at all, thrashed him regularly between the ages of four and twelve, with an orange utility cord and always for petty offenses like having untied shoelaces or eating his cereal incorrectly. At night, she burst into his room while his was sleeping and whaled on him without waking him first because, rape-baby that he was, she should've had an abortion. In the darkest moments of our investigation, when we needed something to make us smile for God's sake, we joked about putting her on the witness stand first, wearing a T-shirt that said, *Exhibit A*. By the time Tyrone turned seven, he tried to hang himself, an obvious cry for help that CPS ignored, sending him back home after his allotted days in the county-run juvenile mental hospital. When we confronted his caseworker—we'll call her Exhibit B—she'd shrugged. "That kind of thing happens in black households all the time," she said. "A dime a dozen."

Tyrone's biological father had allegedly raped his mother, denied Tyrone from day one, and was now a junky, whom Albert, our private investigator and the most resourceful man on our team, couldn't find for nearly a year. Tyrone's father's name wasn't listed in any phone books. He didn't have even the slightest cyber footprint. Finally, Albert and Max tracked the father down by knocking door to door at the apartments where Tyrone's grandmother heard the father lived. She didn't know the name of the complex, only that it was near the Dennis the Price Menace Liquor Store. Since we'd found him, he had called Rob several times, weeping and begging to see Tyrone. Tyrone had said, *No way, no fucking way.* And Rob and Max—ever vigilant and earnest about their jobs as Tyrone's defenders, and both of them large men—had thrown up a wall, their bodies prepared to block the father's efforts to visit his son in lockup if it came to that.

Tyrone stared in my direction. Not exactly a direct beam, but canted to the right. Or maybe I was the one diverting my gaze.

I nodded my head. "That's what the Bible says."

He looked at Max, then leaned forward a little more and turned again toward me. "It say you got to forgive in order to be forgiven."

I nodded.

"I've been thinking on that," he said, his hands pumping the air. "I need my kids to forgive what I done, so I need to forgive my daddy."

Max propped his forehead against his fists and stared down at the table. I knew, from previous interviews with other defendants, that this was the stance Max took whenever he thought he might tear up but, by God, wasn't going to. His cheeks puffed, and his face turned red from the effort.

Tyrone looked at me, his eyes square on mine now. "That right?"

"That's what it says," was all I could manage without my voice cracking.

"Okay." Tyrone nodded. "Okay."

"You don't need to worry," Max told him. "We aren't letting him anywhere near you if that's got you troubled."

Tyrone made a gesture that looked like a rap groove or maybe a Crips sign—his fingers crimped as if double-jointed and his hand flicked, scooping the air. "I'm gangsta with that," he said.

Rob cocked his head to the side, as if he was deaf and simply needed to angle his ear toward Tyrone in order to understand him. *How's that? What?*

I looked around the room for an interpreter.

Max parked his big fists firmly on the table. "That's right. He isn't getting anywhere near you. No worries."

Tyrone jacked up his chin. "I'm gangsta with that."

Max's brow wrinkled. "You want to see your dad?"

The rap groove again. "Fuck it," Tyrone spat at him.

"Okay, okay." Max held up his hands, palms forward, signaling everyone to halt. "No visits from dear old Dad."

"Fuck it. I'm gangsta with that," Tyrone shouted.

It felt like we were trapped in that Progressive car insurance commercial where the elderly guy keeps talking in some sort of jazz-speak—*Okie-McSmokey Skiddlely-Doo*—till Flo shakes her head and admits, *Yeah, still no idea what you're saying.*

"You want to see your Dad," I tried. Decisively. Not a question, but a statement of fact.

"Fuck it," Tyrone said again, but calm this time. He settled back in his chair and flashed his smile.

Max nodded and wrote a note on his legal pad. "Got it. We'll set that up." He looked a little sheepish, then with a zigzag of his own chin and a shrug of his shoulders, he added, "Fuck it."

Laughter snorted from my mouth. The hopeless, egregious ineptitude of a team of middle-aged, middle-class, overly educated white people representing a young African American man from the hood lit up the room. Everyone howled. A real New Year's hullaballoo.

Though it wasn't funny. Not at all. In the county where Tyrone would be tried, African Americans comprised only two percent of the total population. Most of them weren't registered voters—why would they bother in Texas?—so they wouldn't receive a summons. If they owned a car and received the call via their vehicle registrations, the six dollars a day jury salary was a pay-cut they couldn't afford and so they wouldn't appear. Even if they did, during voir dire, when the prosecutor asked if anyone had experienced a negative run-in with the law that might prevent them from taking seriously every police officer's testimony, the African Americans would likely all raise their hands and be dismissed for cause. Tyrone's jury of his peers would look a lot like his defense team.

When we got ready to leave, Tyrone hugged my neck, said, "No shit, you're divorced?"

I nodded.

His face turned dark, like he was getting ready to kick some holy ass on my behalf, getting his game on. "He didn't hit you, did he?"

I shrugged. "He was smart. He had alternative methods."

Tyrone squinted, leaned toward me. "You behaved?" he asked. "You didn't deserve it?"

Which sounds like a horrifying question given its implications and Tyrone's history. Then, again, it was the same question I'd asked myself for years. And it was the same question society implied whenever they argued that women stick around 'cause they like it.

"Angelic," I said. "A real saint."

"Serious now," he said, smiling again, "I got people. What you say his name was?"

I grinned. "Nice try," I said.

"Fear of God and all that," he promised.

I nodded. "Sure: repentance, forgiveness." But in my head, I was thinking what a damn shame it was I hadn't taken my husband's last name when we married. That way, he'd be easier for archangel thugs to hunt down and knock unconscious with a box-fan. At the very least, I wouldn't mind my ex bumping into Max or Rob or Albert in a dark alley. Out loud, I said, "Only, my ex is agnostic. He doesn't believe in any of that."

"Yeah—" Tyrone paused, "—but you do."

At that moment, his face staring at me was that of the little boy whom TYC workers recognized from a second-grade photo—a kid smiling, all flash and bravado, because he didn't want anyone to notice the case of ringworm so thick it covered his arms and torso, because he didn't want anyone to suspect how his cousin and his cousin's friends rain a train on him in the family garage every afternoon. What I know about forgiveness today I learned from murderers. If I was going to tell Tyrone's story and tell it true, I'd have to forgive his mother, and her mother before her, and her mother before her. Forgiveness lies at the bottom of a rabbit hole deep and dark, and once you dare to jump in after, all you can do is fall.

A. G. MOJTABAI

Trew Reade: A Reporter's Story

His name's always been a joke.

"Great name for the business," the managing editor said right off the bat. "Direct from Central Casting. Born to report." It took only the one interview: Trew was hired on the spot. And he was given a byline right away.

What Trew remembers best from that first meeting was the editor's desk ornament—a clear Lucite replica of an open book with its title turned to the viewer:

MY LIFE STORY
By Bob Baxter,
Managing Editor

The open pages were blank. What were you expected to make of it? Surely he didn't mean to suggest a life empty of event? More likely, it was Baxter's way of saying that his life was perfectly transparent, an open book—

which proved to be far from the truth. Two years ago, Baxter became a guest of the government. He's in the Pen at present. ("Eating our tax dollars, sucking on the Federal tit," in newsroom parlance.) Seems Baxter had been busy on the side, up to his neck in some sort of Ponzi scheme. All those reporters around him itching for a story, and not one of them had an inkling!

That Lucite book of Baxter's should have been fair warning. Surface and substance were rarely the same; transparency could be the most cunning of masks. Yet, as Trew was to learn from practical experience, however doggedly he worked to ferret out the facts, the momentum of breaking news (always something new), deadlines, and cutoffs for reasons of space, routinely got in the way and dictated the shape of the story. And there were other pressures. Sometimes he felt that he was not so much writing a story as negotiating it, haggling for every inch of print and even for content. What's even more compromising—he wonders how often he's come to simply avoid the hassle by making the anticipated adjustments on his own before ever submitting the story. But, then again—isn't this part of learning to be a professional? That's how he squares it with himself at least. You can't fight everything.

Being assigned the city beat meant covering crime scenes, commissioners' meetings, school boards, and local elections, as well as courthouse proceedings, trials, and appeals. When he shifted to the police beat, part of his assignment took him to the death house in Huntsville to witness the send-offs. Texas kept him busy and, after he was asked to become a stringer for the Associated Press, his reputation spread beyond the state. He had to admit that he liked his smattering of fame; it gave him an opportunity to be heard—plus, a little extra on the monetary side never hurt—although it wasn't long before he realized that no recognition or payment could compensate for the toll he paid in sleepless nights or the tremor that gradually overtook his writing hand. His motives weren't pure (were motives ever?) yet they weren't entirely, or even largely, self-serving. He could have refused the executions, but reasoned: If this is what we do, someone has to record it. To let it be known.

When exactly was it that his role as witness began to feel like that of an accomplice? A feeling, not a fact—not rational, as Trew repeatedly reminded himself.

So he'd kept on, stayed with it as long as he could stand it, reporting from the death house, bearing his crumb of witness for the human ant-heap. It was too much—it was not enough.

Strange to say, it was not a flawed "procedure" that brought him to finally quit, but one that was technically perfect, without a glitch. Not a heave, not a cough, not a sputter. The prisoner had declined to make a final statement. His crime was vicious, his guilt not in question. The execution process was as smooth and efficient as putting a pet to sleep. Yet, somehow, this one proved to be the final straw for Trew.

It had been a long time coming; few were surprised. Trew had stayed with that assignment for more years than any other reporter, bar none. What was a surprise was his transfer to Features at his own request, well away from the blare of big ink news. If anyone was disappointed at the abrupt close to his promising career, it remained unvoiced. It was only Trew himself, and only at moments, when his withdrawal struck him as a failure of nerve.

In any case, Trew is out to pasture now. He'd thought of this as recovery time at first—not a permanent retreat. It's grown on him, though. And he still has hopes of writing something of note, someway, probably off-assignment, sometime.

His writing hand has been steadier since the transfer. The tremor (for which his doctor never found an organic cause) is no longer a quaking; it's still there, but muted now, hardly noticeable to anyone who hasn't been alerted to it beforehand. But Trew, himself, is never allowed to forget. He frequently drops things, his grasp no longer firm and decisive. And, known only to himself, there's some residual numbness in the heel of his palm and fingertips. He's definitely lost feeling in that hand. It's just the one hand, although it happens to be the one he writes with.

Be that as it may. . . . He covers the counties these days, local events like this one. Seems sometimes like he's moved from Death-the-real-thing to Life-the-game. Hard focus to soft. It's a trade-off. He puts in more miles but the stress is way less, no question. He doesn't get bogged down in endless retrospection, taking himself to task, as he used to, about a question he forgot to ask or an extra witness unvisited. The story doesn't repay that kind of attention. And it turns out he actually prefers hanging around in the boonies to being out and about in the city. "Getting to know every dog and cat on a first name basis," as he likes to say. Away from the punishing pace, all those egos colliding and crashing, a safe distance from the City Desk and Aiden's hammering away at every last thing.

Last week he'd covered a grocery sacking tournament in a town outside Lubbock. When he first heard of the contest, he'd laughed it off, but after interviewing the champion sacker (best on "structure," though not the fastest), he'd learned a few things and passed them on to his readers. Like making a "wall of protection" with the canned goods at the bottom of the sack and placing the lighter soft stuff inside that wall, or insulating the ice cream and frozen food by surrounding them with napkins and toilet paper. Who knew?

Has he ever made that atom's worth of difference he once thought—hoped—he might? He'd started the ball rolling on the story of Lee Somers, an innocent man put to death by the State; but innocent people were still being put to death. In what he calls his "personal life," Trew knows he's never lived, or loved, at full stretch. He doesn't spend all that much time regretting the fact, yet imagines that he might someday; there might come a day when he'd want to have wanted more. What that "something more" would be, whether it even exists, he's not sure.

Right now, even now, he can't forget the death house, there's still this humongous weight he needs to get off his chest. . . .

Painting and repainting the walls of the execution chamber (on the advice of a psychologist) to a "soothing" green did little to alter things. Nor did it ease matters much that the drug dispensing apparatus and operator remained hidden behind a one-way mirror so that all you could see was an IV tube trailing from a small square opening lower down in the wall. It did help—a bit—that the curtain was only opened after the IV needle was successfully inserted (after antiseptic was carefully applied to the injection site); if there was a struggle to find a vein, that was something he did not have to witness.

Most of the condemned men were black men or brown, had little schooling, came from broken families, the wrong side of town. Innocent, or guilty, or swept along—who could say with the necessary certainty? Unable to afford their own lawyers, they'd relied on court-appointed public defenders who were overburdened and cash-strapped, uncaring or careless. Trew studied the numbers but, after presenting them to the editorial staff, was greeted with: "We know this. Is life unfair? You bet. Tell us something new." All he could do was to keep on witnessing for as long as he could stand it, writing up the executions one by one, keeping a blank numerical tally, a sum total of completions, relying on the condemned man's last words to do the rest.

That was standard operating procedure, the "execution protocol," providing a pause for a final statement before the drugs begin to flow or the switch was thrown. Although some prisoners opted for silence, there was always the opportunity to have a say—to be listened to for once. Some professed innocence with their last breaths. Others begged forgiveness. Again and again you'd hear: "I'm not the same man anymore." Many were eager to end the years of waiting and appeal, wanting simply to get it over with, this—the only way out. All welcomed release from prison. Some claimed to be homesick for heaven and thanked the members of the tie-down team, the men who had so swiftly and efficiently strapped them in. Some thanked the warden, though often bitingly.

As for the official reports, there was a little of what the transcriber called "Allah mumbling," which remained untranslated. In English, the four-letter words would not be written into the record and, anyway, could not be printed in a family newspaper. The curses were to be expected—but there were, in far greater measure, blessings—words of hope to those waiting on the row, and reminders to their families to hug the little ones at home, words of farewell: "Keep strong. Hold your heads high . . . Be seeing you. I'll be waiting on the other side." Then the warden would tip his glasses—that was the signal.

Sometimes the prisoner tried to communicate what he was experiencing to the last threshold of awareness. "It's coming . . ." "It's overwhelming." Some said they could "taste it"—

"This is for real," one spoke in an amplified whisper. His head turned and he stared right at Trew, as if speaking only, in confidence, to him: "I feel my heart going . . ." Their eyes locked. Trew had to cough and face away, feeling his own heart stutter in mid-beat.

Some deaths were easier than others. The serial killer in for a string of gruesome murders showed not a shred of remorse.

A white man, pale and narrow-shouldered, with wire-rim specs, he seemed well suited to his job as an accountant, but a highly implausible murderer. "Nobody's bullet-proof," he explained. "Might think they are. I taught them different." Then he smiled beatifically as he urged the warden to "pull the trigger" and wished "peace, true peace" to everyone invited to this occasion.

One prisoner, who suffered from a lisp and facial tic, sent out a written statement beforehand, to make sure that each word counted. "I'm innocent," he began. He'd been waiting for eleven years for this moment. Trew missed some of the words as they were being spoken, but he had the man's speech in hand:

"My truth will last out your truth. I have no kin, no friend. No fear. Go ahead, Warden, give them what they want. You don't want me here and I don't want to be here. Take me away from this place. Go ahead. Finish it off. I'm ready."

A few chose to sing their last words—unmelodious scraps of country-westerns or hymns. One man sang something in Latin, letting everyone know that once upon a time he'd been an altar boy. All Trew can remember are the rhymes: hominum, terminum, dominum . . .

And yet, despite all his death-penalty misgivings, Trew persists in thinking it a privilege to have your last words listened to and recorded. He actually envies it in a way. He wanted, needed—still needs—words carefully considered, words passed on as an inheritance to those left behind. Something more than the usual silence and the tacitly understood "It was fun while it lasted."

He had only to recall his dad's last words:

"That nurse has the cleanest nostrils I've ever seen," he said—and spoke no more.

It would not do!

Of course, no one had ever dreamed this would be his final say. He'd gone into the hospital expecting only minor surgery. The nurse in question had just stepped out of the room.

Two orderlies had entered, loaded his dad onto a gurney and taken off on a fast glide, disappearing down the corridor leading to the elevator and the operating room. It was far too smooth for sadness. And it was all over before they knew it.

That was the last Trew saw of his dad alive. His family had always been "non-affiliated," and at the scattering of the ashes, friends and family did their best to avoid any trappings of a traditional graveside ceremony, each of them straining to say something original, something amusing to remember, but Trew felt certain that "dust unto dust" was on everyone's mind.

At the prison death house, people wept and prayed. The family members of the victims spoke of "closure." Once in a while—but not as often as people might suppose—one of the watchers would faint. He'd seen people on the victims' sides clap, or give one another high-fives when it was over. That didn't happen often, but it did happen. As for Trew, he'd be ready to split as soon as the snoring (in the new, improved way) or the thrashing (in the old days) ended. His deadline gave him a perfect excuse to scram . . .

It's close to two a.m. now. Hours and hours yet to get through . . . His watch is slow, must be the battery running down. He carries a spare: he'll change it. The metal expansion band is nipping his wrist—normally, Trew takes it off when he goes to bed. There's really no need for a watch here, what with the hours, minutes, seconds, fractions of seconds continually flashing on the big screen. He'd be lost without a wristwatch, though. It's another one of those habits.

*

Right now he's struggling to get back on assignment, wondering: What have I missed? How many down?

When he asks the cameraman for the local television affiliate (name's Vince, if memory serves) what's new, he's equally blank, as if he might've been napping. His camera's aimed and ready, though, perched on its tripod. "Just waiting for something to happen," he explains. "No use wasting film."

But, no sooner done explaining, he's on his feet, fiddling with the focus on his lens. And now he's shooting. When he's done Trew reminds him that he'd just said nothing was happening.

"What roused you?"

"Background . . . interesting . . . Have a look."

He lets Trew peek through his viewfinder. Caught in its frame: a boy, holding what looks like a cicada by one wing, using the insect as a fan, the other wing beating frantically against the boy's cheek.

"What people won't do!" Trew exclaims. "Imagine trying to stir up a breeze with a little thing like that—" He feels compelled to say something, to keep the words moving—anything to keep himself awake.

*

Two a.m.: This is one of those times when if you stare at a blank wall, it stares back at you. Because nothing is happening. Really, nothing. Only a cleaning woman, a Latina with a long braid down her back, rattling her buckets, brooms, and mops, moving through the crowd of sleepers and watchers, stooping to gather loose trash on her way to the washroom. Another Latina pushing another trash bucket on wheels clatters after her, an angry clatter from pushing her cart with more force than necessary, as if she too wants to make a statement.

Who tidied up in the execution room—after? Trew wonders for the first time. He never lingered long enough to find out. Was it a man or a woman? And how did he, or she, feel about the streaking of the window on the side where the prisoner's family gathered—the slobber from kisses, the smudges from the press of palms?

It must have been just another one of those messes, just another one of those jobs, minimum wage and outrageous hours, and best not to look too closely at what you're trying to erase.

BRUCE BOND

The Border

1.

Begin with a face, this casting pool set in bone,
　　　　where the other faces graze the surface

and slide, and who remembers what it was to begin,
　　　　who back then, if anyone, we were.

Always the shroud of a stranger across the chill
　　　　of the looking glass, and I am looking more

and more like my father and know I never get there.
　　　　The face on television says, we should open

our borders to Christians only, and somewhere a lonely man
　　　　says, yes, I feel that way. And one flame

flows into another, and who can tell them apart.
　　　　Who has not filled the empty holy landscape

of the margins. Everywhere the smoke of cities
　　　　and exclusionary spaces, where if you knock

the bodies on video feeds they sound like glass.
　　　　What a sound bite needs is a larger story with small

and smaller pieces, a girl, say, who stares
　　　　into the camera before the pan and fade,

though we know she is out there, the face among faces,
　　　　the Eucharist of imagined life.

2.

Let me begin again. Time is priceless,
and we are always in the middle

of some covert conflict somewhere, caught
in the river of thousands pouring into thousands,

gathering in the makeshift city of widows
and tents, and there are limits to a body,

a nation, a sea. There are rivers drawn as mirages are
across the names of other waters,

and what is the use of words and images that come
so far and no farther, of the protest

song and broken camera abandoned in the sand.
Whose grains are these in the storm

blown back across our footsteps,
where the new planes carry their payload,

undetected, and have no people in them.
The words *Christian* or *fire* or *covert conflict*

have no people either, only jaws
to consume the bread of imagined life.

And as we talk, the body of us, in us, divides—
it must—longing to be whole.

3.

Long ago they cut my father's body open to accept
the harvest of a stranger's heart.

When he woke, the hospital room smelled of chrome
and disinfectant, and he thought,

surely this is paradise, and his palpitations
spiked. Somewhere there is a flashlight

in the tunnel of your chest, a voice that cries,
who's there, and no one answers. In time,

it says less and less, camouflaged in fibers;
the beam dims; words go deaf; the gape

of the ribcage swallows the Eucharist
in silence. Who is left to say where the stranger

draws its boundaries. Vein after vein
nets the vital muscle, and even the blood

of the incision is, as they say, connective tissue.
The bruise shade of the liver,

the spleen, the thyroid that is an outpost of the brain,
they are all braided like strangers

at the foot of a tower on fire. Like anger
flowing into anger and who can tell them apart.

4.

America has no face. Let me begin again.
It is neither driver nor the mother

on the bus who pulls the string, not the chime,
not the echo, never the house

particular with debt and pills and bad news
from Ferguson or Beirut or some such holy land,

and the candidate who would wear our features says,
I open my heart, but homes are homes,

and I turn on him and lock my door behind me.
A Christian nation has no Christ,

and Christ no nation. I am looking
for a better song. I cast my vote

into the water to watch it slice across the larger picture.
One nation under God, a child says.

Beneath her hand, the anonymity of the personal,
the vital muscle, the fist, the first

to fear, the last to explain. Lord of the body,
peerless, eyeless, compelled.

I search the names on the ballot for the nameless.
I make my pledge.

5.

To judge another's words by what we know about the speaker
is to know neither speaker nor word.

So says a schoolbook a boy finds boring
and then he gets a beating from two strangers,

and as he hangs by his hair in the grasp of one,
he says nothing, he is losing faith in words,

he goes home and, once again, nothing, and over dinner,
nothing, and night after night, he lies

awake, and nothing comes. I am looking for a better song,
the kind that moves across the borders

in the old language. Or wades against the water
beneath the guns of the lookout, and what remains is

the vast unfathomed reaches of a sky. I am sorry
for everything I did and did not do,

I told my father in the end, and he was confused.
I still see that face among the many he wore,

buried in a music I could not hear, and I needed
my own to hear it. It felt enormous, this tune, and I

was small and smaller, and he was crossing over,
and he looked at me, my grief, as if it were a stranger.

6.

In the song of the Eucharist of imagined life,
a girl stares into the camera, and the liquidation

of eyes and money spills from the anonymity
of the personal into the great collection plate.

Protesters take their guitars to the river, and one
tune flows into another, and whatever music does

and does not do, the girl who sings feels small and smaller,
and who are we to know. Somewhere

a theorist is writing a paper and feels it too: the longing
for greater detail, larger scope. Somewhere

a man eats the bread and feels absolved and little
changes or all things small and who are we to know.

Begin with a face. Yours or another's. Little changes
gather downstream, beneath the eyes, and they have seen it,

the power of a song, how it just might pull a body through
the mirror, out some painful story or door,

into another. The refugees' song carries something
of language over the river, and the river closes behind them

like a wound. It forgets. And in the song you hear it
running. And sometimes in their eyes, you see.

M. M. DE VOE

Baptism

I am trying not to think of myself outstretched on the quilt, tasting flannel in my mouth. My skin still smarts. I'd howled, not so much from the pain, but because it was humiliating for a young lady wearing Sunday best to lie face down with her behind raised to her father. Our house is in the country, far from the college town where my dad works. No one to hear you scream. The memory of the fourteen smacks—one for each year of my life—echoes in my ears. When I got up off the bed, I could hear my brother, Michael, laughing at something on TV in the next room.

I hadn't wanted to do this, my father had said. I did not reply.

My mother had brought the belt to him, buckle clinking.

"Melanie needs punishing."

He'd taken the belt from her. Told me to lie down. Told me to raise my own skirt. Did not even ask me why. Simply hit me, fourteen times.

Up to six I showed great self-control. By seven, I had failed. I had become a bad kid, according to my mother. According to our church. I was spanked monthly, sometimes weekly. But it has been a long time. By twelve, I had learned to control myself.

He told me to stop crying or I'd get more. I concentrated on my plan to poison the coffee I always brought him to eat with his donut after church, and the tears receded. Afterwards there was the awkward moment of getting up from the bed, pulling my skirt down, wiping the mascara from under my eyes. Trying to find some dignified way of leaving the situation.

I did not run, though I had not been spanked for two years. That last time, I had put a wad of bubble gum into my little brother's hair in response to him sticking a wet finger in my ear. When my dad asked, "Do I have to get the belt?" I did not reply, merely smashed the flat of my hand onto the pink lump on Michael's head. That time, my mother had looked on as my father dragged both of us from the car, leaving the motor running. My brother and I were laid out over the edge of the bed, bottoms up. While waiting for the whisk of leather through polyester loops, we even smiled at each other: early Schadenfreude, each glad the other was also getting punished.

Nine swats for me. Seven for Michael and his gummy hair. His kicking feet had left rubber marks on the floor. I had to wait through Michael's seven swats because I was older.

When my dad was done, my brother and I were crying. Perhaps my parents thought it was remorse.

It was humiliation. Hatred. Our father, who swings the belt. And pain. Because the belt hurts, it does. But deep down, I figured I deserved it, after all I'd defied my father by rubbing gum into my brother's hair. The punishment was certainly warranted. My mother celebrated the lovely young lady I became right after, not knowing that the veneer of good girl hid a seething lava pit of bad girl just beneath. She thought the spankings had worked. Indeed, perhaps they had, in their way.

But.

This time, I felt naked and female. The panties I chose to wear that morning were lacy and thin, and I was sure he could see the line of my bottom through them. Lying there, I was being punished doubly. Once, for what I had done, and twice for who I had become. I felt sexual and pretty and ashamed to be either.

Did he avoid looking at me?

Was that why the belt had fallen so erratically—onto my thighs and my back? Was he saving me some shame? Or was he simply so angry that I was no longer little, that he found extra rage to channel into the beating?

"Church in thirty minutes!" my mother shouts after me as I leave the house, limping a little. I slam the screen door and run out into the yard. The horses across the fence whicker, and I imagine my parents weeping when they realize I've stolen the roan and run away to a big city: Houston, or Dallas, or San Antonio. The barbed wire and electric fence look painful, but nothing I can't handle, even in this outfit. My Sunday shoes aren't for riding, but I can always kick them off. "I want you in the car in twenty! Don't make us wait." On the driveway, I am comforted by Ghost, the wild tabby cat I sometimes feed. I lean close and drag my nails through his thick gray coat. He purrs and stays. I am able to tell him everything, right there on the gravel. The oak trees rustle above us as I rub his shoulders, stroke his back, his belly. His yellow eyes are rimmed in black fur like eyeliner from a Cosmo Girl ad. I'm rubbing too hard. I'm hurting him. He meowls.

"Sorry, Ghosty," I say. "It's not your fault my parents suck." Standing makes me wince. The pond behind the house catches the morning sunlight. A glance at my watch tells me I still have a good quarter of an hour before I am required in the family sedan. I squint and wander towards the sparkling water, careful to avoid the mud.

"Hey, Ghost," I call the cat. "Let's go for an adventure." Ghost tangles his body between my ankles. I lean over to pull a burr from his coat. After removing one,

I find another, which I also remove. His coat is now silky, but leaves a film of dust on my hands.

"I'm going to kill you, Ghost, what do you think of that?" I say. He rubs himself on my legs and purrs. "Isn't this a beautiful day to die? Come on."

I walk to the edge of the pond, where at night drunk college boys guzzle beer and shoot off shotguns. I'd climbed out the window to join them the night before and I was stupid enough to write about it in my journal before going to sleep at 3 a.m. Despite its new hiding place behind my Bible, my mother must have found it and read all about me this morning while I was in the shower. She is a professional snoop: I can't escape her any more than Moriarty can escape Sherlock Holmes. I commit the crimes. My mother snoops them out. My father dispenses the punishment. The clearing in the reeds had seemed so isolated last night, with nothing but the stars on their velvet blanket spinning above me as I lay with my back against Steve Fairfield's legs. It was a magical place: it had transformed me into an adult: clever and pretty and self-possessed and wise. The pond had glittered, and enchanted frogs and winged fairy-mounts chirped and buzzed to our laughter and drinking games. In the light of day, the spot is a two-minute walk from my front door, and the pile of empties mocks me: our carefully arranged trophies transformed into common litter. The cat stalks the pile, sniffs it.

"Ghost," I say. "You put yourself at risk by following me here. I'm a bad person."

But I'm not. I'm an Honor Student. I tell Ghost all the awards I won in the last four months, and there are many. I tell him how much my teachers like me, and how they say I'm going to be someone someday. A dragonfly skates over the water, and I hear shouting from the house, though I can't make out the words. The air is dank and smells of rotting reeds. Last night it was filled with cigarette smoke and something sweeter. There were purple pills and white tabs on silver foil. I took no drugs and waved away the joint—how do I explain that to someone who was upset that I tasted a beer? Fourteen swats . . . I might have talked to my mother, but she handed the belt to my father and walked away. He hit without asking questions.

I pick up a glass bottle and someone's long shoelace and tie them together.

"I'm going to make you a raft, Ghost," I say, "so you can sail out into the middle of the pond and drown yourself. Won't that be nice?" My hands shake as I tie the knots. I loop together four bottles and wrap the string around a plank. The ground is spongy and my heels sink in. I hum a stupid song about rainbows that I learned in church choir, and I pick up the docile cat. He's heavy.

"Okay, Ghost, are you ready?" I push the makeshift raft out onto the water using one of my Sunday shoes, and almost slip in the mud. Ghost struggles in my arms but I hold tight. His fur is wet from dew, and I wonder if my new Gap blouse will look stained. Will the preacher comment? Will he call me unclean? The raft floats a foot away from the shore. I count off.

"One . . . two . . . three!"

I heave the tabby out over the water at the raft. I expect him to float out to the middle of the lake and drown in my place.

He twists as cats do, half-flying half-falling, to land on all fours on the rickety raft. Without stopping, he leaps—splashing down in the shallow water before scampering onto the mossy shore and far, far away from me.

The little raft jams itself into the weeds ten yards from where I pushed it in. It no longer bears any resemblance to a raft, just a pile of empty bottles and a dirty shoelace and a plank. Trash. Trash. Just trash.

My mother calls my name. I walk to the car where my family waits to drive me to church. Ignoring her questions, I sit in the back seat with my brother and stare out the window counting exit ramps, saved.

J. SCOTT BROWNLEE

Small Town Agnostic's Prayer

For a long time I prayed.
I looked up & waited.
Lord, you never answered
though I kept listening.
Lord, the sky remained
slick, dark, & unknowable.
Still, I kept on praying.
Still, you did not answer.
I went to a performance
of what death would be
at Kingsland First Baptist:
Heaven's White Gates
& Hell's Flames.
I remember how after
a boy from high school
came & witnessed to us—
knelt beside my scared
mother & brother & me
to help us accept You.
Six months later he fell
asleep driving his pickup
to see his girlfriend. The cab
entered a tree or else split
around it, & I'm willing
to bet as that chassis melted
he felt You or nothing.

Either way, he is dead
whereas I am alive
on this highway driving
back to You or nowhere.
The cicada song roars
like a plane overhead.
The sparse traffic ignites
the horizon tonight
& I think of fire, how
I learned hell was infinite
distance from You—which,
revising, I've realized must be
ironic. You were there in that
truck sitting right beside him
when his head tilted down
at his eyes' relaxing into
something like prayer.
You were how a coyote
will lead a dog miles
from home before giving
the ambush signal, or the way
an owl once dragged a jack-
rabbit into an oak over me
with a single talon. You
were asphalt the parched
buck mistook for water
on account of mirages
imagined by him. You
were saving nothing.

J. SCOTT BROWNLEE

Dog Star

Canine sphere caught in the spin of the still-
turning earth, has your prodigal orbit
decayed enough yet for the words
of your father the wolf to reach you?
You outshine Ursa Major & her galaxies,
nexus splitting dim suns like Esau & Jacob
after Jacob's blessing rendered birthrights
worthless. In the low-income housing
the halogen parking lot lights erased you
but I still took a compass & badly
drawn map with some Twix bars
to share with the hungry children
who knew how to find you in their step-
parents' yawns between Camel filters
& the run-a-muck cats who escaped
the pound crying out shrill lovemaking.
You were brightest at dusk when the bull-
frog chatter proved the purest music.
We deduced you in April through Oakley
sun shades at the varsity game clinching
our division on account of a home run
my friend Quentin hit—the first one
of his life at 5'2" & 100 pounds
after a meal—95 before it: David made

Goliath. You confounded the underdog's
undertaker, & the dead dreamt your blue
hallelujahs each night before their ascension.
How can I wander from my only life
into the dark matter circling the next
without first saluting your green
conflagration? You flare through my torso
& up into my skull where you tell me
I'm made, I am fearfully made by the dark
itself, riddlesome dark without hands,
dark ejecting a red jet of algorithms
whose faint blueprints assemble the sub-
atomic core of God's consciousness.
You remind me dark balances Eden
& Adam with an anti-Eden & an anti-Adam—
every possible path preferable to just one
line of 1s & 0s. At the center of it burns
an anti-Godhead: alpha leading a wolf pack
of stars before you stretched to oblivion.

JESSICA WILBANKS

Made in Nigeria

Excerpted from *When I Spoke in Tongues: A Story of Faith and Its Loss.*

The face of Christianity was changing. Long ago the first Christian missionaries had trickled into the headwaters of the Niger River in twos and threes, clinging to British trade ships and braving malaria to spread the good news to the so-called Dark Continent. But now, just over a century later, private jets left Murtala Muhammed International Airport in Lagos on a daily basis, ferrying Nigerian evangelists toward waiting crowds of thousands at churches in Europe, the United States, and elsewhere in the now-secular West. Pastor Enoch Adeboye's church, the Redeemed Christian Church of God, captured my attention more than any other.

The pastor had grown up in a mud hut, the first son of his father's third wife. His family were Christians, but whenever sickness or catastrophe struck, they went to the traditional healers for help. Legend had it that when Adeboye was taken to one of these healers as a child, the healer prophesied that he would be a great man, far outshining the other stars in the constellations. Pastor Adeboye had been the first in his family to own a pair of shoes, the youngest instructor in the history of the Nigerian university system, and the first to grow one of Nigeria's small Pentecostal churches into a global megachurch with five million members in Nigeria alone. I'd never heard his name before, but *Newsweek* had ranked him alongside Osama bin Laden and President Barack Obama in a list of the world's fifty most influential people. I felt a strange sense of pride in Enoch Adeboye's story, as if he was a cousin or an uncle or some distant relation. He seemed to be the embodiment of my favorite of all of Jesus's promises—that the poor would one day be made rich.

The Redeemed Church seemed to be growing the most quickly of all of the "mushroom churches," as the Pentecostal denominations were dubbed by Nigerians. There were six thousand separate congregations in Nigeria, and over three hundred in North America. Reporters hadn't been able to verify the church's claim that six million people attended their yearly Holy Ghost Convention in Lagos—but if it were true, that made it the largest Christian gathering in the world.

When I found out that the Redeemed Church had spread all the way from Nigeria to Houston, I woke up early one Sunday morning and pulled out various dresses, checking hemlines and necklines until I found something that seemed modest enough to wear to a service. The Pavilion of Redemption rented a fifteen-hundred-square-foot storefront space in an industrial patch of southwestern Houston, about a half hour from my inner-loop apartment. The neighborhood was dotted with gas stations, cash advance depots, and stores advertising prepaid cell phones. As I slowed down on the largely empty highway and searched for the address, I noticed a Korean Pentecostal church and a Spanish Pentecostal church occupying the same block. Finally, on the corner of Bissonnet and Southwest Freeway, I spotted the logo of the Redeemed Church—a purple circle with a small white dove at its center.

When I opened the door of the storefront church, the tiny, carpeted room was filled with men and women and children, most in traditional Nigerian dress. Someone had used plastic columns and artificial plants and curtains to set a kind of stage apart from the rest of the room. I tried to hide in the back of the church, but a stern teenage boy in a pin-striped suit escorted me to the very front row. Family after family came over to greet me before the service started, asking my name and what I was up to in Houston. The worship service began with a squeal of music—guitar, a keyboard, and tambourines. If it wasn't for the presence of the talking drums—hourglass-shaped drums used for traditional Yorùbá songs—I could have been in the church I grew up in. Much of the music was the same, and the lyrics in the songs were so simple and catchy that I was still able to keep up.

The pastor of the church was a slight man in an ill-fitting Western-style suit, but his voice was like a thunderbolt. He changed tones easily, moving from a gentle tone to a fierce one as he prayed over the congregation, and then picked up his gentle tone once again as he announced that there would be no sermon today, as it was the first Sunday of the month. Instead, the service would be devoted to testimonies of the ways the Lord worked in our lives. He warned the congregation that this time was meant to be used solely for testimonies, rather than songs. "If you want to sing, then join the choir!" he said sternly.

For over an hour his parishioners came up to the altar, one after another, young teenagers in fashionable Western clothes and plump grandmothers in *dashiki*. Everyone started the same way, by praising the Lord, and then launched into stories of how God had touched them. The first person was a delicate-looking teenage girl with wide brown eyes. She announced that by the grace of God she had just graduated from high school. Then came a woman who talked about accidentally leaving her wallet on the hood of the car, going to her job as a prison guard, and then coming back out and finding to her delight that it was still on the hood. "It was God!" she exclaimed loudly, and the whole congregation clapped and whooped. Multiple people who thanked God for not getting a ticket when a police officer pulled them over, two more recent graduates who thanked God and their families, a man from Dallas who told of how God came to his rescue when he was trying to turn a rented moving van around in the mountains of West Virginia and got stuck. Another man told the story of finding a wallet and driving to the address listed on the license to return it to a white American woman, who initially refused to open to door to a black man. "Thank God for not making me a thief!" he said.

Afterwards, while members of the church milled around, squeezing toddlers' cheeks, packing up instruments, and swapping Tupperware containers of hard-to-find Nigerian culinary essentials like yam flour and *gari*, the pastor listened to me prattle on about my research and then flashed a smile, and shook his head, waving away my attempts at an explanation.

"You are welcome here," he said. "All blood runs red in the kingdom of God." And then he invited me to the Redeemed Church's weekend-long Holy Ghost convention the following month, where six thousand Nigerian Christians from all over North America met on a plot of land outside of Dallas for a prayer and miracle service.

It hadn't really made sense for me to go. The convention was in the middle of June, during a heat wave that was epic even for Texas, and my ancient Volvo lacked air-conditioning and leaked oil on long road trips. I could barely afford the gas, much less a hotel room, and besides all the hotels in a ninety-mile radius seemed to have been sold out months before. But I finally dug out my credit card and paid the registration fee. A few weeks later, I left my cat a heaping bowl of food, packed a plastic grocery bag full of peanut butter and jelly sandwiches, and piled a yoga mat, pillow, and sleeping bag in the back of the car. As I followed the highway outside of Houston and eyed my oil gauge, I whispered a half-ironic prayer that everything would work out.

The moon was only a fingernail as I followed the long dark roads of the tiny town of Floyd in East Texas, but as I approached Redemption Camp the flood lights illuminating the parking lot lit up the sky to near daylight. Just past a low-rent trailer park called Mockingbird Estates, a long line of traffic snaked past the sprawling cemetery of a hundred-year-old white clapboard church with darkened windows and uncut grass. As the deeply grooved dirt road doglegged to the right I braked slowly so as not to spit gravel on the small, hand-lettered sign in front of the church. *Floyd United Methodist, a Church for the Future.* And then in smaller type, *Rev. Bill Shaddox.* I wondered what the minister thought of his new neighbors. Rev. Shaddox also probably believed that God's hand was alive in the world, but he was probably well aware that if he went to his bishop saying God had spoken to him and given him a message, the bishop would think the time had come to pack him off to the retirement home.

A whistle blew and a teenage boy in a bright orange vest waved me forward. A hundred yards farther up, dun-colored trailers and modest ranch-style houses gave way to lush cornfields and trees tented with kudzu, and Redemption Camp finally came into view for the first time. I had expected an enormous megachurch, but there wasn't much to see—just a vast expanse of asphalt dotted with stadium lights and an enormous white canvas tent perched on a concrete foundation. The tent looked empty and unoccupied, but as the line of traffic crept closer, the piercing noise of the cicadas gave way to snatches of hymns, the deep-throated trills of a preacher's voice booming from a speaker inside the tent and low murmur of *amens* coming every minute or so, like a drumbeat. Just past the parking lot, rows of picnic tables were set up and women in traditional Nigerian dress sold *jollof* rice, bean cakes, and peppered chicken at steep prices. Families in African garb—shiny fabrics of orange and red and purple topped off with towering headdresses for the women—and families in Western church clothes crowded around the tables drinking Coke and Fanta from glass bottles.

I followed a crowd of people into the tent and found a seat on a folding chair toward the back, so far from the stage that I had to squint to see beyond the blurs of color. On the projector screen above the stage was a gravelly voiced white woman with thickly applied makeup and a southern accent. She looked to be in her early fifties. Like so many other Pentecostal pastors, Sheryl Brady's life was her testimony, and she spent the first portion of her sermon establishing her credentials. She spoke quietly and seriously of pain and torment. She had dropped out of high school at fifteen, cut down by a series of three losses. Her father had died of a heart attack, and her sister had died of hepatitis, and then her mother had been in a terrible car accident. Sheryl married at the age of seventeen, shy and quiet, and had three children before she was twenty. For years she lived from paycheck to paycheck, left out of God's promises, unsure of his plan for her life. Not until her forties did she become a pastor and a conference speaker. Her destiny, she said, had been locked up inside her, and it was only through her faith in God that she was able to draw it out. Now she stood in front of us, an intimidating, perfectly coiffed presence, a lady preacher who shouted like an old-school revival minister.

She read from that chapter from the Book of Luke—the one where Peter, one of Jesus's disciples, went fishing with Jesus. Jesus called him his rock, but he was just as much of a doubter as Thomas. Even after seeing miracle after miracle—loaves to fishes, water to wine—he just couldn't open his mind up enough to take in the true nature of the kingdom of God. In this particular story, Peter had been fishing all day and had caught nothing at all. He was back on the shore, cleaning his nets, when Jesus beckoned him out again. He probably hadn't wanted to go, but he listened to Jesus and let down the nets. He caught so many fish his nets nearly broke.

"Look under your boat," she exhorted the congregation. "If you look under your boat, you will see the hand of God holding all those fish back. Jesus was there that day to teach Peter that being a professional fisherman meant absolutely nothing. God is in charge. It doesn't matter how much you study, how much you prepare. Doors will not open for you unless God ordains it. You won't catch a single fish unless God wills it."

Toward the end of her sermon Pastor Sheryl ran her eyes over those many thousands of people and got quiet. Too quiet. She asked us if we were tired, worn out by work and family responsibilities. She looked at us hard and dared us to say it wasn't true.

"Well," she said, "what do you have to show for all that work? Do you have any power? Do you have the ability to heal? Can you lay hands on your body and cast the sickness out? You are closer than you think you are. You have these gifts. Just look under your boat. What does the Bible tell us? Not by might, nor by power, but by the Holy Spirit. You are closer than you think you are to that power," she said, and a hush went through the congregation. "That's why I came to Floyd, Texas," she said in a voice as low and throaty as a lifelong smoker. "To tell you that you are closer to that power than you think you are."

*

In a strange coincidence that my mother would have immediately labeled a sign, the first person I met when I pulled up at Redemption Camp again the following morning was the brother of James Fadele, the pastor who had helped establish the United States branch of the Redeemed Church. Pastor Fadele had been charged by Pastor Adeboye with turning what had been a few years ago a sorghum and wheat field into the denomination's North American headquarters. Thanks to his brother's introduction, within twenty-four hours I found myself sitting in Pastor Fadele's palatial home as the stout pastor explained how he found himself in the position of bringing God's word to the heart of East Texas.

"It doesn't come all at once," James Fadele told me, hopping back and forth between tending to his daughters and helping a visiting pastor from Delaware set up a website for his church. He was trying to explain how God's blessing worked. "If it did, God knows we'd run from it. God dips you in, little by little, to see what you can stand."

Pastor Fadele had grown up in the same family compound outside of Lagos where Pastor Adeboye had grown up. Unlike Adeboye's family, Fadele's family was Catholic. "Well, not exactly," Pastor Fadele said, correcting himself. He explained that his father had attended Catholic services, but refused to officially convert to Catholicism because it would have meant abandoning two of his three wives. As a child Pastor Fadele was a strong student and a devout Christian, winning a scholarship to an American university. After graduating he took a job as an engineer at Ford Motor Company, and then racked up a number of advanced degrees while he tried his hand at various businesses: first detailing cars, then running a few Wendy's franchises. On a visit to the US, Pastor Adeboye encouraged him to start a church, and after initially making some excuses, Pastor Fadele started a small congregation in the basement of his Detroit home. Around that same time, Adeboye had received word from the Lord that Texas was destined to be the North American headquarters of the Redeemed Church. The prophecy was confirmed when a white farmer approached a small group of Redeemed pastors as they sat in a restaurant in Dallas. The man told them that years before, God had instructed him to purchase a hundred acres of pastureland in Floyd. God told him that the land didn't belong to him, but rather a group of "church people." And then he offered to sell it to the pastors for the same low price he had originally purchased it for. Adeboye soon appointed Pastor Fadele as the head of the Redeemed Church's North American division, and Pastor Fadele approached his new mission in the same way he had tackled his engineering degree and fast-food franchises. Within a year construction had started on the plot of land that would slowly become the mirror image of that eighteen-thousand-acre plot of land in Nigeria, just north of Lagos, where a million worshippers gathered every year for the church's annual convention.

Pastor Fadele told me he had been the one who urged his boss to invest in internet technology, including a state-of-the-art website that live-streamed Pastor Adeboye's sermons during their Holy Ghost Services in both Lagos and Texas. It was on that website, back in Houston, that I had first been seduced by the church's mission and vision: "to make heaven" and "to take as many people with us as possible." They pledged to plant churches within five minutes walking distance of every city and town in developing countries, and a five-minute driving distance of cities and towns in developed countries.

"You Americans don't talk about that," he said, removing his delicate glasses to run a handkerchief over them. "You talk about pearly gates and eternal rewards. But Africans believe that we can build a piece of heaven on earth, in our daily lives. Teachers can build heaven at school. Parents can build heaven for their children. And churches can make their congregations a place where God lives and breathes. In Africa, we believe that we can call heaven down to meet us. God wants us to be whole. He wants us to prosper. We don't have to wait until we die to live in glory, here on earth."

I asked Pastor Fadele about his reception from the white community in Floyd. I myself was dubious. Not that long ago, the road connecting Floyd to the county seat had a banner over it that boasted "Blackest Land, Whitest People." Floyd was settled by hearty pioneers from the Deep South, lured east by the rich Texas Blackland Prairie. They'd brought their conservative brand of Christianity, and their slaves, if they were wealthy enough to have them. Many of the black residents of Floyd could trace their lineage back to the days when cotton was king and slave labor was the cheapest way to get that cotton out of the ground. Like most other small towns in this part of the world, the history of Hunt County was rife with lynchings and other hate crimes. Just six years before the Methodist church up the street was founded, a mob of two thousand white residents overpowered a group of officers and seized a young black man who had been accused of assaulting a white woman. The next morning they burned him alive in the south side of the town square. Years later, the white residents of Floyd seemed to have nothing but suspicion for their Nigerian neighbors.

"I don't like to be called a racist, but I don't like to be overrun, either," Luanne Moody told a reporter from the *Dallas Morning News* who knocked on the door of her mobile home in Floyd seeking her opinion of the church. "I don't have any problem with black people. . . . I just feel uncomfortable in large numbers of them."

"I'm not a racist," echoed her neighbor, Tina Causey, a sixty-nine-year-old housecleaner, when a reporter from the *New York Times* came calling. "I just don't like a majority of anybody."

"We'll give them some time," Pastor Fadele laughed, smiling so wide his dimples showed. "Right now they're peeping out the windows, asking each other, where did all those Africans come from? Where did they get those clothes? But then they'll hear the music, they'll feel the Spirit, and they'll come. And we can't wait to have them."

Pastor Fadele rummaged through his briefcase, found the program for the convention, and flipped it open to the governor's letter welcoming the church members to the convention, thanking them for their service, and wishing them success as they worked to lay a strong spiritual foundation for the community. The Hunt County Judge wrote a letter as well, offering his prayers that the conference be both divine and sanctified, and asking the Lord to shower the group with peace and holy tranquility. Maybe Pastor Fadele was right. There weren't many other white people at the convention, but I'd read an article about a church in London, founded by a Nigerian pastor, who regularly hosted four thousand people for its Sunday services.

When I was done asking my questions, Pastor Fadele wanted to know why I'd come to Redemption Camp and why I was so interested in the way they worshipped in Nigeria. I stuttered out an answer, telling him that I had grown up in the church but had gone away from it, and now I was curious about the faith again.

He shook his head knowingly. "God is stirring your heart," he said, and asked me if I'd ever considered traveling to Nigeria. "You won't know what God is doing in my country unless you stand with a million Nigerians at the Holy Ghost Service," he said. "I have a feeling that if you will go there you will come back changed."

I'm sure my neck flushed, the way it always does when I'm overcome with some strong rush of emotion. I hadn't thought of going to Nigeria until Pastor Fadele said those words, but as soon as that idea was out there in the world it became my idea, and the path immediately unfurled in front of me. I'd find the money. I'd go to Nigeria and immerse myself in the faith I had left as a child.

Months later, when I lobbied my graduate school adviser to change my thesis to an exploration of Nigerian Pentecostalism, I'd make the case that there was a story here, a story that I—being a former believer myself—was highly qualified to tell. I'd position myself as a researcher, an intellectual, not a spiritual seeker making a religious pilgrimage. But even then I sensed that there was something else going on, something that had to do with that wonder-working power that I had sung about as a child. That inchoate thing that surged through the congregation when the worship service had reached its peak, that sudden fierceness in my mother's voice when she prayed over a fever, binding it up and sending the spirit of sickness straight back to the Devil. That strange, upside-down sort of power that I had so craved as a girl. The power that stemmed from obedience and transcended race and class and status. I felt that old longing swell up inside me—a longing to join up, a longing to submerge myself into the body of Christ and forget myself and my own desires.

At nine o'clock on the final night of the revival, praise choirs from congregations all over the country poured in from all sides of the tent. Pastor Fadele took the stage and introduced his mentor to the gathered crowds. "Here is Brother Enoch Adeboye," he shouted. "Made in heaven, born in Nigeria, exported to the world!" At the sight of the General Overseer of the church, the man they affectionately called Daddy G.O., the tent erupted into an ocean of sound. Pastor Adeboye was a tall man with a broad forehead and a ready smile, and he wore a bright-blue pin-striped suit with a dark-colored bow tie. As he preached the music slowly swelled up behind him, keeping step with his throaty, British-inflected voice as he called heaven down to meet us. Again and again he talked of power—the electric pulse that lived in each of us, divinely implanted there by God, doomed to go unused unless we activated it. He promised that if we took full advantage of that power, every evil thing in our life would be neutralized, and we would come into the full manifestation of what we were intended by God to become. Every few minutes he interrupted his sermon with flashes of prophecy that God had given him. There was someone among us tonight who had a bad back. God was about to set that person free. Another person had been out of work for many years. A job would come to them very soon. "Those of you who have any form of sickness," he said, "tonight God will set you free!" I found myself listening carefully every time he prophesied, half-expecting to hear him name my problems. *There is someone here tonight who walked away from God long ago. Turn her around and set her on the right path.*

As Pastor Adeboye's sermon wound to a close, the music climbed to a crescendo. That was when he started whispering into his microphone, luring lost souls. That was the moment when he stepped on the gas. Trumpets and piano notes guided his voice like an arrow into a place beyond the brain. Grey-haired grandmothers began kicking off their pumps in a Pentecostal fury and danced across the floor; children threw up their hands to God as if they had suddenly been unshackled. Pastor Adeboye's voice sharpened and crackled and he pleaded with us all to come back to God and cast off our evil, doubting ways. He reminded us of everything the Lord had promised. The poor will be rich, the meek will inherit the earth, and the lost will be found. Those who were slighted and disrespected on earth would receive their just rewards. Pastor Adeboye said that God had arrived before us at this campground and had been waiting for us. "Now the two of you are about to meet!" he shouted.

Later that night, I'd sit in my car for hours as dawn cracked open over the Texas countryside and the long, rumbling pack of cars wound their way through the dirt roads of Hunt County until they reached the interstate. Back at my motel, I'd nod to the elderly proprietor when he glared at me—no doubt a loose woman coming home from a nefarious liaison. In my tiny room I'd pull the blinds closed and curl up on the overly firm double bed, opening my laptop to capture all my impressions while they were still fresh on the surface of my mind. I'd write about the scene as if I was outside of it, unaffected by it. But there in the tent, I'd watched uneasily, holding my pen tightly. I hadn't counted on the music and the way it swelled open a hollow place deep inside my chest. When people started rising around me like prairie dogs popping up out of their holes, I stayed seated until I felt a hand on my shoulder. The woman next to me, a young mother whose baby son was bound on her back in a colorful *kanga*, met my eyes and beckoned me up. My throat seized up, and I started to wave her away. But it was one-thirty in the morning, and the woman had the same sweet half-smile my mother had, so I rose obediently, my pen and notebook clattering to the floor.

She and I were two small bodies in the midst of thousands, swaying in a sea of buzzing voices. I could feel all the faith and passion I had as a girl, right there beneath the surface of my skin. My brain reminded me that I didn't believe in any of this anymore, but when the music tugged at me, I didn't fight it. I lifted my face to the sky. For the first time in years I heard the raw, raucous beauty of those strange heavenly languages, swelling to fill all the space available in that tent. I couldn't understand a word of it apart from a few scattered phrases, *Holy* and *Jesus*, but it didn't matter. I knew they were calling on the Lord in tongues, singing their love for him and calling on him to fulfill all his promises. It would have been so easy to open my mouth and join those other babbling voices in a mass of praise, but my mouth stayed closed. Instead I breathed all that frantic worship in and held it inside my ribcage. My neighbor squeezed my hand and I squeezed back. Then she lifted both our hands to the sky, as if to get a little bit closer to the place where she thought God's power was.

Love and Hope

RICK BASS

Pagans

There once were two boys, best friends, who loved the same girl, and, in a less-common variation on that ancient story, she chose neither one of them, but went on to meet and choose a third, and lived happily ever-after.

One of the boys, Richard, nearly gambled his life on her—poured everything he had into the pursuit of her—Annie—while the other boy, Kirby, was attracted to her, intrigued by her, but not to the point where he would risk his life, or his heart, or anything else. It could have been said at the time that all three of them were fools, though no one who observed their strange courtship thought so, or said so; and even now, thirty years later, with the three of them as adrift and asunder from one another as any scattering of dust or wind, there are surely no regrets, no notions of failure or success or what-if: though among the three of them, it is perhaps Richard alone who sometimes considers the past, and imagines how easily things might have been different. How much labor went into the pursuit, and how close they all three passed to different worlds, different histories.

*

Richard and Kirby were seniors in high school, while Annie was yet a junior, and as such, the boys were able to get out of class easier than she was—they were both good students—and because Kirby had a car, an old Mercury with an engine like a locomotive, he and Richard would sometimes spend their skip days traveling down to the coast, forty miles southeast of Houston, drawn by some force they neither understood nor questioned, traveling all the way to the water's edge.

The boys traveled by themselves at night, too, always exploring, and on one of their trips they had found a rusting old crane half-sunk near the estuary of the Sabine River, saltbound, a derelict from gravel quarry days. They had climbed up into the crane (feeling like children playing in a sandbox) and had found that they could manually unspool the loopy wire cable, and with great effort, crank it back in. (When they did so, the rusting, giant gear teeth gave such a clacking roar that the nightbirds roosting down in the graystick spars of dead and dying trees on the other shore took flight, egrets and kingbirds and herons, the latter rising to fly long and slow and gangly across the moon; and as the flecks and flakes of salt rust chipped from each gear tooth during that groaning resurrection, the flakes drifted down toward the river in glittering red columns, sifting fine as sand, orange wisps and strands of iron rust like magic dust being cast onto the river by the conjurings of some midnight sorcerer. Was I falling in love with her, Richard wonders now, or the world, or both?)

With such power at their fingertips, there was no way not to exercise it. Richard climbed down from the crane, muck-waded out into the gray slime salt-rimed shallows—poisoned frogs yelped and skittered from his approach, and the orange sky-dancing flames of the nearby refineries wavered and belched, as if noticing his approach and beckoning him closer; as if desiring to stoke their own ceaseless burning with his own bellyfire.

That first night at the crane, Richard grabbed the massive hook of the cable's end and hauled it back up to shore and fastened it to the undercarriage of Kirby's car, then raised his hand over his head and gave a twirling motion.

Kirby began cranking, and the car began to ascend in a levitation, rising slowly, easily, vertical into the air. Loose coins, pencils, and Coke cans tumbled from the windows at first, but then all was silent save for the steady ratchet of slow gears, cranking one at a time, and the boys howled with pleasure, and more birds lifted from their rookeries and flew off uneasily into the night.

It was only when the car was some twenty feet into the air—dangling, bobbing, and spinning—that Richard thought to ask if the down-gears worked—imagining what a long walk home it would be if they did not—and imagining, too, what the result might be if one of the old iron teeth failed, plummeting the Detroit beast into the mud below.

The gears held. Slowly, a foot at a time in its release, the crane let the car back down toward the road.

The boom would not pivot—had long ago been petrified into its one position, arching out toward the river, like some tired monument facing the direction of a long ago, all-but-forgotten war—but there were hundreds of feet of cable, so that they were able to give each other rides in the rocket car now, one of them lifting it with the crane while the other gripped the steering wheel and held on for dear life, aiming straight for the moon, and praying that the cable would hold.

They soon discovered that by twisting and jouncing around in the passenger seat, the car could be induced to sway further, and to even spin, as it was raised—the Coriolis effect swirling below like an unseen, unmapped river—and it took all of an evening (the spinning headlights on high beam, strafing the mercury-green bilious cloudbank above, where refinery steam crept through the tops of the trees) before they tired of that game (startled birds flying right past the sky-driver's windows, occasionally). They began hooking onto other objects, attaching the Great Claw of Hunger, as they called it, to anything substantial they could find: pulling half-submerged railroad ties from out of the sandbank, the old bumpers of junked cars, twisted steel scrap, rusting slag-heaped refrigerators, washers and dryers.

As if in a game of crude pinball, or some remote-controlled claw-clutch game at an arcade, they were able to lurch their attachments out into the center of the river; and with a little practice, they learned how to disengage the hook midair, which led to satisfying results—dropping junked cars into the river from forty feet up, landing them sometimes back on the road with a grinding clump of sparks, though other times in river's center amidst a great whale-plume of splash.

A sculpture soon appeared in the river's middle: a testament to machines that had been hard-used and burned out early, spring-busted not even halfway through the great century: the steel wheels of trains, cogs and pulleys, transmissions leaking rainbow sheens into the night water, iridescent sentences trailing slowly downstream in perhaps the same manner in which shamans once tossed entrails to determine or sense the world's flow and coming events. Within a few nights they had created an island in the slow current's middle, an island of steel and chrome that gathered the bask of reptiles on the hot days, and into the evenings—turtles, little alligators, snakes, and bullfrogs. There was no notion of choice, then—no *either* Kirby, no *or* Richard. There was just joy.

Nights were the best. There were still fireflies back then, along the Sabine, and the fireflies would cruise along the river and across the toxic fields, swirling around the angel-ascending car, the joy ride: and the riders, the journeyers, would imagine that they were astronauts, voyaging through the stars, cast already out into some distant future.

In September the river was too low for barges to use, though when the rains of winter returned the river would rise quickly (flooding the banks and filling the cab of the crane), and the riverboat captains working at night would have to contend with the new obstacle of the junk-slag island, not previously charted on their maps, and they might or might not marvel at the origin or genesis of the structure, but would merely tug at the brim of their cap, note the obstacle in the logbook, and pass on, undreaming, laboring toward the lure of the ragged refineries, ferrying more oil and chemicals, hundreds of barrels of toxins sloshing quietly in the rusty steel drums stacked atop their barges, and never imagining they were passing the fields of love. . . .

Richard and Kirby bought an old diving bell in an army-navy surplus store for fifty dollars—they had to cut a new rubber gasket for the hatch's seal—and after that, they were able to give each other crane rides into the poison river.

For each of them it was the same, whether lowering or being lowered: the crane's operator swinging the globe out over moonlit water the color of mercury, then lowering the globe, with his friend in it, into that nether world—the passenger possessing only a flashlight, which dimmed quickly upon submersion, and then disappeared—the globe tumbling downcurrent then, and the passenger within not knowing whether the cable was still attached or not, bumping and tumbling, spotlight probing the black depths thinly, with bright brief glimpses of fish eyes, gold-rimmed and wild in fright, and the pale turning-away bellies of wallowing things flashing past, darting left and right to get out of the way of the tumbling iron ball of the bathysphere.

The cable stretching taut, then, and shuddering against the relentless current: swaying and shimmering in place, but traveling no more.

Then the emergence, back up out of total darkness and into the night. The gas flares still flickering all around them. Why, again, was the rest of the world asleep? The boys took comfort in the knowledge that they would never sleep: never.

On their afternoon school-skip trips together, the three of them traveling to the Gulf Coast, they would wander the beaches barefooted, walking beneath the strand line, studying the gulf as if yearning to travel still farther—as if believing that, were they to catch it just right, the tide might one day pull back so far as to reveal the entire buried slope, entirely new territory—though this was not a clamant yearning, for already, so much else was just as new. It was more like a consideration.

Beyond the smokestack flares of the refineries, there was an abandoned lighthouse, its base barnacle-encrusted, out on a windy jetty, that they enjoyed ascending, on some such trips, and once up into the glassed-in cupola, they would drink hot chocolate from a thermos they had brought, sharing the one cup, and would play the board game of Risk, to which they were addicted.

And slowly, within Annie, a little green fire began to burn, as she spent more and more time with the two older boys; and more quickly, an orange fire began to flicker, then burn, within Richard, as he began to desire to spend more and more time in her company.

Only Kirby seemed immune, his own light within cool and blue.

They played on.

*

By mid-September Kirby and Richard were bringing Annie out to play the bathysphere game, and to view their slag island. They would come out on lunch break, and would skip a class before and sometimes after, to buy them the time they needed. There was a bohemian French African oceanography teacher who was retiring that year, and who could see plainly what Richard, if not Kirby, was trying to do, chasing the heart of the young girl—the junior. The teacher—Miss Counteé, who wore a beret—would write hall passes for all three of them, knowing full well they would be leaving campus, issuing the passes under the stipulation that they bring back specimens for her oceanography lab.

They drove through the early autumn heat with the windows down and an old green canoe on top of their car. They paddled out to the new slag island and had picnics of French bread and green apples and cheese.

They piled lawn chairs atop the edifice. And even though the water was poisoned, the sound of it, as they lay there in the sun with their sleeves rolled up, and their shoes and socks off, eyes closed, was the same as would be the sound of waves in the Bahamas, or a clear cold stream high in the mountains. Just because the water was ugly did not mean it had to sound ugly.

Richard knew that to the rest of the world Annie might have appeared slightly gangly, even awkward; but that had nothing to do with how his heart was leaping now, each time he saw her—and after they began traveling to the river, he started to notice new things about her. Her feet pale in the sun, her shoulders rounding, her breasts lifting. A softening in her eyes, as the beauty in her heart began to rise out of her. And many years later, after their lives separated, he would believe there was something about the sound, the harmonics, of that ravaged river, and her ability to love it, and take pleasure in it, that released something from within her: transforming in ancient alchemy the beautiful unseen into the beautifully tangible. And Kirby would agree with him: that there had been alchemy, in those days, and even amidst so much poison.

The water lapping lightly against the edges of the green canoe, tethered to one of the steel spars mid-pile. Umbrellas for parasols: crackers and cheese. Annie's pale feet browning in the sun. Perspiration at their temples, under their arms, in the small of their backs. Richard felt himself descending, sinking deeper into love, or what he supposed was love. How many years, he wondered, before the two were married and they would browse upon one another, in similar sunlight, in another country, another life? He was content to wait forever.

It was, however, as if Annie's own fire, the quiet green one, would not or could not quite merge with his leaping, dancing orange one. As if the two fires (or three fires) needed to be in each other's company, and were supported, even fed, by each other's warmth—but they could not, or would not yet, combine.

Without true heat of conviction, Annie would sometimes try to view the two boys separately, and would even, in her girl's way, play or pretend at imagining a future. Kirby, she told herself, was more mature, more responsible—he could run an old crane! As well, there was an instinct that seemed to counsel her to both be drawn toward, yet also move away from, Richard's own more exposed fires and energies. . . .

It was too much work to consider, it was all pretend anyway, or almost pretend. They had found a lazy place, a sweet place, to hang out, in the eddy between childhood and whatever came next. She told herself she would be happy to wait there forever: and for a while, she believed that.

*

Occasionally, the befouled river would ignite spontaneously; other times, they found that they could light it themselves by tossing matches, or flaming oily rags, out onto its oil- and chemical-slicks. None of the three of them were churchgoers, though Annie, a voracious reader, had been carrying around a Bible that autumn, reading it silently on their picnics, while crunching an apple. The bayou-breeze, river-breeze, stirring her strawberry hair.

"I want to give the river a blessing," she said, the first time she saw the river ignite. The snaky, wandering river fires, in various bright petrochemical colors, seemed more like a celebration than harbinger of death or poison, and they told themselves too that they were doing the river a favor, helping to rid it of excess toxins, through such incinerations.

They loaded their green canoe with gallon jugs of water the next day, tap water straight from their Houston faucets and hoses.

The canoe rode low in the poisoned water on their short trip out to the iron-and-chrome island, carrying the load of the three of them as well as their jugs of water. The gunwales of their green boat were no more than an inch above the vile murk of the river, and they sat in the canoe as still as perched birds to avoid capsizing, and let the current carry them to the island of trash.

Once there, they spent nearly the rest of the afternoon scrubbing with steel wool, and pouring the clean bright water over the crusted, rusted, mud-slimed ornamenture of bumpers and freezers, boat hulls and car bodies. They polished the chrome appurtenances and rinsed the mountain anew. They waded around its edges, oblivious to the sponges of their own pure skin taking in the river's, and the world's, poison.

When they had it sparkling, Annie climbed barefooted to the top and read a quote from Jeremiah: "And I brought you into the plentiful country, to eat the fruit thereof and the goodness thereof; but when ye entered, ye defiled my land and made mine heritage an abomination."

On her climb up to the top, she had gashed her foot on the rusted corner of one sharp piece or another. She paid it no mind as she stood up there in her overalls, her red-brown hair stirring in the wind, a startlingly bright trickle of blood leaking from her pale bare foot, and Richard had the uneasy feeling that something whole and vital and time-crafted, rare and pure in the world, was leaking out of her through that wound, and that he—with his strange vision of the world, and his half-assed, dreamy shenanigans—was partly responsible: if not for leading her directly astray, then at least leading her down the path to the flimsy or even unlatched gate, and showing her a view beyond.

And Kirby too, viewing her blood, felt an almost overpowering wave of tenderness, and with his bare hand quickly wiped the blood from her foot, then put his arm around her as if to comfort her, though she did not feel discomforted: and now the two of them sank a bit deeper into the fields of love, like twin pistons dropping a little deeper, leaving Richard off-balance for a moment, for a day, poised above, distanced now. . . .

*

There was no clean water left with which to rinse or purify themselves, after the ceremony. Instead, they burned handfuls of green Johnson grass, wands of slow-swirling blue smoke. Like pagans, they paddled back to shore, mucked across the oily sandbar, and while Richard and Kirby were loading the canoe back onto the car, Annie went off into the tall waving grass to pee, and when she came back she was carrying a dead white egret: not one of the splendid but common yellow-legged cattle egrets, but a larger and much rarer snowy egret (within their lifetime it would go extinct), whiter than even the clouds—so white that as Annie carried it, it seemed to glow—and it had died so recently that it was still limp.

She laid it down in the grass for them to examine. They stroked its head, and the long crested plumes flowing from the head. Perhaps it was only sleeping. Perhaps they could resuscitate it. Kirby stretched the wings out into a flying position, then folded them back in tight against its body. Nothing. Annie's eyes watered, and again Kirby felt the overpowering wave of tenderness that was not brotherly, but stronger, wilder, fiercer: as if it came from the river itself.

It seemed that the obvious thing to do would be to bury the egret, but they couldn't bring themselves to give such beauty back to the earth, much less to such an oily, drippy, poisoned earth, and so they took the canoe and paddled back out to the island, and laid the bird—fierce-eyed and thick-beaked—to rest in the crown of the island, staring downriver like a gunner in his turret, with the breeze stirring his elegant plumage, and a wreath of green grass in a garland around his snowy neck.

This time on the way out they remembered their oceanography assignment, and scooped up a mayonnaise jar full of water and sediment that was the approximate color and consistency of watery diarrhea, and swabbed a dip net through the grass shallows, coming up with a quick catch of crabs and bent-backed, betumored mullet minnows, and then they loaded the canoe and drove back to school, through the brilliant heat, the brilliant light, the three of them riding in the front seat together.

When they got back to school—a feeling like checking back into a jail—they hurried up the stairwell with their fetid bounty, late to class as usual, and placed their murky-watered bottles on the cool marble lab table at the front of the room for the rest of the class to see.

Miss Counteé made alternating clucking sounds of pleasure and then dismay as she examined the macroinvertebrates as well as the crippled vertebrates, murmuring their names in genus and species, not as if naming them but as if greeting old acquaintances, old warriors perhaps from another time and place—and the other students got up from their seats and crowded around the jars and bottles as if to be closer to the presence of magic.

Richard and Annie and Kirby would still have the marsh scent of the river upon them, and the blue smoke odor of burnt Johnson grass, and sometimes, for a moment, Miss Counteé and the students would get the strange feeling that the truly wild catch that had been brought in resided not in the mayonnaise jars, but in the catchers themselves.

Miss Counteé took an eyedropper and snorted up a shot of dead Sabine, dripped it onto a slide, slid it under a microscope, and then crooned at all the violent erratica dashing about beneath her: the athleticism and diversity, the starts and stops and lunges, the silky passages, the creepings and slitherings, the throbbings and pulsings.

The river was dying, but it was still alive.

*

By October the leaves on the wounded trees at water's edge were turning yellow, and Annie was riding in the bathysphere.

It was different, in the daytime. As the sphere tumbled, she could orient herself to the surface by the bright glare above—the bouncy, jarring ride to the bottom, the tumultuous drift downstream, and then the shuddering tautness when the cable reached full draw. Usually she was busy laughing or praying for her life, but sometimes, at full stretch, she considered sex.

It was different, in the daytime, when the crane lifted the sphere free and clear of the river: different, in the birth back into that bright light, water cascading off the bathysphere and glittering in sheets and torrents of sun diamonds (the awful river transformed, in that moment, into something briefly beautiful). Sometimes, to tease her, the boys would let her remain down there just a beat or two longer, each time: just long enough for the precursor of a thought to begin to enter her mind, the image that—despite their obvious affection for her—something had snapped within them. Not quite the thought, but the advancing shadow of the thought—the chemical synapses stirring and shifting, rearranging themselves to accommodate the approaching, imagined conception—of the boys, her friends, climbing down from the crane and getting in the car and driving off. Not *abandoning* her, but going off for a burger and fries. And then forgetting her, perhaps, or getting in a wreck. Something. Anything.

Not quite loneliness, and not quite desperation. But not quite the old security she'd known all her life, either. She loved it, and was terrified by it.

Always, the boys pulled her up and reeled her back in, before the thought of abandonment came, and the thought beyond that—the terror of utter loneliness, utter emptiness.

None of them questioned the fact that the crane was there for them, a relic still operating for them. They didn't question that it was tucked out of the way below a series of dunes and bluffs, away from the prying, curious eyes of man, and didn't question the grace, the luck, that allowed them to run it, day or night, unobserved. They didn't question that the world, the whole world, belonged to them.

There were still a million, or maybe a hundred thousand, or at least ten thousand, such places left in the world, back then. Soft seams of possibility, places where no boundaries had been claimed—places where reservoirs of infinite possibility lay exposed and waiting for the claimant, the discoverer, the laborer, the imaginer. Places of richness and health, even in the midst of heart-rotting, gut-eating poisons.

For the first time, however, Richard and Kirby began to view each other as competitors. It was never a thought that lasted—always, they were ashamed of it, and able to banish it at will—but for the first time, it was there.

*

The egret fell to pieces slowly. Sunbaked, rained-upon, wind-ruffled, ant-eaten, it deflated as if only now was its life leaving it; and then it disintegrated further, until soon there were only piles of sun-bleached feathers lying in the cracks and crevices of the junk-slag island below, and feathers loose too within the ghost-frame of its own skeleton, still up there at the top of the machines.

As the egret decomposed, so too was revealed the quarry within—the last meal upon which it had gorged—and they could see within the bone-basket of its ribcage all the tiny fish skeletons, with their piles of scaleglitter lying around like bright sand. There were bumps and tumors, misshapen bends in the fishes' skeletons, and as they rotted (flies feasting on them within that ventilated ribcage, as if trapped in a bottle, but free, also, to come and go) the toxic sludge of their lives melted to leave a bright metallic residue on the island, stained here and there like stripes of silver paint.

*

Sometimes they would be too restless to fool with even the magnificence of the crane. Bored with the familiar, the three of them would walk down the abandoned railroad tracks, gathering plump late-season dewberries, staining their hands with the juice until they were as black as if they had been working with oil. Kirby or Richard would take off his shirt and make a sling out of it in which to gather the berries. Their mouths, their lips, would be black-ringed, like clowns.

She beheld their bodies. They filled her dreams—first one boy, then the other—as did dreams of ghost ships, and underworld rides. Dreams of a world surely different from this one—a fleshing, a stripping back to reveal the bones and flesh, the red muscle, of a world not at all like the image of the one we believe we have crafted above.

Unsettling dreams, to be shaken off by her, with difficulty, upon awakening. Surely all below is only imagined, she tried to tell herself, only fantasy. Surely there is only one world.

The berries they brought home were sweet and delicious, ripe and plump. The dreams of gas flares, simmering underworld fires, only an image, possessed nothing of the berries' reality. Only one world, she told herself. There is nothing to be frightened of, no need to be cautious about anything.

*

The cracks and fissures of chance, the ruptures at the earth's surface claiming the three of them, then, as surely as all must be claimed—those crevices, crevasses, manifesting or masquerading as random occurrence rather than design or pattern, but operating surely, just beneath the surface, in intricate balancings of need-and-desire, cost-and-recompense—an alignment of fates as crafted and organic, almost always, as the movements of the tides themselves. There was a school Halloween dance that autumn, a party, which Kirby was unable to attend, due to some family matter that had arisen just that week. The crack or crevice, seemingly without meaning.

It was a low-key evening, filled with chaperones, and with the elementary and middle schools combining, that evening, with the high schoolers. The party was filled with Twister and Pin-the-Tail-on-the-Donkey and Bingo and bobbing-for-apples. There was a haunted house, and masked children of all ages in all manners of costumes ran laughing and shouting through the school hallways, and the high schoolers hung back for a while, but then gave themselves over to the fun.

There was dancing in the basketball gym, with some of the children and adults still wearing their masks and costumes, though many of the teenagers had taken off their masks and were now only half-animal—tiger, fairy, princess, gorilla. Their faces were flushed, and the discrepancy between what their hormones were telling them—*destroy, rebel*—and what the rigid bars of their culture were telling them—*no, no, no*—was for the liveliest of them like a pressure cooker.

Annie was dressed as a princess, and Richard a red devil. They sat for a while and watched the other children dance. Annie waited, and was aware of no pressure. It's possible she could afford to step aside of the drumming, mounting pressure her peers were feeling because she had Richard and Kirby in her life, and Richard at her side, much as a young girl might have a pet bear or lion in her backyard. She turned and smiled at Richard, serene, while the records played and the little monsters ran shrieking, bumping against their legs. The scent of sugar in the air. The aura dense around them of all the other itchy, troubled, angst-bound teenagers, wanting sex, wanting power, wanting God, wanting salvation—wanting home and hearth, wanting the open road.

There was no need yet for Annie to participate in any of that confusion. Everything else around her was swirling and tattering, but she was grounded and centered, and she was loved deeply, and without reason. She smiled, watching Richard watch the dancers. She reached over and took his hand in the darkness and held it, while they watched the dancers, and while they felt the palpable fretting and shifting of their peers. It was lonely, being sunk down to the bottom of the world, she thought, but comfortable, even wonderful, to have each other.

"What do you think Kirby's doing right now?" she asked, twisting his hand in hers.

*

They left the party, and went out for an ice cream sundae, and enjoyed it leisurely, watching the rest of the city zoom by out on the neon strip of Westheimer Road, a busy Friday night, hearing dimly even in the restaurant the whooping and shouting from open car windows, and the screeching of tires, and gears accelerating.

They enjoyed the meal with no conscious forethought of where they were going next—though if anyone had asked them, they would have been able to answer immediately—and after a little while, Kirby drove past, finished with his family engagement, saw Richard's car, and he pulled in and joined them.

With Richard and Annie still wearing their costumes, they journeyed to the east, riding with the windows down as ever, and with the radio playing, but with a seriousness, a quietness, the three of them knowing with the somehow-heavy knowledge of adults that they were ascending now into the world ahead, as if to some upper level, a level which would sometimes be exciting, but where more frequent work would be the order of the day: less dreaming, and more awareness and consciousness. Carve-and-scribe, hammer-and-haul. Almost like a war. As if this unasked-for war must be, and was, the price of all their earlier peace, and all their peace-to-come.

Richard and Annie held hands again in the car on the way east, and the three of them knew by the way the allure for the crane was dying within them as they drew nearer to that sulfurous, wavering glow on the horizon that they would soon be moving on to other things, and in other directions. It was almost for them then—for the first time—as if they were pushing into a heavy headwind.

It was getting late. The city's children had finished their trick-or-treating, and as they passed through a small wooded suburb sandwiched between shopping malls, they stopped and went up and gathered several gutterstubbed candle remnants from the scorched mouths of sagging, sinking, barely glimmering pumpkins.

One pumpkin had already been taken out to the sidewalk for the garbage men to pick up the next morning, and they resurrected that one, placed it on the front seat between Annie and Kirby, and fed it a new candle, coaxed it back to brightness as one might offer a cigarette to an injured or dying man.

They rode through the city and then east toward the refineries, with their runty candles wax-welded all over the front and back dashboards, with the windows rolled almost all the way up now, to keep from extinguishing the little flames—the light on their faces wavering, as they passed through the night (to the passengers in the cars and trucks they passed, it seemed strangely as if Kirby and Richard and Annie were floating, so disorienting was the sight of the big car filled with all those candles—and they kept heading east, toward the flutterings and spumes of the refineries' chemical fire, toward that strange glow that was like daytime-at-night.

It was the night that Annie and Richard went down into the bathysphere, and into the river, together, with Kirby above them, working the manual crank on the crane like a puppeteer. They were still wearing their costumes—there was barely room for them to squeeze in together, and Annie's satin dress spread across the whole bench, and Richard's devil's tail got folded beneath them—he rode with his arm around her, and hers around him, for stability as well as courage, as the globe was lifted swaying from the earth—that first familiar and sickening feeling of powerlessness, as the ground fell away below them—and they rode with an array of candles in front of them.

Their faces were almost touching. *This*, Richard was thinking, *this is how I want it always to be.*

They glimpsed the stars, swinging, as Kirby levered them out over the river, and then there was the thrill of free-fall—"Hold on!" Richard shouted, covering her with both arms and shielding her head—and the concussion of iron meeting water, the great splash—candles went everywhere, spilling warm wax on their hands and wrists, their faces—one landed on Annie's dress and burned a small hole in her dress—and then, once underwater, the globe righted itself and settled in for the brief ride downstream; and with the candles that were still burning they relit the scattered ones, and leaned forward, and cheek to cheek studied the interior of the foul river as they tumbled slowly through its center.

"What if the cable snapped loose?" Richard asked, "when we hit the water so hard?"

Not to be outdone, Annie said, "What if some old bum, as a Halloween joke, sawed the cable down to its last fiber, so that when we reach the end, it will snap?"

There was a long silence as Richard's imagination seized and worked with that one for a while, until it became too-true.

"What if we were stranded on a desert island?" Richard asked.

"How about a forested island?"

"Right," Richard said. "What if? And what if we had only a little while to live?"

"The last man and woman on earth," Annie said.

"Right." *Man and woman.* The phrase sounded so foreign and distant: light years away, still.

"Well," said Annie, "let's wait and see." But her arm tightened around his significantly, and Richard found himself urging the cable to *break, break, break.*

The cable reached full stretch; there was a bumping, and then the globe was swept up and out, tumbling them onto their backs—as if a carpet had been pulled from beneath their feet—and again the candles fell over on them, as did the hot wax, and this time no candles stayed lit, so that they shuddered in darkness, and felt the waves, the intimate urgings of the injured river, washing over and around their tiny iron shell.

The force of the current made eerie sounds, murmurings and chatterings against their craft, as if it, that sick river, had been waiting to speak to them for all their life and had only now gained that opportunity—and they lay there, reclining in each other's arms, safe from the eyes of the world and its demands, its appetites, for paradox and choice; and just as the air was beginning to get stuffy and they were beginning to get a little light-headed, they felt the surge begin: the magnificent power, the brute imprecision of gears and cogs hauling them back upstream, just when they would have imagined (convinced by those fast murmurings and chatterings) that there could be no force stronger or greater than that of the river.

Gradually they broke the surface—through their portal, still lying on their backs, and arm in arm, but relaxed now, they could see the plumes and spray of water as they were birthed back to the surface; they could see the crooked, jarring skyline of the refinery fires, and farther above, the dim stars just beyond the reach of the gold-green luminous puffs of steam that marked the factories.

There was not much time now. Soon they would be up and free of the river, swinging, and then Kirby would land them on the beach. They were hot now, sweating, and there was barely any air left. Annie leaned over and found Richard's face with her hands, and kissed him slowly, with both hands still on his face. He kissed her back—took her face in his hands and tried to shift, in order to cover her with his body, but there was no room—for a moment, they became tangled, cross-elbowed and leg-locked like some human Rubik's cube—they broke off the kiss quickly, and now there was no air at all—as if they had each sucked the last of it from out of the other—but they could feel the craft settling onto the sand beach now, and knew that in scant moments Kirby would be climbing down and coming toward them; that there would be the rap of his knuckles on the iron door, and then the creak of the hatch being opened.

Time for one more kiss, demure and tender now, and then the gritty rasp of the hatch: the counterclockwise twist, and then the lid being lifted, and Kirby's anxious face appearing before them, and beyond him, those dim stars, almost like the echoes or spent husks of stars. Cool October night sliding in over their sweaty faces.

Richard helped Annie out—her dress was a charred mess—and then climbed out behind her, marveling at how delicious even the foul refinery air tasted, in their freedom. Kirby looked at them both curiously, and started to speak, but then could think of nothing to say: and he felt a strange and great sorrow.

They left the bathysphere as it was, sitting hatch-opened and still attached to the crane with its steel umbilicus; for any number of reasons, none of them would ever go back, would never see how the crane would eventually tip over on its side, half-buried in silt; nor how the bathysphere would become buried too.

They rode back into the city, still in costume and with the pumpkin and candles glimmering once more, silent and strangely serious, reflective, on the trip home: Annie and Richard holding hands again. The candle wax was still on their faces, and it looked molten upon them in the candlelight.

On the drive home Annie peeled the candle wax from her face and then peeled off Richard's as well, and held the pressings carefully in one hand.

When Kirby pulled up in front of her house—the living room lights still on, and one of them, mother or father, waiting up, and glancing at the clock (ten minutes past eleven, but no matter; they trusted her), Annie leaned over and gave Richard a quick peck, and gave Kirby a look of almost sultry forgiveness, then climbed out of the big old car (they had extinguished their candles upon entering the neighborhood) and hurried up the walkway to her house, holding her long silk skirt bunched up in one hand and the candle wax pressings in another.

"Well, *fuck*," said Kirby, quietly, unsure of whether he was more upset about what seemed like to him Annie's sudden choice, or about the fracturing that now existed between him and his friend. The imbalance, after so long a run, an all-but-promised run, of security.

"Shit," said Richard, "I'm sorry." He lifted his hands helplessly. "Can we. . . can it. . ." *Stay the same*, he wanted to say, but didn't.

They both sat there, feeling poisoned, even as the other half of Richard's heart—as if hidden behind a mask—was leaping with electric joy.

"I'm sorry," Richard said again.

"The two of you deserve each other," Kirby said. "It's just that, I hate it that—" But the words failed him, there were none, only the bad-burning feeling within: and after sitting there a while longer, they pulled away from her house and drove for a while through the night, as they used to do, back before she had begun riding with them. And for a little while, they were foolish enough, and hopeful enough, to believe that it would not matter, that they could get back to that old place again, and even that that old place would be finer than any new places lying ahead of them.

*

The romance lasted little longer than did the carcass of the egret. The three of them continued to try to do new things together—they did not return to the bathysphere—though Richard and Annie went places by themselves, too, and explored, tentatively, those new territories. Always between or beneath them, however, there seemed to be a bur: not that she had made the wrong choice, but rather, that some choice had been required—that she had had to turn away from one thing, even in the turning-toward another—and that summer, even before the two boys, two young men, prepared to go off to college, while Annie readied herself to return for her senior year of high school, she informed Richard that she thought she would like a couple of weeks apart, to think things over, and to prepare for the pain of his departure. To prepare both of them.

"My God," Richard said, "*two* weeks?" They had been seeing each other almost every day. Their bodies had changed, their voices had changed, as had their patterns and gestures, and even the shapes of their faces, becoming leaner and more adult-like, so that now, when Annie placed the old wax pressings to her face, they no longer fit.

"I want to see what it's like," she said. "Maybe everything will be just fine. Maybe we'll find out we can't live without each other, and we'll end up married and child-raising and happy-ever-after. But I just want to know."

"All right," he said, far more frightened than he'd ever been, dangling from the crane. "All right," he said, and it seemed to him that it was as if she was climbing into the bathysphere alone, and he marveled at her bravery and curiosity, her adventurousness, and even her wisdom.

*

There is still a sweetness in all three of their lives, now: Kirby, with his wife and four children, in a small town north of Houston; Richard, with his wife and two children; and Annie, with her husband and five children, and, already, her first grandchild. A reservoir of sweetness, a vast subterranean vault of it, like the treasure-lair of savages—the past, hidden far away in their hearts, and held, and treasured, mythic and powerful, even now.

It was exactly like the treasure-trove of wild savages, they each realize now, and for some reason—grace? simple luck?—they were able to dip down into it back then, were able to scrape out handfuls of it, gobs of it, like sugar or honey.

As if, still, it—the discovery of that reservoir—remains with them, a power and a strength, so many years later.

And yet—they had all once been together. How can they now be apart, particularly if that reservoir remains intact, buried, and ever-replenishing?

Even now, Richard thinks they missed each other by a hair's breadth: that some sort of fate was deflected—though how or why or what, he cannot say. He thinks it might have been one of the closest misses in the history of the world. He has no regrets, only marvels. He wonders sometimes if there are not the ghosts or husks of their other lives, living still, far back in the past, or far below, or even farther out into the future, still together, still consorting: other lives, birthed from that strange reservoir of joy and sweetness, and utter newness.

And if there are, how does he access that? Through memory? Through imagination?

Even now, he marvels at how wise they were, then, and at all the paths they did not take.

RICH LEVY

Kindred Spirit

I like this time of night
when everyone else is asleep or fidgeting

and know my mother liked it too.
She was always awake

when we drifted off
in our shoebox of a house,

my father snorting like a hooked fish
(the Greatest Generation vs. the unconscious),

my sister laughing and shifting
on her narrow bed.

I could hear mother's bathwater running,
her footsteps in the hall,

her sigh as she lowered herself into the tub,
could see a sliver of light beneath the door

before I fell into dreams.
She's dead now, but wasn't this comforting?

And aren't I comforting others too
as I cruise the house,

locking doors, wiping countertops,
putting away the last of the bread and the milk,

trading sleep for a swept floor
and a few minutes

among the dozing, like
a self-conscious apple in the fridge?

These nocturnal gambols
are a secret I shared with my mother

only in the solitude of memory,
and now I'm sharing it with you.

OCTAVIO QUINTANILLA

Psalm 2

Last night I fell asleep
holding my father's hand, Lord,
and I woke with ashes in my mouth.
He tells me he's ready to die,
ready to let the shadow of his ghost
perch over the house he built
with his own two hands.

But the watery gray of his left iris
tells me a different story.
He wants to keep hearing
the rooster's crow at dawn
calling him to work.
Wants to listen to his wife's slow heartbeat
as she makes him a cup of coffee
long before he rises.
He wants to keep seeing the everlasting, Lord,
and in this way,
reach the knowing that You've reached.

Impossible, I know.

I must remind him to stay alive,
for my mother's sake,
who will die in a country
where her last thought
will be of another.

And so I say, keep your ear close
to my brain, Lord.
Listen for the small motor of grief.
Shut it down.
As others have used You for their own purpose,
for once, let my will bend Yours.

PETER HOHEISEL

An Old Lady Hunting Treasure

Not ready yet, for heavenly treasures,
each morning, she is out there
in front of the Sandy Shores Hotel
sweeping Corpus Christi beach
with her metal detector.

In a blue baseball cap
And plastic shoes,
The breeze flaps her
Print dress, outlining
Her slender body.

She is that age beyond
Age,
Is everything she is going to be.

I asked her what
Were the most
Exciting gifts
That her mesh basket
Had scooped from the sand:
"old silver coins, one was 1853.
And rings, one with rubies in it,
Lots of class rings."

MONICA MACANSANTOS

Homing In

Your child would've been twenty-one today, had she survived the fire. There would have been one more bed in your house in the suburbs, one more person living the American Dream. Back in the old country your house was made of wood, and it went up in flames, like the life you abandoned for good. Your husband's scars haven't faded. He couldn't save your one-year-old daughter—the flames lapped at him like tongues of faith. It's the will of God, you both say, as you listen to Joel Osteen preach to a stadium of followers. "Offer up your lives to the Lord and the Lord will set you free!" he yells, and you answer "hallelujah!" as you recline on your expensive leather couch, watching the Reverend on TV. You've learned not to despair. In your mind, the tongues of faith lap at your daughter's flesh like cool water that drowns the willing. I look out your window and my ears are drowned by the peace of the suburbs. This is where you have built your home.

MONICA MACANSANTOS

Christmas House, Vallejo, California

After your daughter's fiery death,
Your house bathes in the fluorescence
Of mourning.
A giant snowman grins
At the evergreen highway,
A long-lashed horse pauses in mid-air.
Santa's elves spill out on your lawn,
Bearing gifts, frozen in their mirth.

My aunt drives me here one night
On our way back to the suburbs.
She is familiar with these roads,
Knows the path to the light:
She leads me, an exile, to the silence
Of candle-lit dinners
And freshly mown lawns.
Later tonight,
I will speak to her children
In the borrowed tongue.
This is how we conquer the wilderness:
We move on, travel light.

But then your house blazes into our path.
We pause to gaze at the ornaments
Of a childhood long past:
A pink ballet dancer,
A soldier with lovesick eyes.

Light, like memory,
Must be encased in glass
To endure a darkness
That falls like snow.
But glass is heavy.
We choose to travel light.

ROBIN GARA

When You Ask Me If I Believe

I might tell you a story
my mother told me long ago
back when her abled hands dealt out cards
explained the rules
enjoyed the game.

One summer day
When tomatoes bloomed red in her garden
I asked her if she knew what would happen to us
when we died.

After a pause
she shrugged and said
well
we won't know till we get there
will we?

Even now
her words somehow
comfort.

That day I learned
that every rock I pick up, examine, dry off,
and look at again
will be enough.

The clouds that drift by as I lay under
or fly over
will carry me
to that place where there is no explanation
and
There is no need.

NAOMI SHIHAB NYE

Shoulders

A man crosses the street in rain,
stepping gently, looking two times north and south,
because his son is asleep on his shoulder.

No car must splash him.
No car drive too near to his shadow.

This man carries the world's most sensitive cargo
but he's not marked.
Nowhere does his jacket say FRAGILE,
HANDLE WITH CARE.

His ear fills up with breathing.
He hears the hum of a boy's dream
deep inside him.

We're not going to be able
to live in this world
if we're not willing to do what he's doing
with one another.

The road will only be wide.
The rain will never stop falling.

YVETTE R. BLAIR-LAVALLAIS

Wading in the Water of the Trinity River: A Womanist Perspective

As a writer, theologian, and womanist preacher, I am fascinated by water towers. Anytime I journey through Texas, I am intentional in photographing water towers, particularly those in small towns—towns with only one or two exits; towns that extend an invitation to road-tired travelers with bright neon signs of fast-food eateries and billboards for "the cleanest restrooms," and world-famous kolaches. In what I consider my pastoral anthropology, this sense of discovering truths about communities, I tend to look for how water towers are situated within these towns. These water towers are tall, prominent landmarks that lend themselves to being more than just a visible sign of the town's name painted across the frontal and rearview; they are symbolic vestiges that hold history about the people who settled there. What life was like—and what it wasn't like.

The primary role and focus of a womanist is to examine the life of a community and identify what social injustices exist, and how to eradicate those injustices so that everyone experiences equality. It is rooted in the experiences of black women solving everyday problems. It differs from feminism in that it is not solely focused on the rights of women. It also has another major distinction in that it is an approach that happens through the lens of black women. Historically, black women have been the most marginalized group in any community, and therefore, can pinpoint injustices in ways that are often overlooked, unnoticed or neglected by others.

This term womanist was coined by the literary giant, Alice Walker, whose work *The Color Purple* rose to critical acclaim after the book became an award-winning movie. It was in her 1983 critically acclaimed work, *In Search of Our Mothers' Garden: Womanist Prose*, that this term was breathed into life, following its incubation and infant appearance in an earlier work by Walker. It is derived from "womanish," a Black folk expression of mothers to female children suggesting being grown, responsible, and acting beyond the age of a young girl, acting womanish.

It is in that thought, that I, as a womanist preacher, seek to approach the homiletic text in a responsible manner, desiring to know more than what's on the surface, and going into the deep exegetical work of looking at the biblical text through a lens of liberation.

*

Because when black women are freed and liberated, we are all liberated.

And that deep examination of going beyond the surface is akin to pastoral anthropology—and deep in the heart of Texas, what with all its water towers and water wells, lie some interesting truths about how water has been filtered and processed and streamed through our communities. Water towers are the tributaries that help quench the thirst of parched souls under shade trees, in A-frame churches, and in blighted neighborhoods in the south and posh gated communities in the north. These water towers and wells hold their own narrative about how this most basic and most valuable life-saving resource is distributed among the least, last, and lost, and the inequities that exist between the marginalized and the mansion-dwellers. If manna from heaven is our daily bread, where is the water that everyone needs to wash it down?

Biblically, water symbolizes new birth, baptism, being replenished. Visually, that's easy to imagine along the beautiful hiking trails in Travis County, where Lady Bird Lake, named for the former First Lady of the United States, the wife of Lyndon Baines Johnson, is clear and pristine, and attracts thousands of hikers each year. But juxtapose that against the tiny town of Sandbranch, an unincorporated marginalized town against the backdrop of Dallas, resting against its horizon, where some of the least and last call home. There is a paradoxical twist as to whether any persons are lost, because they are easily found in this impoverished community that was seemingly forgotten; because for years they were discarded beneath the pile of abandoned promises and used tires. Yet at the same time, it is arguably one of the uttermost ends of the world, that is, one of the communities included in The Great Commission when Jesus told eleven of his disciples to go and make disciples of all nations, baptizing them in the name of the Father and of the Son and of the Holy Spirit.

*

Except there is a water issue that makes this problematic.

When Jesus was baptized, and God said, "this is my beloved son, in whom I am well-pleased," it's hard to imagine Jesus being immersed anywhere in Sandbranch because the town continues to struggle with access to clean water. It's also hard to imagine him being baptized in Dallas, the third largest city in Texas, whose Trinity River is not befitting of its name. It crests during heavy rainfalls and rainstorms, and produces a stench along the corridor that divides the city along southern and northern lines. The highly celebrated Dallas skyline is most visible from the Bottoms of the Trinity (a neighborhood so named because of its geographical location), where churches, mostly small, line streets that are home to abandoned houses, and are at the vortex of sewage and homelessness.

And that's problematic.

With churches dotting the freeway and stained-glass windows looking onto the banks of the Trinity River, it's a shame that congregations cannot perform outside baptisms and wade in the water of the Trinity. After all, it bears a biblical reference that suggests at least that this water is home to God the Father, God the Son, and God the Holy Spirit. On the other end of the metroplex, in Fort Worth, or Cowtown as it is affectionately called by the locals, this same Trinity River is home to ducks and geese who are eager to greet visitors as they meander through the park.

Water, sparkling clear and clean, has become synonymous with economic value. Cities promote their waterparks, river walks, ponds, man-made lakes and other bodies of water as major attractions for visitors and residents alike. Water is a metaphor for a community that has experienced its comeuppance; a city that proudly boasts its superior water system; a town that generates revenue for family-themed parks like NRH2o (North Richland Hills) and Hawaiian Falls. Yet on the southern side, there is Bahama Beach Waterpark, situated in a mostly depressed end of town where for four months of the year, church summer programs tout this as a field-trip destination, gather their children and spend the day.

One cannot help but ponder how this same scenario would play out in Katy or Channelview, where homes are nestled along the Gulf Coast, with glimpses of the ship channel in view all around Houston. More than these being idyllic neighborhoods where great stories are penned, landscape portraits painted, and backdrops created for prom goers or outdoor nuptials, these real-life experiences are part of watershed moments—real and metaphorical.

Farther south, in San Antonio, is the home to the state's oldest church. According to newspaper clippings, the San Fernando Cathedral is nearly three hundred years old. Construction began in 1738 and was completed in 1750. A careful reading on the website reveals that this community of believers, who started with a group of fifteen families from the Canary Islands (a watershed moment), is the oldest continuously functioning religious community in Texas. And that's a big deal, because Texas is a big state, and to know that the founding families were from a geographical region of *water* is an indication that this church embodies the *living water* of Christ, and has done so for nearly three hundred years, with intentionality in responding to the needs of the people in and around the church.

If the Guadalupe River, which is a focal point of San Antonio, boasting beautiful landscapes, with a history of feeding the city—all the way back to the late 1600s—ever needed a nickname, one could offer up the Trinity River, because this river offers itself as a source of waterpower. Its water tower, with its name plastered across it, might best represent freedom, liberation, and wading in the water. Not the troubled water like the lyrics to the black spiritual, "Wade in the Water," implies, but the wading that children and adults can enjoy in nearby communities like New Braunfels, Gonzales, and Kerrville, because of the economic and perhaps equitable distribution of this resource.

And that's a solution. Isn't that what the Trinity, the Holy Trinity of God the Father, God the Son, and God the Holy Spirit would demand?

I still grapple with the disparities in the water systems of communities in Texas. Until the early 1990s, an Oak Cliff neighborhood called Alameda Heights still used well water. In this mostly impoverished area of black and elderly residents, the injustices of natural resources were overlooked. Backyard cookouts were plentiful, but backyard pools were noticeably absent. They finally have a water pump station that distributes water directly into that community.

If water is meant to replenish and rejuvenate dry communities, many who are economically starved and disproportionately underrepresented when it comes to clean, flowing, natural resources, then the water towers don't necessarily offer a true and fair picture of what it means to experience what I like to call communal baptism—that deep sense of caring for your neighbors and loving them as yourself, whether they attend your church or not; loving them enough to liberate them from the environmental injustice of lack of clean water.

If water is meant to quench the thirst of parched souls who are bone dry and weary from being on the south end of town, where justice doesn't always flow like a mighty river, then it means caring for those neighbors enough to ensure that they are able to wade in clear, clean water, even if there are no waterfalls like White Rock Lake, where egrets bathe. It means unbottling and opening the valves so that the water that feeds the daddy longlegs and revelers along the bustling Sixth Street of our state's capital can also be enjoyed by heavy-burdened mothers of newborns in Stop Six and Lake Como, whose front porches are littered with bottles of Dasani.

Finally, if our communities are going to experience rebirth, it most certainly cannot happen with dirty, unfiltered water. Even birds refuse to wade in dirty water, and for good reason.

Known and Unknown

OWEN EGERTON

The Martyrs of Mountain Peak

Kent is dead. All the kids at the camp are crying and singing and praying. They don't know that it was my turn, not his.

Rich is standing in front of us leading the songs. The ten kids who had Kent as a counselor are huddled in the front row. Already seven of them have announced that they've given their lives to Christ—although one is actually regiving his life, since he already gave his life to Christ as a sophomore, but since then he's been smoking pot. None of the kids I counsel have given their lives to Christ, but they look pretty sad.

We're singing "Desperado," but with the words changed. The lyrics are flashed on a screen.

> *Desperado, why don't you come to love Jesus,*
> *You know that he sees us*
> *For so long now...*

It was Kent's favorite song. Pricilla Brone is helping Rich by leading the girl echo parts. She's got tears on her face and her hair is all shiny. She's so pretty it hurts to look at her, especially when she sings. When the song ends, Rich asks us to bow our heads and pray. All two hundred and six teenagers close their eyes and bow their heads, even the kids who hang out at the cigarette pit and usually make fart noises during the prayers.

"God, Father, Daddy—thank you for letting us know Kent. We're going to miss him," Rich says. "But we know that now he's with you and your Son in Heaven. Thank you, Daddy. Amen." People are crying and hugging, just like last week.

"Let me tell you a little bit about where Kent is now," Rich says, his eyes twinkling. He's smiling like a TV dad. Everyone wants Rich to be their dad. He's kind and funny and tells great stories. Better than my dad back home in Houston who's always grumpy and sleeps all weekend.

"Heaven is a lot like Camp Mountain Peak, only better. You can bet Heaven's got horses like we've got. The angels help on the ropes course and the apostles run the four-wheelers and maybe Mary and Martha are scooping Kent a Snack Shack ice cream special right now. I bet Kent is playing disc golf with his halo—oh sure, and they've got a video arcade like us and a thirty-person hot tub like ours and an Olympic-size pool—maybe bigger even, and in Heaven I bet they even have a forty-yard, two-story-high waterslide. Only the one in Heaven won't have a low panel on the curve."

A few kids sob out loud. Kent had been trying to beat the Camp Mountain Peak speed record on the waterslide when he died. According to the slide's digital timer, the record is 23.2 seconds, which I set way back in June. Kent was obsessed with beating it. He was competitive like that, which is totally not the point of Camp Mountain Peak. Rumor has it that when the panel gave he was wearing a Speedo and had greased up with baby oil. Total pride. For one thing, counselors aren't allowed to wear Speedos or two-pieces in the swimming area. When I was a camper here five years ago, not even kids could wear Speedos or two-pieces, but they've laxed. And baby oil? I mean, what's Christ-like about baby oil? I was going to die on the ropes course, fully dressed.

"No, the waterslide that Kent is riding right now is faster and wilder than our slide and no chance of falling out, and even if he did, he'd just fall on a cloud instead of down a cliff. You know Kent is just loving that." Kids nod along. Rich crouches down and kind of whispers so all the kids have to lean in to listen. "He's looking down right now on us here and feeling sorry for us. Probably wondering why we're so sad when he's having such a blast. Probably hoping that we're buying a ticket for the Camp Mountain Peak he's at. Only we can't afford that camp. We can't even make a down payment. The price is way out of range. You know why? The price for that camp is perfection. Anyone perfect out there?"

All the kids shake their heads back and forth.

"Didn't think so," Rich says and stands up. "But it's okay because you know who bought the ticket for us? Jesus did. He is perfect and with his own blood Jesus bought us all a pass to the best camp you can imagine, and it doesn't last just two weeks, it lasts forever and ever." He stretches his arms out, trying to show how much forever is.

"And you got to know," Rich says, looking real profound. "The waterslide is the only route from the ledge to the pool, and just like that Jesus is the only path that splashes into Heaven. Nothing else works. Jesus is our waterslide."

I'd heard this several times before, though the part about the waterslide was new. Every two weeks a fresh group of teenagers from all over America comes to Camp Mountain Peak, and every two weeks a counselor dies. It's become an unofficial policy. Always an accident. One of us just acts a little less careful and the rest of us let it happen. It started early in the summer.

The first session was lame. Two hundred or so kids and twenty counselors. We prayed so hard. I remember praying until my head ached, but only one of my kids stood up on the last day to say he had opened his heart to Jesus. Overall only eleven kids stood up. Eleven kids! That sucked. Rich still got weepy and smiley and told the whole camp that the angels were celebrating, so we played "Celebrate" by Kool & the Gang and dropped balloons, but all us counselors were pretty bummed.

Session two was feeling a lot like session one. The kids loved the four-wheelers, the theme parties, the hot tub, the rappelling lessons, but didn't give a spit about the Lord and Savior. They were too busy making out behind the dining hall to care about God bearing the burden of their sin. I had this one kid from Denver in my cabin who said that his hobbies were "pounding beer and pounding babes." I caught him having sex with a girl in the hot tub after hours. I told him that every time he puts his penis in a girl who's not his wife he's putting a nail into Christ. But he still didn't give a squat.

Then on the last day of the session, Will died. Will was a counselor who also took care of the horses and he was practicing a stunt for the Farewell BBQ and Hoedown when he got thrown. It was horrible. Like someone punched the whole camp in the stomach. We went ahead with the BBQ and Hoedown, but it was no fun.

That night, standing in front of all the kids, Rich looked tired and sadder than I've ever seen him. "You know what, I don't feel much like talking tonight. But you know what? Will would want me to tell you about Jesus." Rich didn't move on the stage or crouch or whisper or spread his arms at all that night. Just stood in the center and talked. "That's what he'd want. Because, yeah, we've got some fun stuff up here, we sing some fun songs and the ribs tonight were pretty excellent, but the only reason, the only, only reason, is so we can tell you about Jesus. And Will would gladly die if it meant that just one of you would have a chance to meet Jesus."

I mean, kids were falling over themselves to give their lives to Christ. One hundred and ninety-seven kids stood up and told everyone how they now love Jesus. And the ones who didn't stand up felt pretty stupid and probably came to Christ on the bus ride home. Even my hot-tub kid from Denver stood up, all crying. He told me he was never going to pound a girl again.

"Except your wife," I said, and we laughed. I gave him his own *Adventure Life New Testament* and hugged him goodbye. That was the best.

After the kids left and before the next group rolled in, we counselors started talking. Rich was right. It was worth dying to see kids loving Jesus. We stayed up real late in the Coffee Haus, just the counselors, praying and singing and reading *Acts* aloud. And it was like the Spirit was leading us. There were four more sessions in the summer, so we drew lots like the disciples did to replace Judas. I got session six, the last session of the summer. All the counselors were crying and smiling. They laid hands on the four of us and prayed. Pricilla Brone had her hands on me. They were warm. I was so happy, so filled with the spirit, so ready. I could hardly wait till my session. It was like promising to die made God more real. I could touch God. I was scared, sure. But Jesus was scared. He cried in the garden. I was scared like he was. At dawn we all climbed to Christ's Point and sang hymns.

After that we never spoke of the agreement, not letting our left hand know about the right hand. In fact, by the middle of session three, I was beginning to think nothing would actually happen, but then Crick Peppers "accidentally" locked herself in the kitchen freezer. In session four David Blankins forgot to open any of the garage windows while doing repairs on an idling four-wheeler. Becky Towt choked on a doughnut in session five. I have no idea how she managed that. My plan had been to forget to strap in on the ropes course on day ten of session six, but Kent had to go and slip out of the waterslide and fall off a cliff.

*

The kids I counsel are all somber as we walk back to the cabin.

"He must have been going damn fast to fly out like that," one of the kids says.

"I heard he shaved his legs to make him slicker," another says.

"Shit man, he was brave."

I pray for these kids a lot. Every morning I wake up before Morning Bell and pray God will crack their hearts open like walnuts. I love them. How can you not love someone you're planning to die for? I used to imagine them all crying after I died on the ropes course, sorry they hadn't listened or gotten to know me. I pictured them standing up on that last day and telling everyone they love Jesus and then coming back to Mountain Peak years later with their kids or grandkids and pointing out the spot I died at and holding hands with their grandkids and everybody praying and thanking God for me.

I tell them to head back to the cabin and I'll be there in a minute. I don't have to worry about them sneaking out. Nobody sneaks out after a death.

I go walking toward the ropes course.

The stars are amazing up here. The camp is dark. They turn off a bunch of lights when things are sad so the kids can see the stars, especially the shooting stars. So many stars, and Jesus made them all. He knows them all by heart. He knows every single hair on my head. He knows I'm walking now, he is right here with me. But I can't think of anything to say, cause I'm kind of mad. God knew about that low panel. He knew about the baby oil. He knew it was my turn, but he let Kent put on that Speedo and shave his legs and fall out.

At the Buenas Vista View I stop and look out over the valley. It's windy, a little chilly, but I don't care. It was at this spot I opened up my heart to Jesus five years ago. I didn't need a dead counselor. I just heard all about the Father's love and my sin and how they whipped Jesus with this nasty whip with glass in it and then Rich said that if we wanted to have some time alone we could go off and I walked out here and I prayed for a sign and God sent a shooting star right over Camp Mountain Peak. It was wild. Like God ripping the sky just for me. It turns out that you can see like three or four shooting stars every five minutes, but still. I've come back every summer since then. I was a camper twice and a junior counselor twice, then last year Rich made me a full counselor. This place is more home than home. It's my favorite place in the universe.

I walk on to the ropes course. It's spooky at night, all the trees and ropes making shadows. It's real dark too. Smells like pine needles and bark. I think I'm alone but then I see Pricilla sitting on the observation deck, dangling her legs. I go and sit by her and for a while neither of us says anything. Finally she says, real quiet, "So I guess you won't be dying then, huh?"

"I guess not," I say. Her hand kind of touches mine, just the fingers. A wind comes by and a few leaves float down.

"So, you want to pray?" she asks.

"Sure," I say. We bow our heads and our faces kind of get close, real close, touching and . . . I don't know. We just start making out. Like totally making out, tongues going all over the place and hands under clothes and yeah, Jesus sees, but I'm like, yeah, look at this Jesus, this is a tit, Jesus, and my hand is on it. And she's touching my hair and my arms and my legs and between my legs and it's like praying but faster and more heat and she's touching my zipper and I'm touching her zipper and there might be a billion shooting stars but I don't care. Then Rich shows up with his flashlight and catches us. Pricilla starts buttoning up real fast and I'm trying to hide the bulge in my jeans.

"Sweet Jesus," Rich says.

*

I'm staring at the wall in Rich's office. He has a picture of every summer staff since 1970 and above them a wooden plaque that says, "The harvest is rich but the workers are few."

Rich isn't saying anything yet. He's just rubbing his eyes. He already talked to Pricilla. I waited outside. I heard her crying. Rich looks real tired.

"You know the rules, I know you do."

I nod. My throat feels full, like it's packed with wet sand.

"You left your kids unattended. They were worried, you know. They came and found me. I was worried. Then I find you and Pricilla. On a day like this, too."

I try and say something but I can't talk.

"I'm sending you home, okay. I'm sending you home tomorrow and I don't think you should come back next summer."

I think I'm going to bawl, I mean just wail. But I don't. I get cold.

*

I walk back to the cabin. A couple of kids are sitting on the porch. They don't look me in the face when I tell them to hit the sack. They just mumble and stay where they are. I walk inside and lie down on my bunk.

I can still hear them talking on the porch, but I can't tell what they're saying. I lay awake for an hour or two till everyone is sleeping and breathing heavy. The cabin smells like cedar and sweaty laundry. I've always loved the smell. It smells safe. But now the smell makes me feel ashamed. Everything does. Shame like a real hard blush, like a blush that's going to stain my skin. Then I think about Pricilla and her hands and I immediately pop a woody, then a lot more shame. So to stop the woody I think about my mother. Then I think about Kent's mother. She sent that care package with the Rice Krispies treats. When I close my eyes I see Kent. He's at the bottom of the cliff all bent up and in his Speedo and there's no blood, but his skin looks funny and you can tell he's dead. Bastard. So I imagine myself down there instead. I imagine the falling and the landing and the cracking. Then the woody starts to come back, which is weird, so I get up and go out on the porch.

I look out on the dining hall, the volleyball/basketball court, the crafts store, saying little goodbyes to everything. I see a few kids sitting in the cigarette pit. It's way past curfew, almost morning, so I head over there to tell them to go back to their cabins, and they all look a little green, a little fuzzy, even their cigarette smoke is green and fuzzy. I recognize Will first. Then David and Crick, and Becky and last of all, Kent, still in his Speedo, still smelling like chlorine and baby oil. All just standing around, smoking. Sitting behind them, lighting one cigarette from the end of another, is Jesus. He looks totally different than in the movies, shorter, kind of dirty, but you can tell it's him. You just know.

"Hey, guys," I say, and I'm breathing fast. They don't look at me. Just sit and smoke.

Kent says, without looking up, "Turns out we're wrong about the whole Jesus thing."

"What do you mean?"

"Jesus doesn't save," Becky says, still sounding like she's got a doughnut in her throat.

"He doesn't?" I look over at Jesus, who just shrugs.

"Maybe Buddha does," Crick says. "Or Shiva."

"My money's on Zoroaster," Becky says.

"I've never even heard of Zoroaster."

"Narrow is the way," Jesus says with a shake of his head and a chuckle. "Want a smoke?"

Oh God, Jesus is talking to me. Looking at me. Jesus is asking if I want a cigarette. This is everything. Jesus is hanging out with all these guys, awarding their devotion, like he hung out with Peter and John and James, making them fish for breakfast.

"Can I stay here?" I ask. "Can I stay with you guys?"

"You got to be fucking kidding me," Kent says.

"You . . . " I point at Kent. Sitting there all smug and bruised, just a few feet from Jesus. "You stole my place, Kent. That's my place."

"You want it? Come and take it."

I run at him. He doesn't move, just takes another drag on his cigarette. I slam into him, only it's more slamming through him and for a second my stomach drops and knots, like I'm standing on the edge of a canyon. Below me are miles of nothing. Then I'm past him and I smack into a pole.

When I open my eyes I see Jesus. He's looking down at me, and he looks sad. Disappointed, I guess. Me trying to fight Kent's ghost, me and Pricilla. All these thoughts I'm not supposed to have. He died for me and this is how I thank him?

"Jesus," I say, "I'm sorry." He looks so sad.

"Jesus, please forgive me."

He smiles. His teeth are black. "No," he says.

"I have to ride that fucking waterslide a hundred times a day," Kent mumbles. "Ungrateful bastard. A hundred times a day."

As he's speaking the clouds begin to go pink and their green bodies start fading.

"Jesus?" I say, getting to my feet. But Jesus is making eyes at Becky. "Jesus!" They fade away as he scoots over to light her cigarette. The green flame is the last I see of them.

I'm still standing there when Rich comes out of his office, same clothes as the night before, his eyes red like he hasn't slept a wink.

"Grab your stuff. We're leaving in five minutes."

*

Pricilla and I sit in the back of the camp van as Rich maneuvers the windy road with the mountain slanting up on one side and cutting down on the other. As we pass the sign that says GO WITH GOD, Pricilla starts to weep a little. I take her hand.

"I had a dream about Kent," she whispers. "He was smiling and flying. He had this white robe and was so happy." She smiles. "And we were singing, him and me. We were singing 'Jesus Loves Me.'"

I think of telling her about green Jesus and the smoking and the canyon feeling inside Kent. But why? It won't make her happier. Doesn't make me happier. And maybe it never happened. Maybe I dreamt it all. And Jesus is just as he has always been. Loving me. Watching over me. Maybe this is real faith, believing when you know it's not true.

Rich's head bobs to the side just a little as she and I start softly singing.

"Jesus loves us, this we know . . . "

I see Rich's head bow and I think he's praying. Then the van drifts and hits some small pines on the side of the road. Rich jerks up and pulls on the wheel and we're skidding.

Pricilla squeezes my hand. A wheel catches the edge and the van tilts so hard I hit the ceiling. Through the windshield I can the see the valley and the trees and some sky, and we're falling and turning and, floating inside the van, like the inside of Kent. Just before we hit, I swear I hear Pricilla whimper, "Save us Zoroaster."

NOEL CROOK

Smith Canyon

That summer when loss took me by the throat
I came home to the parched Texas hills, in late
August a bleached bone-color, the grasses sallowed,
white caliche roads shrouded in thin dust.

I drove to the canyon—a great scar, beautiful
in the way of a scar, in the story it tells—
where a child can trace the stone swirl of a mollusk
big as her father's foot, and the cliffs are whales

that swim endlessly, tattoos of humped and eyeless
trilobites embellishing their flanks;
where along the steeper sides the untouched ledges
tease with their pale stippling.

The mind canvasses them, lies along them,
crouches in crevices cool with the chalky smell
of millennia. Comanches camped here,
chipping arrowheads at the water's edge.

Under the persistent wheeling of the buzzards,
I walked the rocky shore, sank deep in the dark water
until green and fingering reeds brushed my hair, glad
that once the cliffs had whispered

with the scuttling of a million blind crustaceans.
I was their sister, the warm sun whitening
my bones, the curve of my spine
another decoration on the limestone floor.

CHRIS ELLERY

Calf

"You shall go out leaping like calves from the stall."
Mal. 4.2

Chester stood at the fence in the morning
stroking the nose of a calf,
some agreement of animal energy connecting.

The boy who watched them, caring for both,
wondered about this world
where you love an animal you raise for slaughter.

All day the man and the boy hauled hay,
stacking the bales in Chester's barn.
The boy inhaled the dust and darkness.

Fresh-cut hay, animal dung.
The dry old barn with its own way of knowing,
storing up wisdom from fodder.

When they pitched the last bale
it was already dark.
Every inch itched, every muscle ached.

But he forgot his fatigue when Chester patted his arm:
Pup, that's a good day's work.
The boy leapt onto the bed of the flat-bed truck

for the ride home to supper.
The wheels raised dust on the River Road.
The boy inhaled the night, the pine and the water.

MARK SANDERS

The Ghosts on Farm Road

Steam lifts off the stock pond, and,
though I don't know why they are there,
the dead have come again to bother me.
The horses, who bump the fence, impatient,
do not see them, do not care the dead are there—
what might the dead do? Stop the sun?
The horses paw the feedlot dust and snort,
whatever, whatever.
                                        Yet—
the wisp that dances most wildly
is the sister whose health would not permit dance
in the first place; no wind this morning—
the intimate absence of breath she knew.
There her ghost is, skating and twirling.
And there my father, hunkered to the water,
too heavy to move, big man bearing the burden
of his bulk upon the bulk he had been handed.
My mother, too, between the two, there, thin
and aspiring skyward into the nothing
they all became. Puffs of steam mouthed in cold.

Once—how long has it been?—I had ridden horses up
switchbacks in rocky terrain, kneeing them onward,
posting in the saddle to lessen the jolt the ride made.
In those days the dead hid behind stones big as houses,
big as grief, trees black and contorted as from nightmares;
they moved inside clouds that streamed in rivers above the river.
I feared the ghosts would spook the horses,
but they trod, trod on, and the rocks they kicked down
tilted the balance of sloping daylight until,
now, in current darkness, they are here,
having found me again at last.

Good morning, good morning, *whatever*,
you troublers, hitch and hassle and snag.
The horses need me now. I have work, always work.
See me roll my sleeves. Now stand back.
Let me get on with it.

ROBERT OKAJI

La Grange

Sorrow's pith: the swirling mass and its cycle.
What falls rises. What rises falls. Rain, rivers. Hope.
The city plucks out its eyes and swallows the gray whole.
She wades to the kitchen, lights a Salem, then the burner.
Where in this wind does the hummingbird hide?
The old clock on the shelf still ticks ebony notes.
A voice drifts by: *Is anyone there?*
I have tea she says. Strong like me, and bitter.

D. G. GEIS

A Stockyard Liturgy

For Temple Grandin

O Lord—
If history is a slaughterhouse,

May our paths always curve
And be trod without diversion.

Let no sharp angle impede our progress
Or uncertainty give us pause.

Permit us to stream freely
Down the conveyer

And grant us one final hug
Before we are stunned.

As blood flows freely
Along the path

Of least resistance,
So may the meat hook

Of inevitability
Lift us high above all butchery,

And our ending,
God willing—

Be both sudden
And humane.

William Virgil Davis

Lazarus Alive

Covered with a cakey dirt and maggot
mix, as if he really were somehow
strangely reborn, he stepped out slowly
in the brittle air, to light so sharp
and bright he had to shield his eyes.
And even he quickly held his nose.

At first he seemed surprised—or just
confused. It wasn't what he'd thought
it ought to be—the afterlife he'd so often
worried over. Somehow, now, nothing
about it seemed to make sense. He sat
stunned and silent in the opened tomb
and stared at them. And they stared back
at him.

He must have wondered what
they wanted him to do or say. They knew
that he couldn't explain it—even if he
wanted to. It was such a new miracle.
He didn't try to walk or talk. He closed
his eyes, already ready to start dying again.

CAROL COFFEE REPOSA

Lighthouse, Port Isabel

We enter
A chrysalis
Of peeling plaster,
Plod up the spiral staircase,
Pant toward sea and sky.

Suddenly I'm in
A Christmas Carol, watching the Ghost
Of Christmas Past drag Scrooge
To an unwilling glimpse
Of keepers joining hands

During a storm,
Kindness in a gale
While rogue waves crash
Against the tower,
Blur the flashing lamp.

We reach the top,
Take in a breathless Gulf
Tranquil at the moment
Despite tempests come and gone,
Battles fought.

Ships were lost here, many drowned,
But still I think this beacon
Is perfection, sending out
Its swirling slice of light
Forever
Into dark.

BRIAN VAN REET

The Window

Staff Sergeant Fitzpatrick tried to hold the memory, his eyes moving from the menu to his fiancée, to a rusty freight passing through the outskirts of Marathon, dotted with trailer parks and cement factories, into the Chihuahuan Desert. Overhead, the late-morning sun heated a corrugated tin roof, supported at the corners by twisting columns of mesquite. In the distance the train clicked lazily through a crossroads, bell clanging, the sound of steel on steel taking its time to echo and reach the little café where Fitzpatrick and his fiancée, Sadie, sat at a table on the flagstone veranda.

"I'll have the chicken enchiladas," he said.

The waitress nodded at him. He should have gotten a salad, had put on a few pounds since his days playing high school ball, but what the hell. Sadie, more beautiful than he was handsome, remained absorbed in the menu.

"I think I need another minute," she said. "Sorry."

After the waitress left, Sadie set down the menu and sighed in exasperation. "I never know what I want. What's wrong with me?"

"Nothing," Fitzpatrick said. "Take your time." He watched her study the selections intently, as if what she ate for lunch today might actually make a difference in the grand scheme, wondering about the contrast between the morbidity with which she regarded this decision, and the spontaneous, joyful proposal she had made a month ago, after only knowing him for the winter.

"Okay." She folded the menu as the long train receded over the horizon, becoming inaudible. A ratty mockingbird landed nearby and approached their table, turning its head from side to side, strutting with avian confidence. Soon the waitress returned.

"I'll have a fajita salad and a beer," Sadie said. "You want a beer?"

"Sure," Fitzpatrick said. "I'll have a beer."

*

They ate, finished their first round, and ordered another. The waitress popped the tops with an opener from her apron and set the bottles on the table. An SUV, one of the newer, hybrid models, mountain bikes racked in tow, passed on the road and pulled into the dusty lot beside the café. The doors opened and a couple got out. Fitzpatrick chewed his final enchilada and washed it down, observing the approaching twenty-somethings. The driver was a thin guy wearing a large red beard and a stocking cap; his passenger, a woman with pale skin, a bob haircut, and a stud through her nose. They claimed the other table on the veranda. Sadie glanced over while continuing the conversation.

"I'm thinking of hiring my cousin for the photography," she said. "Or is that a bad idea?"

"Her stuff online was good. Maybe she'll give us a deal."

Sadie nodded and made a note in her planner. The waitress arrived to take the newcomers' order. The mockingbird followed her to the threshold, and she shooed it off when she returned with the drinks.

The tables of sun-bleached wood were large and close. As they drank and talked, Fitzpatrick overheard the guy with the red beard ask after the pierced girl's brother. What caught his attention was the mention of boot camp.

"I don't hear from him too much," the girl said. "He never was much of a writer. They've only given them phone time once or twice so far. But yeah, I can tell he's already turning into a real jarhead. The last letter he wrote, he mostly bragged about how many pushups he can do now."

There was sarcasm and resignation in her voice, a mix of lament and attack. She sounded like she regretted everything she was saying immediately after saying it. "I hope he doesn't make it through. For his own sake. Jesus. Dumb kid—some people need saving from themselves."

Fitzpatrick and Sadie made eye contact. He grinned, a funny half-sneer he sometimes made, then squinted at a far-off point in the desert. With a look of beautiful ferocity, she tilted back her second beer and finished it.

"Ready."

He nodded and got the waitress's attention. They split the check and walked past the other table to the parking lot. He started his jeep and pulled onto the road. Sadie frowned out the window at the veranda, the transmission eased into second, and they passed out of view of the café. Fitzpatrick turned on the radio. She turned it down.

"I hate that you have to go back there," she said, "and they get to sit around and play armchair quarterback. Never making one sacrifice for all this."

"You don't know that," he said.

"Whatever. They're hypocrites."

"So's everyone."

"Why are you always taking other people's sides?"

"Because you're being unreasonable. Can you please buckle your seatbelt?"

She scrunched up her face, changed her voice, and did her best impersonation of the pierced woman. "Jesus. Stupid kid. Some people need to learn the art of sniping irony. Some people need a Xanax lobotomy. Some need to be spayed or neutered for their own protection." She dropped the act, reached behind her, and buckled her seatbelt. "I'd rather be unreasonable than a pretentious bitch."

*

An hour later they passed through the gates of Big Bend National Park. The beer buzz from lunch had turned into a mild headache, dry mouth, a general feeling of dehydration. Over the course of the hour Sadie had not let the argument drop, going silent for a while only to begin again with complaints about their narcissistic, callow, ungrateful generation—the worst yet, she claimed. Fitzpatrick agreed that people were generally self-centered to the point of being evil—take the Stanford Prison Experiment, for example, or the one where the researchers had little difficulty convincing subjects to administer what they believed were lethal electric shocks to fellow human guinea pigs—in the name of science, of course. But he doubted our nature had been getting much worse over time.

"Look at the Assyrians," he said. "They used to skin and boil their enemies alive."

"What's that got to do with anything?"

"All I'm saying is, it's not that things aren't bad now. But at least they're less brutal."

Sadie laughed like she felt sorry for him. "And you say this, a twenty-six-year-old about to go fight your second war. Will you at least admit maybe you're wrong? Maybe things are worse."

"Maybe. But I've only seen what I've seen. And I've never seen anyone skinned alive."

She shook her head and watched out the window as the road took a long curve. Thirty miles in the distance, the clustered, towering spires of the Chisos came into view, a fractured volcano rising in a hazy plain. The intermediary landscape held the stark majesty of vast, empty places. Fitzpatrick found it beautiful but also troubling, a landscape composed mostly of nothing.

They passed through the badlands of the park, the road snaking by sandy washes and ragged arroyos. The car hummed along and blew cool air on them. Ocotillo plants rose from the earth like inverted brooms, growing in clumps alongside the occasional yucca, cousin to the pineapple, fitted with a rosette like a crown of waxy knives. Neither plant was much taller than a person and would provide no shade. It was spring, but even so, crossing this desert in the heat of the day would be a task he would not wish on anyone. There would be no resupply of water for twenty miles. In an earlier time the prospect of the arduous crossing would necessitate a long detour through chains of mountains encircling the plain on either horizon. As it was, the car made the direct route effortless.

*

Arriving in the basin a thousand feet above the plain, surrounded by peaks and ridges, they bought iced tea at the general store near the visitor's center. Leaving the car for a new place lightened the mood, and the earlier argument was dropped. They sat on a bench in front of the store, sipped their drinks, and watched a school group dressed in neon being shepherded into an exhibit on desert wildlife. A stuffed mountain lion perpetually snarled through the plate glass behind them. After stretching their legs, they checked in, got the key to their room, and drove around the cul-de-sac, scanning the ring of lodges for their number. They parked nearby and began unloading the car.

"All right, there's a grill," Fitzpatrick said.

"I told you there would be."

In their room they set to work putting away their stuff.

"What do you think about going to the hot springs? Then we could check out Terlingua and get some dinner. It's a ghost town—a tourist trap, really. But charming in a kitschy sort of way."

He said that sounded fine, and they dressed in swimsuits, massaged sunscreen into each other's backs, and took off down the blacktop out of the basin. They descended to the desert floor and followed a gravel road to the trailhead set in a grove of cottonwoods. From there it was a short hike to the river, passing stone buildings abandoned a century before, once a health spa run by a German immigrant until Pancho Villa killed the tourist trade. Tamarisk trees with bright green leaves bobbed in a light wind, and Fitzpatrick remarked on an enormous stand of palms growing in a tight circle. He and Sadie followed the rocky trail, the Rio Grande to their right, a sandstone cliff to their left. The cliff overhung the trail and was dotted near the top by insect-like constructions, the mud nests of an unseen flock of swallows. Before long they reached the hot springs, a single pool twenty feet in diameter, built into the riverbank with stones and cement.

In the pool sat a balding man in his forties, strapping, sunburned, gap-toothed. Beside him, his wife, who had a face like Miss America. They drank from a magnum of red wine, raising plastic flutes to lips stained brown and purple. Their two boys, who looked to be identical, blond twins, waded in the river below the pool. Fitzpatrick and Sadie set down their gear, removed T-shirts, and kicked off their shoes.

"Look, Dad, he's doing it again!" One of the twins pointed at his brother, who had crossed the international boundary and climbed the opposing bank, peering into a dense, jungle-like mass of cane, giant reeds topped with white flowers.

"Boy, get back in that river," the man called, setting down his drink. "Ranger'll lock your ass up." The boy crowed and splashed back into the water, rejoining his brother in the geopolitically liminal shallows. "Shoot," the man said, shaking his head at Sadie in an indirect, western greeting, a mix of wariness and affection.

She and Fitzpatrick eased into the pool. A slight steam came off its surface, smelling of sulfur. Fitzpatrick lay back, submerging all but his buzzed head, which he rested on the side of the pool. He dug his fingers into the soft, black sediment on the bottom, taking up handfuls of the stinking mud and dripping the warmth on his chest. Then he sat up and turned to look over the edge. A cut in the retaining wall funneled the constant outflow of the springs down a little channel, making a waterfall into the Rio Grande. He straddled the wall and climbed over, careful not to slip on rocks overgrown with algae. He sat in the middle of the waterfall and watched the twins play, enjoying the incongruousness of hot and cold, the springs cascading off his back, his feet dangling in the river. Sadie poked her head over the side.

"Whatcha doing?"

"Dare me to run to Mexico," he said.

"You wouldn't."

He stood on the mossy rock and took a low dive into a hole near the bank, stroking perpendicular to the current until it became too shallow to swim. He picked his way over the polished rocks onto the Mexican side, stood there for a moment, crossed his arms, and looked with ironic pride at Sadie, challenging her to something more. The twins made clucking, whooping noises.

After he swam back to the United States, they gathered their things and hiked to the trailhead. They changed in a facility and made the drive to Terlingua, where they sat on a creaking porch of grey planks and watched the horizon as the sunset overtopped mushrooming thunderheads. Later they ate chicken-fried steak inside someone's idea of an old-time saloon, while locals played sad country songs. Full of drink and dinner, they made out in the parking lot, pressed against his jeep. By the time they returned to their lodge the moon had risen over the Chisos Basin. Fitzpatrick piloted the car into an empty space. Beside them was the SUV from lunch.

"Look," he said.

"Great. You sure it's the same one?"

"Unless someone else has a 'Born Again Pagan' bumper sticker."

*

They woke early the next morning and did it again before showering and eating breakfast. He was in great spirits, cooing to her, pinching her ass when she turned her back. They did the dishes together, packed lunch, and headed out. The plan was to hike to the Window. The trail began in the basin near the cul-de-sac of lodges and traversed a steep, exposed slope covered in patches of blind prickly pear and althorn, like living barbed wire. The century plants were Fitzpatrick's favorite.

"They only bloom once," Sadie said. She stopped to point out one whose giant stamen had emerged from the center of low-slung agave leaves. Buds like cauliflower sprouted laterally from the upper reaches of the stalk, twenty feet in the air. Sadie explained how after blooming and scattering its seed, the plant browned and died but did not wilt, its fibrous skeleton standing as evidence of a final, reproductive effort, the simultaneous transformations of sex and death. The slope was dotted with any number of these brittle corpses.

Fitzpatrick photographed one of the larger ones from several different angles. Hearing someone approach on the trail, he stopped, and the family from the hot springs, absent the mother, passed going the other way. Fitzpatrick said hello and asked the man if he would mind taking a picture of himself and Sadie. His twin sons running amok, the man finally snapped the picture after fiddling with the camera, and at the same time his boys succeeded in toppling the century plant Fitzpatrick had just photographed. It might have been standing there a decade or more, longer than the boys had been alive, a fact their father pointed out while scolding them as they went on their way. Fitzpatrick felt a short-lived but powerful swell of hate after the dead plant fell, hatred of people, generally, their destructive urges, but kept his mouth shut and channeled it into motion on the descent of the hillside.

They moved fast and had gotten in a good workout by the time the trail leveled-off near the bottom of the basin, running beside a dry creek bed shaded with oak and juniper. The air was still at the bottom. Sadie led. Far above, fang-like peaks were joined by panoramic battlements of igneous rock. Dark stains on the mountainside marked the path of dry waterfalls. Near the trail, a boulder as big as a house had fractured off Emory Peak during the last ice age and tumbled to rest in the lowest point of the basin. The final quarter mile, they walked over the slickrock canyon, the soil eroded to reveal scalloped stone polished to a waxy sheen.

The canyon grew deeper and narrower until they rounded a bend and were confronted with the Window, a rectangular notch in the rim of the basin. Through this aperture one could see fifty miles and a thousand feet down, wind and air.

"Dare you to fly to Mexico," Sadie said.

Fitzpatrick looked at her.

"Hey," she said. "Kidding." She walked closer to the edge. "Isn't it something?"

He grunted in agreement and sat down, catching his breath, leaning against the canyon wall to unpack lunch. The slickrock was cool and pleasant to the touch, and the view was amazing, but as he ate he kept imagining a wall of water bearing down on them through the narrow canyon, descending past the low-point boulder in a rush of flash flood, ending in a column of whitewater jetting through the Window like a colossal rainspout. The fall would be long and terrifying. He ate his sandwich and tried not to look bothered; it was a stupid thought. There wasn't a cloud in the sky.

*

That evening they fired up the grill in front of their lodge. In a cooler they'd brought steaks, beer, and the makings of potato salad. Fitzpatrick cracked a beer after washing his hands of the rub he had patted into the meat: olive oil, black pepper, and truffle salt. He was lighting the charcoal when the SUV pulled into a nearby space. The man with the red beard smiled graciously and approached the grill. His female companion went the opposite way and disappeared inside their room. Fitzpatrick didn't realize it, but he was scowling nervously. The man nodded at the burning coals and introduced himself as Vern.

"Richard." Fitzpatrick extended his hand, and the two shook. "I think we crossed paths in Marathon, the other day."

"Right, right. Small world. But I guess most people who stop there are headed here. How many are you cooking for?"

"Two," Fitzpatrick said.

"You mind if we share the grill? Doesn't look like there's another one nearby. We can contribute coals."

*

Vern took a sip of the beer Fitzpatrick had given him and slid his spatula under a soy burger, laying it on the grill opposite steaks that sizzled and dripped trails of liquid flame. He did the same with a ground beef patty for his girlfriend, Liz, who sat watching from the steps to their lodge.

"Smells great," he said. Liz rose and ambled over to mix herself another drink from the bottles of bourbon and Coke sweating on a nearby picnic table. The sun had just finished setting. An aircraft moved overhead in twilight, blinking near Mars above the rim of the basin.

"Good stars tonight," Fitzpatrick said.

Liz agreed and moved beside Vern at the grill. Sadie came out of the lodge holding a battery-powered lantern which she set on the picnic table, taking up the beer she'd left, shooting a glance at Fitzpatrick. He could tell she wasn't happy about sharing the space, although nothing had been said. He finished his third of the evening, crumpled the empty can, and tossed it in the bin chained to the grill. Watery blood began to rise from the tops of the steaks, and he flipped them.

"Those look good," Liz said, frowning a little. "We should've done steak."

*

The Milky Way stretched across the black sky like a smear of bioluminescence. Empty plates and beer cans littered the picnic table where the two couples sat and watched moths feverishly batter the cool blue lantern. The level in the bourbon bottle had dropped by half, accelerating its decline after Fitzpatrick switched from beer at Liz's invitation. Sadie sat between them. She had not said much over the course of the evening. The talk ranged from the idiosyncrasies of Texans to the best brand of mobile phone, to favorite books and movies, to how much they all looked forward to trips like these. Lately it had died down and they drank silently, watching the stars and listening to the wind in the desert, the dark flutter of bats preying overhead.

In addition to her brother in the marines, Liz had a father who was retired navy. She'd guessed Fitzpatrick was military by the security decal on his windshield: "DOD," a bar code, a serial number. Then came the usual questions—where had he been stationed, for how long, and what was it like?

Then, "Do you mind if I ask you a personal question?"

Fitzpatrick said no, drawing the word out in polite cautiousness, beginning to guess what might be coming. He experienced a twinge of déjà vu; something like this had happened several times before, but never with such a casual acquaintance. Blame the booze. He crunched an ice cube between his teeth and resigned himself to being a natural curiosity.

"Did you ever, you know . . . kill anyone?" she said. "Over there."

Sadie let out an incredulous hiss.

"Yeah," Vern said, rising to his feet. "I don't really—"

"It's okay," Fitzpatrick said. "I don't mind."

*

He awoke the next morning trying to piece together the fight that had erupted after he and Sadie had left the picnic table for their lodge. She had wanted to know why he had answered that horrible woman—he'd never even told her that. Fitzpatrick said she had never asked and he would tell her whatever she wanted to know.

"I don't need to know the details," she said, shutting and locking the bedroom door. He asked her to open it but she wouldn't. Soon he heard her running a bath, and was too tired to carry it any further. That was about how it had gone.

The morning light shining through the kitchen blinds hurt his eyes, and he itched himself, worn springs sighing below his bulk as he shifted on the unfamiliar sofa. A blanket lay mussed around the cushions. It hadn't been there before; during the night she must have come out of the bedroom to cover him. He wondered why she didn't want to know, whether he had done wrong by answering.

He thought about the story he didn't tell them after answering Liz's question with a simple "yes." He didn't volunteer any more than that, and neither Liz nor any of the others had the balls or the desire to ask further. The party had broken up soon after. But if they would've asked, he would've told. Told them of another morning patrol on a four-lane highway north of Baghdad, every klick of it by now familiar. His platoon clearing the road for a supply convoy due in a few hours. They drove slowly past donkey carts laden with plastic jugs of gasoline, crumbling tenements painted blue and white, rocky fields dotted with squatters' shacks of mud sculpted over empty tins of vegetable oil. Through a palm grove and across an irrigation canal smelling of sewage, and they came upon a man walking the side of the road, trailing an AK-47, its barrel dragging in the dust.

The man was not wearing any uniform and went barefoot, dressed in brown slacks and a collared shirt left half-untucked, yellow stains in the armpits. He paid no attention to the grating rumble of vehicles suddenly trailing him. The barrel of his rifle clattered over the dusty asphalt in a snaking trail. Fitzpatrick got on the platoon net and ordered the other two trucks to block the road while he and his wingman followed at a distance. He switched up to battalion, reported their location, a sit-rep, and asked for guidance. The order came down to disarm the Iraqi.

They halted and dismounted, all but the drivers, and the two gunners who watched down their sights as the trucks crept along.

"Tell him to stop," Fitzpatrick said to the interpreter.

Abdul-Azeem, tall and thin, shouted with gusto over the noise of traffic slowing to gawk in the opposite lanes: "Oguff!"

The man with the rifle continued down the shoulder of the highway, his back to them. He began to babble a stream of Arabic which Fitzpatrick could not understand, but which struck him as different from the cadences he had become familiar with after five months in country.

"What's he saying?" he asked.

"He is crazy," Abdul-Azeem said, his tone disinterested in the way of someone who's seen it all and wants you to know he's not afraid, not even of this. "Maybe he is drunk. Whatever. What he says is shit."

"Can you understand anything?"

The interpreter listened for a moment as they trailed at a cautious distance. Fitzpatrick kept his rifle low and ready, buttstock in his shoulder, the muzzle pointed at the ground between them.

"He is talking to God," Abdul-Azeem said. "Asking for forgiveness, but it is not the way a Muslim should pray. It is a . . . what is it, the opposite?"

"Blasphemy?"

"Yes," he said. "Blastphemy."

"Tell him again to stop," Fitzpatrick said.

The interpreter uttered more threats, and this time the man did stop. He knelt and touched his head to the ground benevolently. He did not release hold of the rifle. Then, in one deliberate motion, he spun and began to lift it. Barely hesitating, Fitzpatrick shot him twice in the gut.

The man bled in the Humvee as they sped to the aid station. Until very near the end he cried vigorously. The gunner lost it and began to kick at him and shout for him to shut the hell up. Fitzpatrick turned in his seat as much as his body armor would allow and said he would court martial him if he didn't stop, and the gunner cursed some more but stopped. The medic rode along and did what he could, starting an IV, applying pressure, but the suicide-by-cop—how Fitzpatrick had come to think of the man over the years—went into shock. When they dragged his corpse from the truck his olive skin was grey and his pupils dilated, frozen open in fear at the moment of death.

*

That morning it was like the argument had never happened. They didn't speak of it, though an undercurrent of tension lingered in their conciliatory lovemaking, in the overeager way they clung to each other. Afterwards they showered and dressed, and he cooked bacon and egg sandwiches. It was the final day of the trip, and though neither was feeling great, they decided it would be a shame to let the opportunity go, and they went ahead with their plan to hike the Lost Mine Trail. Sadie studied the guidebook at the dining table.

"Listen to this," she said, reading aloud. "'Supposedly, at certain times of the year, the rising sun shines on Lost Mine Peak, marking the entrance to a rich mine developed by the old Spaniards.'"

"There's no gold in them hills," Fitzpatrick said, bringing their sandwiches and glasses of orange juice to the table. "The Spanish found out the hard way."

"This is why it's a legend. Anyway, it's supposed to have some of the park's best views."

They ate, drank coffee and water to ease their headaches, and packed a lunch for the trail. On the way out of the lodge they ran into Vern and Liz loading their SUV.

"You guys outta here?" Fitzpatrick asked.

"Back to the grind, brother," Vern said.

Fitzpatrick made a joke about his grinding hangover, which did a little to ease the awkwardness of the morning after. Liz came forward and said goodbye; she needed to go inside and finish with her suitcase. She waved to Sadie and shook Fitzpatrick's hand, touching his shoulder.

"Thank you for your service," she said.

He never knew what to say when people did it like this, ghoulish and self-absolving.

"Don't thank me, thank my recruiter."

*

They left the trailhead and ascended a rocky path through a forest of juniper, oak, and piñon pine. At about a mile the path reached a saddle above a canyon. They stopped to take in the view, looking far into Mexico. Casa Grande Peak stood to the southwest like a rotten molar, its jagged sides dropping sharply into fields of scree and talus broken by patches of clinging scrub. Gradations in brown and red revealed the location of past rockslides, the forces conspiring to shape this frozen landscape. They didn't speak. It was strange. This place was once the bottom of a great ocean.

After the saddle the going became steeper. They climbed a series of switchbacks maintained by terraces of split logs. The last few switchbacks were very steep, treacherous sections made of steps carved in the rock. Fitzpatrick followed, breathing heavily, struggling to keep up. The portion of his shirt covered by the pack was damp with perspiration, but the sweat evaporated from uncovered skin before he could feel it. Finally the switchbacks ended, and they emerged above the tree line to the flat rock of the ridge, exposed more than a mile above sea level. The wind, which had been a mere breeze in the canyon below, became much stronger, and at times he had to hold one hand to his head to keep a particularly forceful gust from lifting the brim of his canvas hat and carrying it off. The last half-mile to the top sloped gently on the broad ridgeline, the way marked by cairns. Sadie, confident and energized, practically skipped over the pitted rock. Fitzpatrick chose his steps more judiciously. She stopped and turned to see where he was.

"Come on, slowpoke!" she teased, calling over the wind. "We're close."

He hurried over the last bit and came to the end of what could be reached on foot, a shelf of rock jutting out of the mountain. At the far end of the shelf, the rock sloped up and curled into a formation like the lip of a toboggan. Sadie headed for it.

"Watch out," he said. "It's a straight drop on the other side. Five hundred feet."

A feeling which had started in him when they'd emerged above the tree line grew much more intense, the sensation of being ineluctably drawn to the edge, moving without moving. He felt unsteady on his feet though they were planted firmly at shoulder width. He did not shift an inch but felt himself rotating, spinning through the cosmos at a million miles an hour on a dozen different axes. The wind buffeted him on all sides, bursting and flurrying unexpectedly, the intimation of an unknown gravity that could exert itself fully and wipe him off the face of the mountain. His head spun. Sadie reached the elevated lip of the outcropping, grasped it with hands stretched overhead, took a toehold, boosted herself up, her head craned over the edge, looking down. Then she inched higher.

"Hey!" Fitzpatrick shouted. The muscles in her shoulders jumped, and she slid back, her sneakers rasping on the rock. He was embarrassed and turned away, but she caught the look in his eyes.

"What's wrong?" she asked.

"I don't know," he said. "I'm feeling . . . it's a funny feeling. Vertigo, maybe."

"I guess we should go down."

He nodded, knowing she was disappointed not to spend more time at the top.

On the return trip they walked hand in hand over the ridgeline until they hit the switchbacks and it became impractical. Then they went single file but remained close, descending into scrubby juniper. In the shade a brace of jays with blue-gray breasts sidestepped in an antagonistic mating dance, holding wings aloft and bristling in a display of false size. Locked in ritual, they paid no attention to the people watching.

The saddle was flat with stones convenient for sitting. They decided to stop there to eat. He dropped his pack, unzipped it, and rummaged through packages of food. Sadie scrambled to the top of a boulder and stood with hands on hips.

"It's just gorgeous," she said. "Look, you can see the Window."

"Where?"

"Down there, the bottom of that cut."

"Uh-huh."

She climbed down from the boulder. He handed her lunch, and they ate and talked. He took a drink of water and breathed deeply, smelling ozone clean and sharp. The vertigo, or whatever it was, had dissipated after they'd descended the ridge, by this time fading to a memory of itself, the ghost of a premonition. He didn't ask, didn't want another argument so soon, but couldn't help thinking maybe some part of her was hoping for the worst, if that could be the nature of the attraction. He tried to put the worry out of mind and follow her plans for the future, turning his face to bask in the sun. Far below, blooming creosote covered the plain in eerie yellow points. It was spring and nearly perfect weather.

JOHN FRY

credo

like a preacher's son returned to God
—but never the church—

hungover from afternoon's endless
lesson in thirst—I do not know

where I am going or how this late
July—below the eyes of Sirius

rabid & bright—I pray you find me
near the strung out corner of Babcock & Prue

where the carne asada smells especially spicy
tonight—since sky's enamel lid slammed shut

I've looked for that angel unawares,
prodigal or pilgrim, saint or sinner, to ask

*

is body the shape of soul—
is soul the shape of body—

when, doubting, he touched to see
seeking the exact location

of soul's shining kingdom
of heaven behind spear-split skin

did Thomas find the aleph—
did Mary feel any pain

when crowning she
pushed out godhead

—Judas kissed Jesus
—did Christ kiss him back

JOHN FRY

to get there

to get there
is a road

(that's a river)

limestone bed
that's a road

(water whispers over)

which the river
that what road

(a kind of sign)

bluff-sung vesper
cedar silent split

(how can I)

over whispers water
choiring latelight come

(if I river, if I road)

never over
but cross

(through)

NAN CUBA

Way-Seeking

In December 2000, I had been researching Mesoamerican spiritual beliefs for my novel, *Body and Bread*, when two archeological sites I was visiting in the Yucatan manifested the sacred. On the first morning of a ten-day trip, I walked from my thatched-roof cottage down a path to Chichen Itza. I had seen photographs and read descriptions, even using those images as models while writing scenes. I had also visited various cities in Mexico, seen European historical sites, and studied my city's Spanish missions. But when I rounded the path's final corner, the stone pyramids rose from arid ground like walls of a mighty cathedral, and I stopped, jolted, teary. Years before, as an unhappy college student, I had wandered into a small chapel on a particularly lonely night, and sitting in the dark, I thought I saw a diaphanous spirit flit across the front of the altar. Now, standing before what had been from AD 750 to 1200 a sophisticated urban center covering an area of almost two square miles, a similar sacred energy felt palpable.

I wandered from one restored ruin to another, silently reading plaques, imagining pre-Columbian Nahua worshipping there: the observatory, *El Caracol*, translated "The Snail" because of its spiral staircase inside the tower; the Temple of the Warriors flanked on its south and west sides by two hundred round and square columns; *La Iglesia*, the Church, whose exterior frieze was decorated with a limestone masonry veneer made up of *Chac* masks, stepped frets, zigzag lines, and pilasters; the Stone Ring thirty feet about the floor of the Great Ballcourt; *Tzompantli*, the Skull Platform, with vertical rows of carved impaled skulls; and the Temple of *Kukulkan*, named for a Mayan deity similar to the Aztec *Quetzalcoatl* or Feathered Serpent (quetzal bird + rattlesnake), who with his opposite, *Tezcatlipoca*, created the Aztec world. This last Mayan pyramid, usually called *El Castillo*, or the Castle, was seventy-nine feet high, but its temple on top added another twenty feet. Each of the four sides was covered in a staircase; each base was 181 feet across, one covered in stone serpent heads. As instructed on the plaque, I clapped while standing in front, and an echo sounded like the "chirp of a quetzalcoatl," meaning the distinctive *kyow* of a brilliant red, blue, and iridescent green quetzal, god of the air and symbol of freedom and wealth. In the 1930s, under the pyramid's north side, a small staircase was discovered that led to another temple below the current one, and inside that area at the top of the stairs, which was the pinnacle of the earlier pyramid, stood a high priest's throne in the shape of a jaguar, painted red with eyes and spots made of inlaid jade. Images had been discovered in various locations of a priest wearing a jaguar skin, assuming the role of God L, the primary lord of the underworld, while he sat on a similar ceremonial bench.

Mayan gods with jaguar attributes could move between the day world, which was the earth and the living, and the night world, which was the underworld of the ancestors. Since the jaguar image recurred throughout my novel as a metaphysical motif, mentioned first as an Aztec mask belonging to the narrator's brother before he committed suicide, I eagerly joined the line at the entrance. People packed the cave-like passageway, silently inching higher while another line descended after viewing the marvel, our shoulders rubbing, elbows bumped. As the air thinned and heat spread like fungus, my breaths shortened until I panted, an invisible fist pressing my chest, my head a detached weight, woozy. Determined to witness what had become a touchstone for my protagonist, I closed my eyes, inhaling, exhaling, stretching breaths, trying to calm but sensing only damp bodies and a tightening; so, I stopped, then bent over, trying to shift blood to my head but finally turning to the man climbing behind me. "I'm going to faint," I muttered, and he grabbed my elbow. We descended like swimmers rising through water, oxygen gradually filtering back into my lungs, until finally, I burst into open light, bystanders oblivious. The kind stranger had sacrificed his place in line, but I had sacrificed a holy encounter, missing this rare clue in my search for an understanding of the spiritual.

I knew the Nahua believed the cosmos was unified by *teotl*, a self-generating, transmuting energy force. *Teotl* was not a god, but a charged current like electricity, and it comprised everything, creating a seamless cosmic totality. Multiple gods were only features of this energy source. Much of its power derived from the cyclical oscillation of contrary yet mutually complementary, interdependent polarities, such as being/non-being, order/disorder, active/passive, animate/inanimate, earth/sky, male/female, life/death. When humans perceived these as dualities rather than aspects of the same regenerating process, *teotl* was masking itself. Nothing was temporal or theistic; everything was *teotl*. A person's goal was to be well-rooted in *teotl*, and in that way, live a balanced life that contributed to a cosmic balance.[1]

My search for more clues took me to Ek Balam, translated "Black Jaguar," a Mayan city surrounded by jungle, dating from 100 BC to its height at AD 700-1200. During our drive there, my guide said restoration had begun only a couple of years before, which meant few tourists came, and in fact, we were the only people there that day. In the Central Plaza, the massive Acropolis pyramid, sometimes called *El Torre*, or the Tower, was 480 feet long, 180 feet wide, and 96 feet high, making it one of the largest structures ever excavated in the Yucatan. Its six levels had housed the city's governors and other dignitaries. Thatched-roof palapas protected multiple facades, and at my guide's urging, I followed him up the stairs toward one.

The stone steps were uneven and narrow, so I was looking at my feet when I moved sideways underneath the overhang. As the vision registered, I leaned back, taking in more, muttering "Incredible," laughing. I could have been standing next to Harrison Ford inside a movie set, searching for the lost Ark. These ancient set designers had sculpted stucco and limestone mortar into a fantastic wall frieze of alto-relief forms and painted over them. Three dimensional glyphs surrounded warriors (a headless one above the doorway), anthropomorphic figures, a woman sitting sideways, skulls, stylized serpents, and plants, towering, I guessed, about twenty feet high and forty feet across. The doorway was bordered by a row of thigh-sized fangs, which also bordered flooring that formed a stage representing a giant jaguar's open mouth to the underworld. Sacrifices had been made there to Ek Balam's powerful ruler Ukil-Kan-Lek-Tok, the highest official during the city's peak in AD 800. A pair of 6.5 feet statues of Winged Guards, with clearly visible hair braids, loin cloth patterns, and carved skulls on their belts, stood on pedestals, protecting this, their ruler's tomb.

Because the Nahua believed each person's lifelong goal was to maintain "balance upon the slippery earth," their religion can be called way-seeking rather than truth-seeking. And in this way, it's more like Taoism or classical Confucianism than European philosophies.[2] Gnosticism, the early Christian sect, was also way-seeking, and like the Nahua struggling for a balanced physical existence, Gnostics wanted to escape the "poverty" of "unknowing." The way to free yourself was to attain gnosis, or self-knowledge, which might be called insight. They believed that you must go on a spiritual quest to discover that you are a child of God like Jesus. When you know yourself at that level, you will also come to know God, because you will discover that the divine is within you and identical in quality with God himself. Therefore, death is no longer a problem, but death is a solution, because the true self will be liberated to a state that's no longer dependent on physical life. Instead of coming to save us from sin, Gnostics thought Jesus came as a guide who opened access to spiritual understanding, much like the living Buddha. In fact, some wonder whether the Hindu or Buddhist traditions influenced Gnosticism, since the religions were not clearly differentiated two thousand years ago. In AD 80-200, when trade routes between the Greco-Roman world and the Far East opened, Gnosticism flourished, and Buddhist missionaries had been proselytizing in Alexandria for generations before that.[3]

According to Ronald A. Barnett, Emeritus Professor of Higher Education at the University of London:

> If we compare the Mesoamerican concept of the prime deity or *God* with that of Judaism, Christianity, Islam, or with the abstract first principle of Hinduism, the Aztec concept does not seem quite so strange any more. For example, *Ometeotl* "invents" or "thinks" itself into existence. Similarly the *YHWH* of the Old Testament means "I am what I am." Like the Muslims with their 99 known names of Allah (+ the 100th mystery name), the Aztecs had many names for the different existential attributes of their prime deity. The Aztecs also believed that the priest was the god's image or replica on earth . . . Compare this with the transubstantiation of the Catholic mass or the idea of God's representative on earth in Christianity.[4]

According to an *American Psychological Association* cover story, "A Reason to Believe," brain researchers think religions are the result of "our cognitive tendencies to seek order from chaos, to anthropomorphize our environment and to believe the world around us was created for our use."[5] Although this may be true, my mystical experiences at Chichen Itza and Ek Balam energized my own way-seeking. Writing my novel helped me accept that some questions will forever go unanswered, finally bringing me to this conversation I am having with you.

---

1. "Aztec Philosophy," *Internet Encyclopedia of Philosophy*, accessed June 23, 2017, http://www.iep.utm.edu/aztec.

2. http://www.iep.utm.edu/aztec, (June 23, 2017).

3. Elaine Pagels, "Excerpt from: The Gnostic Gospels," *The Gnostic Society Library*, accessed June 23, 2017, http:/gnosis.org/naghamm/Pagels-Gnostic-Gospels.html.

4. Ronald A. Barnett, "Mesoamerican Religious Concepts: Part Two," *Mexconnect*, accessed June 23, 2017, http://www.mexconnect.com/articles/546-mesoamerican-religious-concepts-part-two.

5. Beth Azar, "A Reason to Believe," *American Psychological Association*, accessed June 23, 2017, http://www.apa.org/monitor/2010/12/believe.aspx.

ROBIN DAVIDSON

The Black Madonna of Częstochowa

When Russians invaded Poland in 1920, they were said to withdraw their troops on seeing the Madonna's image in the clouds.

At first, when my father dies, I do not sleep. Then I dream each night
of a Polish train headed for Częstochowa.

In my bag I carry a portrait. The Black Madonna, Queen of Miracles, Protectress
of Poland since the 14th century. She is painted on glass

in zinc-based paints, framed in black-stained wood.
The Polish border guard asks for my ticket, opens my bag, unwraps the portrait:
          Bogurodzica. Mother of God. He lets me pass.

          No. I am in an airport
and read the sign aloud *Liberty International Airpoet,*
but the American security agent checking my luggage is not amused.

The zinc's triggered an alarm. He lifts the portrait to the light, begins to scrape
paint from the glass. The blues of her robe, the tiny gold stars,

the reds yellows greens of the garden behind her
become splinters
          weaving themselves into my neatly folded clothes until
          I begin to hum,
Airpoet, Airpoet, fly away home, your house is on fire,
your children are gone. Adorno stands in line ahead of me, turns:

My dear young Ladybug, don't you know a myth when you hear one?
To atone for your nursery rhyme naïveté, I order all planes to stay aloft for the day.

Then the splinters of garden paint become soot that rises,
falls in flakes into my hair.

Neither train, nor plane, nor house
has solid form, and I see the world change, dissolve.

Note: In his dream transcript dated January 1954, Theodor Adorno writes, "I heard Hitler's inimitable voice . . . 'To atone for my only daughter's victimization in a tragic accident, I order that all trains shall be derailed today.'"

Truth and Beauty

JIM LAVILLA-HAVELIN

West News from the Little Bend of South View

for Mobi, Kamala, and Marisol

the urban left had it somewhat easier –
they didn't have to make the choice
    between being peasant or landowner
intelligentsia – worker
is not quite the same
and while we all still struggle with the
    victim or executioner one,
owning land does present some ticklish questions –

I used to have Proudhon's
"Property is Theft"
inscribed on the side of one of my bookshelves
but again, those were books
so, irony or not, having/hoarding
seemed almost acceptable,
less so in these days of the little free libraries.

Yes,
"we were the land's before the land was ours,"
but mostly that meant a suburb backyard
    with willow tree
or various patches of next to no grass
and much concrete in quite a few cities

now, it's acres – enough land that half
we keep wild (if leaving it be can be considered keeping)
and the other half takes more than one day
of mowing on the riding mower

so I know as I know very little else
they are not "my trees"
and not just because
they will outlive me

back then to books, or the people inside them –
to Ed Abbey and to Aldo Leopold
for some help with this,
and to craggy Henry who never claimed
ownership, though he
nearly burned the whole woods down.

The trees belong to themselves – they've made this deal
to grace my vision, shade my eyes, help me see
the grasses and the dirt, the weeds – that we call weeds,
some wind-intentional plants, the ants
and all the other
glorious anarchy of my West.

LAURENCE MUSGROVE

Bluebonnet Sutra

This weekend, the Buddha and I drove
To the Hill Country to see the bluebonnets,
And on the return trip home I asked him
About how he was able to overcome
The suffering so many of us continue to
Wrestle with in our lives, and he rolled up
His window so he could be better heard
Saying, "Our suffering is to a large degree
The result of the fear we feel about being
Ourselves. In other words, much of our
Common suffering is a self-imposed
Despair that we unknowingly practice
In hope that our friends and family
Will rush to our aid, when in truth
The only ones who will ever come
Are a patient heart and a ready mind."

CHARLES TAYLOR

Taking on the Big One

A while it's been
since I opened the
tackle box and tried
to tackle the big

one, the great white
blob out in life's
ocean, Mister Death, with
his swell bloodhound nose

that smells his upcoming
meals miles away. I
usually like to picture
death as a shrouded

stranger hidden behind the
curtains, the toes of
scruffy shoes sticking out,
a passive sort of

guy waiting for the
simmer down before slipping
out and waving down
a taxi for the

next town. Truth is
death's rather an anachronism
as envisioned, a quaint
return to a time

when we were certain
all sorts of spirits
haunted the words or
hid in the basement.

CHARLES TAYLOR

At the Heart of the Heart

I'm looking for
A sacred place
where all sorts
of sticks can
set their killing
fires down and
slap hands together
grinning, glowing, gritty,
like the way
of the dancing
smiling Jesus who
skipped out on
his crucifixion for
the sunrise party;
imagine a spiritual
groove, a virtual
grove, in the
way the Indians
washed free the
war paint to
sit by curling
smoke and talk
with smiling hands
at the marriage
of rivers, an
intersection to end
our bleak and
bloody human traffic.

STEVE WILSON

Call It a Kind of Grace

if, as
summer

heat blossoms

to flame
on the mesa,

cardinals—
their
scarlet

coruscating against sun-

light—within the withered
brushwood

settle and show

NAOMI SHIHAB NYE

Grandfather's Heaven

My grandfather told me I had a choice.
Up or down, he said. Up or down.
He never mentioned east or west.

Grandpa stacked newspapers on his bed
and read them months after the news was relevant.
He even checked old weather reports.

Grandma was afraid of Grandpa
for some reason I never understood.
She tiptoed while he snored, rarely disagreed.

I liked Grandma because she gave me cookies
and let me listen to the ocean in her shell.
Grandma liked me even though my daddy was a Muslim.

I think grandpa liked me too
though he wasn't sure what to do with it.
Just before he died, he wrote me a letter.

"I hear you're studying religion," he said.
"That's how people get confused.
Keep it simple. Down or up."

GARY T. MCDONALD

Novel Excerpt from *Blood* Money

"*Are you washed in the blood of the Lamb?*" He couldn't get it out of his mind. His car radio was dead and that old refrain had been torturing him for the last hundred miles. It started outside Abilene and now he was almost to Big Spring on the I-20 with that God damn hymn chasing him all the way.

Are you washed in the blood,
In the soul cleansing blood of the Lamb?
Are your garments spotless? Are they white as snow?
Are you washed in the blood of the Lamb?

It was what that woman in polka dots had sung while his mother lay in her casket looking vaguely like a figure from a cut-rate natural history diorama featuring Cro-Magnons. Her mortuary "artist" was not going to win any MacArthur Genius grants.

He was unsettled, but not necessarily discontent to see his mother like that. There was a part of him that hated her. She, more than anyone, had mercilessly imbued him with that terrible sense that if he didn't get with the program he was doomed to Eternal Fire. And he'd carried that with him every step of his life. What was the program? It was the hidden message in all those pasteboard signs the numbnuts waved for the TV cameras at Cowboy games.

"John 3:16." The surface message was obvious. If you believe, you're saved. The hidden message was only implied. If you can't believe Almighty God impregnated a mortal woman (like Jupiter did Hercules's mom) and that his son, the Lord, walked on water and ate a meal, talked to people, and walked with them from Jerusalem to Bethany after being dead for three days, after being tortured to death so that *you* could be saved—if you can't believe *all* that, you're screwed. You're going to burn in Hell. Forever.

How much Vipassana meditation was it going to take to liberate him from that particular curse? Who the hell knew?

And Geoff could smell it now. Wasn't that Hell he sniffed? Or was a belt or some other obscure Asian doodad melting down under the Camry's hood, destined to leave him stranded in the middle of West Texas, an eternal hostage to God's wrath? Was it Sherman who said if he owned Texas and Hell, he'd rent out Texas and live in Hell?

Or maybe it was just the oil and gas smell. Big Spring was in the Permian Basin, wasn't it? He'd driven through Midland and Odessa enough to know that smell. Maybe he was okay. If he could just get out of this God damn Texas and make it to his favorite motel in Lordsburg, New Mexico, he was halfway home.

And that thought brought up another memory. Years ago, he had stepped into his younger brother's room after coming back to the family home from the hospital where the kid had just died. On the turntable was Side B of a Jerry Jeff Walker album. The first cut—Guy Clark's "L.A. Freeway." Maybe the last song the kid ever listened to in his short life before he went to the hospital to die.

"*If I could just get off of this L.A. freeway without getting killed or caught, Down the road in a cloud of smoke to some land that I ain't bought . . .* " Presumably, in Texas.

But it was just the opposite for Geoff. If I can just get off this Texas highway without getting killed or caught, get back to my Venice Beach condo that I own outright and where I've got a meditation cushion strategically placed for maximum mind liberation from Bible verses and curses. And his mother's ever-present disappointed look that said she knew for a fact her son was going to Hell.

What a hypocrite he was. The day before his nineteen-year-old brother died, he had held him in his arms and had told him that the universe was so old, Eternity was so long, that our lives are all just a blink of an eye. That once he passed though the threshold to the Beyond, he wouldn't even have time to turn around before Geoff would be there with him along with everyone else he cared to see. Geoff did not believe it then or now, but it had comforted a badly frightened young pot dealer who was soon to meet his Maker. Or not.

That turntable. That Jerry Jeff Walker album. They were both in the backseat behind him now, along with copies of plays and college papers he'd written but had never bothered to cart to LA. And in the trunk, his dad's tough-looking Super Black Eagle Benelli twelve-gauge. What else was he going to do with it? Sell it to some potential mass murderer?

It was a duck hunter's gun, but maybe it would make an impressive statement if Venice erupted again as it did after the Rodney King cops' verdict came in. Maybe he could stand off the justifiably pissed-off urban masses so the Millennial members of his Homeowners' Association would not be raped and pillaged of their Whole Foods wine collections and Love Yoga mats.

On the other hand, hadn't he vowed not to harm any sentient being? Maybe those shotgun shells were so old they wouldn't fire if he pulled the trigger. Best just keep it unloaded and hope for the best.

Big Spring hadn't changed much since the last time he'd driven through. God, how do people live here? Oh, to be back home.

He had risen early that morning, deflated the air mattress he had slept on, rolled it and the sleeping bag up, walked through the completely empty house into the garage, and loaded the bedding and shotgun into the trunk of the Camry. The real estate agent pulled up and he handed off the keys to the family home. He and his sister had spent the last two weeks making trips to Goodwill and the toxic waste disposal site to clear the place out. Still, the toxicity of that house remained. John 3:16.

He would always be a Texan, but knew he'd never be in that house again. Maybe never even in Dallas again. That place where you can't throw a stone in any direction without hitting a Bible-thumping Republican. But now, 560 miles away and counting, that Lamb's blood was still all over him and he didn't know if he'd ever be able to wash it off. And finally breathe easy.

Maybe this new project would help. His agent had called him a week ago. Apparently, Tim Hardesty had called him and made a pitch. Geoff only vaguely knew Tim, who had married Geoff's high school and college girlfriend, Rachel Golden, ten years earlier. They lived in Hollywood, and Geoff saw them maybe once a year. Neither he nor they could stand the long, crosstown trek on LA freeways to get together. But the real reason he avoided them was because he knew in his heart of hearts he was still in love with Rachel.

Both his and her parents adamantly opposed their relationship from the start. His didn't want him marrying a Jew (who would pull him further away from Christ), and hers wanted her to marry a nice Jewish lawyer. They already had a dentist and doctor in the family. No *goy* writers were required. Probably a wise position to take.

But the parents weren't the only problem. Rachel chided him endlessly on his goal of making it in Hollywood. Why couldn't he do something that actually *helped* people? That did not sit well. He needed a supportive partner if he was going to take on the dragon of Show Biz. They broke up.

After college, she worked for various NGOs until she found herself in LA running an earthquake relief organization founded by a Syrian tech billionaire. And Tim, a sometime musician and ancient Greek scholar, for lack of gainful employment, joined her in the effort. Then, at some point, either in earthquake-torn Greece or a year later in Turkey (he won't say which for legal reasons), he found an ancient Greek manuscript. He smuggled it back to LA in the organization's logistical equipment and worked for three years carefully handling the old papyrus and translating the document. He took it to the people at the Getty, who eventually authenticated it as a First Century document. Their PR people did a masterful job of hyping it, and Tim got rich when *The Gospel of Thomas (the Younger)* was published. Of course, Rachel got fired from her organization. The buck stopped with her when it came to plundering host countries of their cultural heritage in the name of earthquake relief. No one else would hire her, but she really didn't need to work. They bought a fabulous house high in the hills not far from the Griffith Observatory.

Not content with being the discoverer of a document that sold worldwide in the hundreds of thousands, Tim decided to indulge his lifelong dream of becoming a novelist. With Random House waiting eagerly, he churned out an action-packed romp based on an episode in his *Thomas (the Younger)* find and sent it off to them. They were not impressed. But they knew they could sell a book with his name on it. So they proposed hiring a ghost writer to "make some tweaks." To protect his artistic achievement, he countered, insisting that he hire and supervise "the editor." The publishers decided that they had nothing to lose.

Tim knew screenwriters, but none that had written a successful novel . . . except Geoff. It was Geoff's *Perchmouth* that had landed him his first Hollywood gig, adapting his own novel for Paramount. It was loosely based on his West Texas deputy sheriff grandfather's investigation and capture of his boss's murderers—Perchmouth Stanton and Ida "Ma" Hunsucker—who went on a Bonnie and Clyde-style killing spree back in 1933. The movie never got made, but Geoff got into the Writers Guild and other assignments rolled in.

Now, years later, with no real screen credits except for an awful Dolph Lundgren flick he rewrote in nine days, sticking strictly to the producer's lousy outline so that the investors would release the production funding (a movie with a 23% audience approval rating on Rotten Tomatoes), his career desperately needed a jump-start. His last spec script was about a Buddhist monk clearing landmines in Cambodia, and nobody had even nibbled at it.

So Tim had called Geoff's agent and offered him 50K to work on *The Blood of Men and Angels*. But the really enticing part was that if either *Thomas (the Younger)* or *Blood* was made for TV or film, Geoff would get the adaptation gig, sole credit, and half from both the sale and the writing fees. The three of them were to meet the day after tomorrow at Tim's palace in the Griffith Park hills.

Geoff was wary at first. He read a PDF of Tim's draft of *Blood*. It was what you'd expect from a novice writer. Full of moustache-twirling villains and bodice-ripping sex scenes. And another odd thing—Tim had simply lifted whole sections of *Thomas (the Younger)* and used them as back story. While Thomas and his former pupil (the young Jewish aristocrat who would become the famous general and historian Josephus) make the long trek from Jerusalem to Rome on a diplomatic mission, Thomas finally shares with him stories of his youth when he traveled with Jesus, how he watched his beloved uncle die on a Roman cross, and his later misadventures with a crazed narcissist named Saul of Tarsus—later the self-renamed Paul, as in the *Apostle* Paul.

It was a weird book. But the backstory compelled him to go out and buy a copy of *Thomas (the Younger)*. And then he saw what all the fuss had been about.

This was the book he had been searching for his whole life. A book that totally debunks the Synoptic Gospels and, thus, Fundamentalism, while portraying Jesus as a Neo-Buddhist, teaching people to meditate and making no claims about an afterlife or his divinity.

It had been years since Geoff had been so excited by a book. And thinking about it had taken his mind off the onerous funeral and house-clearing tasks that tore and weighed on him like an anchor.

Geoff was ready to go to work. He would make the deal. He would get that *Blood* money. He would whip the book into shape. He would avoid any scenes with Rachel. His agent would sell both books to HBO or Showtime or the History Channel or someone. He would adapt the hell out of them. He would revive his career. This time—no booze, no drugs, no weekend trips to Vegas with aspiring actresses. Just a mindful appreciation of each moment, unfolding one after the other, without desire or aversion.

And the compassionate intention of creating something that might lead others to make efforts to find the peace and happiness he sometimes achieved on the cushion.

Vipassana means insight. There was a lot of insight in *The Gospel of Thomas (the Younger)*. If there ever was a gospel inspired by God, this was it. Everything the Buddha said was there—impermanence, no-self, and desire and aversion as the source of all dissatisfaction in life.

Insight is a flash of inner knowing of the Truth, not in the brain, but in the heart. That's what he would live for now that he was escaping his past. For good.

But the Lord would probably not let him go easily. That bloody lamb was still dripping its toxic waste all over him. He'd need a long, hot shower to get clean. And there was one waiting for him. If he could just get off this God damn Texas highway and make it to friggin' Lordsburg.

Just then—disaster. No way he could have seen that Highway Patrol cruiser hiding in the turnout, peeking out from behind a wall of oil drums. And here it came, cherry top ablaze to capture the guy with the California plates and an Obama bumper sticker. And a shotgun in the trunk.

Geoff pulled over and waited, peering into his mirror. The patrolman in the passenger seat took his time heaving his girth out of the cruiser and trundled toward him with his ticket clipboard in his left hand, his right on the butt of his holstered pistol. The safety strap was unsnapped. Equanimity, Geoff, equanimity.

He rolled down his window. The heavy-set officer kept well away from the car and projected his voice.

"Ten miles over the speed limit."

"Sorry. My mind must have wandered."

"License and proof of insurance."

Geoff searched them out. When he handed them over, he noticed the Jesus fish tattoo on the back of the man's hand.

The guy lifted his sunglasses and scrutinized the insurance doc.

"USAA. You a vet?"

"My dad. He was a Marine."

"Officer?"

"I think all pilots were. He served in the Pacific. Died a few years ago."

"Sorry to hear it." He peered through the passenger window. "You moving?"

"Just cleared out the family home. Mom passed a week ago."

At that moment, the guy's partner sauntered up. He was rail thin and had a sour look on his face when he spoke.

"You wanta pop the trunk so we can have a look-see."

Geoff hesitated. Was this legal? The search might be, if he agreed to it. But he also knew from years of driving back and forth from the skeet range with his dad (the only thing they ever did together) that it was perfectly legal to transport an unloaded shotgun in the trunk. Unless some law had changed in Texas recently that he didn't know about. But Texas passing a more restrictive gun law? No chance.

He popped the trunk. And in a flash Skinny Cop disappeared behind the trunk door he raised, then apparently pulled the Benelli straight out of its soft drag bag because Geoff next saw him step around to the driver's door holding the shotgun like Lee Harvey Oswald in that famous backyard picture of him with the Mannlicher rifle.

"Looky here, Sergeant . . . What was you plannin' to do with this?"

Geoff swallowed hard. "Take it home. To LA. It was my dad's."

The heavy-set patrolman spoke up. "He passed on. So he says."

"You ain't heard? They don't allow no guns in California."

Geoff looked over at the sergeant. Went for it. "I noticed your fish tat. On your hand there. *Nice.*"

"Know what it means?"

"You've been washed in the blood of the Lamb. . . . Are your garments spotless? Are they white as snow?"

The man stared at him. Geoff smiled back like a fool. Used his Tibetan mind control. The big patrolman shook his head.

"You know. I think I'm gonna give you a warning this time. Keep your mind on your driving. Swifty, put this man's shotgun back in his trunk where you found it."

"Thank you, Officer." And thank you, Jesus.

He heard a rustle in the trunk and then Skinny closed it with loud bang. He took his license and USAA card back from the Christian gent, started the Camry, waved and pulled out on the empty road, careful not to accelerate in an unseemly manner.

A moment later, in the mirror in the receding distance he could see the cruiser pull pack into its lair. He breathed.

"If I can just get off this Texas highway without getting killed or caught . . . "

And if he could just keep that in his head, maybe he could banish the Lamb for a while. But Geoff knew with crystal clarity that now he owed Him one.

HEATH DOLLAR

A Frontier's Passing

The night was quiet except for the barking of dogs from the pueblo down the road, their distant, hollow calls echoing the emptiness of the land. In the hours before dawn, when the night was blue and cold, and the Milky Way swirled and swarmed above the scrub desert floor, Handley Robertson sat on the porch of a Chihuahuan cantina.

Inside the bar, his friend Jim Bullard drank dollar beer with a Mexican rancher. They talked cattle in Spanish and admired one another's hats. Jim never mentioned that he worked for the U.S. Border Patrol, nor would he. In the back of the bar, three mechanics, covered in grease and surrounded by empty beer bottles, laughed and called one another "*buey*" and "*cabrón*." Along the wall and away from the window, a young woman, more of an opportunist than a prostitute, shared a booth with a middle-aged white man. She was barely twenty years old and had a baby by a husband six months dead, or so she claimed. She had gathered her only available resources, a firm body and a blue polyester dress, and intended to trade that body for hard currency.

The cantina's front screen door creaked open, and the heels of Jim's boots resounded across the wooden porch.

"Handley, why don't you come back inside?"

"Ain't ready just yet."

"Well, what sort of pressing business do you have out here on the porch?"

"Sittin'. I'm just sittin' on the porch."

"Well, come back inside."

"Don't much want to. It's nicer out here. Look how bright Jupiter is."

Handley took a sip of the beer that he held loosely in his hand. Through the screen door he could hear the young woman speak in a calm, quiet voice. She talked of saving her money and going to college, of becoming a veterinarian or a nurse.

Whether the girl could be believed was uncertain. Perhaps it was only the part she played in these late-night dramas, or what the men that crossed the border to seek out such women sought—a pure heart in dire circumstances. Perhaps they thought there would be emotion. Perhaps exploitation thrilled them, thrilled them in a way that they dared not share with others for fear of being called monstrous or inhuman. Perhaps they found secret joy in avenging themselves of the frustrations and heartbreaks, of the loves that dangled just beyond reach, and placed all the sins of women upon a single lamb—all the blackness, duplicity, and humiliation upon her, and washed away the sins of all women in a brackish tide of climax.

For Jim, such a woman was only a tool, a tool as sharp as a scalpel and blunt as a club that he used against another woman on the other side of that border, a woman that never loved him or spoke kindly of him, yet shared his bed and cooked for his children.

"Are you coming in?" Jim asked.

"I'll be there dreckly."

"All right," Jim told him and walked back inside.

Handley sat staring into the night, and his mind savored the fatigue he felt. He found solace in knowing that exhaustion would bring him sleep and that sleep would lend him oblivion for a time. He found no interest in the women; the cantina; the red-lit bordellos of boystown; or even the woman he thought had caused him to come here. He did not grieve her. He only grieved the cycle from which he could not stray, the cycle of failed romances that had extinguished themselves for one reason or another, though the reason was always the same. Like a comet in its orbit, these relationships followed the same awkward path around and around and around. In the end, Handley's sorrow was not for the loss of this woman, but for the cycle she had become a part of.

Framed by the cantina porch, a shooting star streaked through the atmosphere. Handley saw it but did not make a wish. He only looked at the quivering meteor and tried not to think about the woman. Scratching his stubbled chin, he wondered whether the meteor was mainly composed of silicates or of iron. He wondered whether it had survived its impact with the Earth or if it had turned to dust. He fixed his mind on these particulars in order to defy the urge to wish. And then, when the memory of the woman resurfaced above the silicates and the iron, he trained his attention to the sky.

For Handley, the sky possessed great meaning. He was an astronomer working at the McDonald Observatory in West Texas. In that desolate outpost, he traded love's young spring for the divination of the heavens. He would have a difficult time finding a woman willing to sleep alone every night. And living in the empty lands of West Texas, his prospects would be few. In such places, women of talent and mind leave when the first opportunity presents itself and never return to that hostile, barren land whose only fruit is the viscous crude pumped from its bowels. For the women who remain, they find themselves married and with child before they can legally drink.

Thus, Handley sat outside a Mexican bar trying to forget another unavoidable end. This time it had been a beautiful girl named Paloma, a girl with very little to say. After two years, she had nothing to say. The relationship had dissolved. And Handley, sitting on the rude planks of the cantina porch, now found love to seem far more like a tenant of this Earth than of the heavens. He imagined love to be a dove that sometimes came with a wounded wing to call, a bird that rested broken for a time and then flew away.

"Handley, come back inside," Jim said, standing on the porch again, this time with a thumb hitched into a belt loop of his jeans.

"Don't want to."

"Serve yourself. I can't make you."

"I'm thinking about leaving McDonald."

"And where would you go? The next place won't be no different."

"I guess I'll have to learn to accept some things."

"Yeah, and learn to quit feeling sorry for yourself. You ain't exactly underprivileged."

Jim spat tobacco juice into the sand. He stood there like he had more to say but instead patted his friend's shoulder and once again returned inside.

An ocean of light began to claim the stars within its tide. The great cosmic mystery faded at the same rate as the Chisos Mountains began to appear on the horizon. Handley thought about Doppler's redshift, and how Hubble, standing on the giant's shoulders, had concluded that the universe was constantly expanding. He thought about how this redshift notion supported Hubble's theory that all of the forces of the universe had been pressed into a point far smaller than Pandora's box and then released in one colossal blast.

Though he was a scientist, Handley was also enthralled by less tenable cosmologies, such as the Mayan legend about men of straw, the story of Brahma and his creative force, or the tale of two lovers and their idyll with a sensuous garden. He also liked the ancient Greek belief that the world was born of Chaos. And he prayed to both God and Kierkegaard that Nietzsche wasn't right. He didn't want to do this again.

Handley didn't know where the universe began or the universe ended. He only catalogued and chronicled what was happening in the sky above him. On his desk he kept a scripture from the Vedas, "To know is to not know." It sufficed for him far more than speculation. No, Handley had not meant what he had told Jim about leaving McDonald, and Jim knew it. Handley would continue to work. He would continue to discover. And love, were it fated by the comets and portents above, would eventually find him.

In the shallow light of morning, Handley rose from the porch, and the screen door creaked behind him as he walked back into the bar. A young boy was mopping the floor as the sun lit the window. A slow ranchera played on the jukebox, and someone was cooking tortillas and chorizo in an unseen kitchen. Taking a chair at the simple wooden table where Jim still sat, Handley did not mention the dozen empty beer bottles on the table.

"*Dos más cervezas*," Jim told the bartender.

Jim drew two cigars from his shirt pocket and gave one to Handley. They smiled at one another uncertainly and waited for their beer.

ROBIN DAVIDSON

Delayed Baggage, Oświęcim, 2004

Thus men forgot that all deities reside in the human breast.—William Blake

Blake was wrong. We are not gods. We do not have
enough space within, no matter how we modulate our breath,
to hold a world, its diasporas of wars and loves.

I owned a suitcase once I packed with loss.
A gray sweater in braided wool of a man I could not love.
A black wool skirt I could not wear to a friend's funeral across an ocean.
A watercolor drawing of the oldest street of a Polish city I could not keep.
A book of photographs—the faces of dead children—
and stories written in a language I could not read.

We do not have
enough space within, no matter how we modulate our breath.

I dreamt I saw the suitcase fall in flight.
The aircraft's belly opened, the bag dropped,
and it too slowly opened so that each garment, drawing, book
fell and flared—little parachutes floating and falling—
my own small life visibly scattering,
suspended as objects in the twin oceans of air and water.

To hold a world, its diasporas of wars and loves.

I have seen hundreds of suitcases—black and brown and green,
labeled carefully by their owners with names, addresses,
then more carefully by others with numbers randomly assigned.
They stand upright, lie sideways, sit stacked and stored
in a glass warehouse, in a mud and wire landscape,
looking out at the human museum,
waiting sixty years to be claimed.

Note: Oświęcim is the Polish town renamed Auschwitz by the Nazis in World War II.

BLAKE KIMZEY

And Finally the Tragedy

And finally the tragedy. The boy's parents selected a wooden casket with fine-grained eddies streaking its polished sides, ready to be lowered into a family plot when they found him. It wasn't that the boy had been lost and then found dead—that would have been okay. The tragedy was that the boy was found, that he came to, hair matted and sweaty on his forehead. A team of hound dogs with wet salty noses trained on dirty dry field brush found the boy near twilight. The townsfolk were close behind, stabbing lit torches skyward.

The field was blue with moonlight, banded with a stand of trees and a dead creek bed cracked bank to bank. The sounding footfalls of fleeing boar drummed the hardpacked ground. Blackbirds spooked from treetops, feathers shined metallic in flight, and the only thing left in the field was the boy and the townsfolk and the sound of hound dogs panting for water and wind agitating petrified tree branches.

The boy lay in a slight depression of his own making, his chest rising and falling. He had tumbled from the stars, had been swinging satellite to satellite when he fell. We made a ring of silhouettes five or six bodies deep around the boy. When the boy's eyes opened the women hummed hymns and the men nervously worked their calloused hands together. As Reverend, I bent down and looked into his face. His cheeks, where a spray of freckles had been, were now a swirl of galaxies, glowing faint with the matter of the universe. I felt a crush of bodies peering over my shoulders, an expectant congregation. Torches were duffed and the hound dogs bellied to the ground. It was up to me to make sense of the boy, but I found no purchase in what I saw before me. His eyes flickered bright as stars pinpricked in the firmament.

Then the boy opened his mouth, cavernous as a two-story movie theater. I feared he would swallow us whole. Inside his mouth was a projector spinning film. It cast bright yellow light onto the night sky and made a translucent screen of moving images. We pushed our chins upward, as if one body. The reel shone with galaxies blooming like colorful flowers before us. Night became day and day became night and on and on it went. Men grew beards white as chalk that swept the ground and women spun their hair into buns that rose like hives. We lost track of time and the screen slowly dimmed and finally the film stopped spinning. Twilight again. The boy closed his mouth and stood. He started walking through the field toward town, the white church steeple rising over an umbrella of trees. We silently followed in a procession. One by one our bodies turned to dust, salting the wind, and our souls burned in the boy's imagination, forever alight.

Joy and Gratitude

GREG BROWNDERVILLE

Honest Gospel Singing

When I was a kid, I went to church.
I sang in church: from the time I was twelve,
I did a special every Sunday.
And often, when the preacher preached, I nodded yes
like a boat motor
bobbing down the highway toward the lake.

My fancier companions took me to the lake
in high school and college. I remember
floating tipsy, grazing bridges with fingertips.
I remember picnics on the party barge
and being a helpful kid, twisting lids
off jars for women. I remember
some of my life.

But last night, home
for the first time in a long time,
when I walked into my dark boyhood bedroom,
I was slapping blind: my hand
didn't know where the light switch was anymore.

And this morning in church,
when the preacher asked me to sing, I rose quietly
and walked to the front—slow,
like a spooky old man through a kindergarten classroom,
there to learn with the other children
how to sound things out.
And though I started all right, the second verse
wouldn't come home to me. I muttered
melodically. Nonsense syllables.

But the people broke out in tongues—
they wept, and said some mystery words
like *shahn-die*, seconding my gibberish with God's,
because they know. They know
honest gospel singing when they hear it.

NORMA ELIA CANTÚ

Female Energy along the Camino That Is Life

In my life, I have had several spiritual encounters with what I have called the Divine Female Energy of the universe. Here, I would like to tell of three incidents. The first is taken from a book on my pilgrimage along the Camino de Santiago, el Camino Frances, in January 2011. The other two happened earlier, sometime in the 1990s and early 2000s.

Mary in Rabé de las Calzadas

On January 5, 2011, we (Becky, my Camino companion, and I) left the elegant Municipal Burgos Albergue (the pilgrim hostel) and walked toward our next destination, Rabé de las Calzadas, where we stayed at Hostal Liberanos Domine, a private hostel, run by siblings Clementina and José, who welcomed us as if they had been expecting us. It had been a long day that began early in Burgos—it was already 8 a.m. but it was still dark—walking in the rainy early morning to the bank to get some cash, as our Euros were dwindling. We walked the crowded streets as people huddled under colorful umbrellas on their way to work or school. I noted that the fashionistas were wearing wool suits, but instead of skirts or pants, they wore shorts! Like the hot pants of years ago, these young women wear short shorts under suit jackets—in winter no less. Formal wear for the office. One woman especially stood out. At Banco Santander where we went to exchange our dollars for Euros, she walked in obviously cold, in a camel-colored wool suit, with short, cuffed shorts over brown tights and brown leather knee-high boots; her elegant jacket had brown leather elbow patches. Another woman in the street was wearing a blue denim suit with short shorts and black tights and boots. She was very elegantly coiffed, and with fancy jewelry, but no doubt freezing in her shorts-suit. Must be the fashion this winter. I know I couldn't wear it no matter how fashionable. I would be too cold! Of course, what we are wearing marks us as pilgrims, and my REI black pants and layers of wool over long-johns keep me warm. I am thankful for my sock liners, socks, and hiking boots as well as my glove liners and gloves.

But my new yellow poncho makes me feel like SpongeBob SquarePants! In our pilgrim garb, we are anything but fashionable. Luckily, no one expects a pilgrim to dress any differently from the way we are dressed. We bought more tissue packages, for our noses run constantly as we walk in the cold. The rain is merciless. The rain that the fields thirst for poses a problem for the pilgrim. All day, I think of the *poemario* and make up titles for poems, and lines drift in and out. It was cold and rainy as we walked out of Burgos having had a light breakfast at a café near the Banco Santander near Plaza Mayor. We walk along the path and on roads that are muddy, but the path is well marked.

Walking into the tiny town of Rabé and being greeted by José made what had just happened along the path more meaningful. Pleasantly surprised, I didn't understand the impact of his welcome until much later. Before arriving, but close to Rabé and to the hostel where we had planned to spend the night, I had a strange urge to pray the rosary. It is unusual for me to suddenly begin praying anything, much less the old ritual prayers. But on the Camino it happened twice. On this day, I found myself unable to resist the urge, and I thought of my dad, whose devotion to the rosary had been such that in my childhood we would pray the rosary daily in the evening after dinner. His strong voice leading the prayers. Also, during Christmas, or when someone died, it was my father who with his deep sonorous voice led the prayers beautifully and complete with the long litanies. So, I began praying to myself using my hands, as I didn't have any beads, to count the individual Hail Marys of the mysteries, and changing the walking stick from one hand to the other to mark the five mysteries. As I was finishing up the rosary, praying the special prayer my family always prays at the end of the rosary,

> *Dios te salve, reina y madre, madre de misericordia, vida y dulzura y esperanza nuestra, dios te salve a ti amamos los desterrados hijos de eva a ti suspiramos gimiendo y llorando en este valle de lagrimas, ea pues senora abogada nuestra vuelve a nosotros esos tus ojos misericordiosos y despues de este destierro mustranos a Jesús, fruto bandito de tu vientre, o clemente, o piadosa, o dulce virgin María, ruega por nosotros santa madre de dios para seanos dignos . . .*

We walked into the town and I felt a strange joy. As if I had arrived somewhere really special. When José, the hospitalero, handed each of us a small medal of the Virgin Mary, after stamping our credenciales, I remembered my earlier urge to pray the rosary and felt a connection. I asked him why he was giving us the medal, and he explained that he did that with all the pilgrims because the town was dedicated to Mary. I again felt that indescribable joy.

Later I read in our guide that the town's thirteenth-century church is dedicated to Santa Marina. The *albergue* (hostel), named Santa Marina and Santiago, according to our guidebook, honors both Mary and the apostle. I remember the Latin name and in fact I have a card that José also gave us with the image of the Virgin Mary and the name of the private albergue along with the simple medal, a reminder of that special town along the Camino Frances. That night in that holy place, with the feminine energy engulfing my body and my spirit, I fall asleep and dream. Mary, the female energy, welcomed us to her town; I feel joyous and full of energy. I welcome the feminine energy and offer the day's *caminata*, the day's hike, to Mary.

But encountering this female energy that is Mary is not new, and I recall previous encounters: Once in Laredo, Texas, my hometown, and another in Austin, at a retreat hosted by the Indigenous Women's Network. In Laredo, it happened when La Virgen de San Juan de los Lagos came to town on a pilgrimage. The holy statue was brought annually to San Agustin Church—before it became a cathedral—and there were rosaries and prayers along with Matachines dancing into the night. In fact, I was there because I was researching the indigenous-based folk Catholic dance tradition of the Matachines and had been invited by one of the local groups. As the dancers took a break, I walked into the church and seated myself halfway up. The rosary was being led by an older woman, and in no time I fell into the rhythmic prayer song that is a well-prayed rosary. Thoughts of my childhood home surfaced, and I wept. My father would have us kneel in our tiny living room in that old wood-frame house on San Carlos Street in el Barrio Las Cruces as he led the prayers. My tears were more about nostalgia and memory. The memories of my grandmothers—Guadalupe Vargas de Cantú in Monterrey and Celia Becerra de Ramón in Laredo, whom we called "Mamagrande Lupita" and "Bueli," respectively. Neither was too much into church attendance, but both were deeply spiritual and were devotees of the Virgin Mary. I remembered their prayers and the warmth of their hugs. As the oldest daughter of her son, Florentino, I felt I had a special place in Mamagrande Lupita's heart. But as the oldest granddaughter on my mother's side, I also felt that Bueli loved me in a special way. She lived with her daughter, my mother, and our family until she passed when I was twelve. I feel her profound influence to this day. She taught me to read. She taught me to *declamar*, and of course, to pray.

All these feelings flooded over me as I was left sitting there in the half-empty church, as most who had just prayed the rosary moved outdoors to see the Matachines. Then as if I had stepped into a different dimension, I felt a warmth engulf. I felt transported and felt a strong urge to get up and go up to the Virgen whose statue had been placed front and center in the altar space and was surrounded with white flowers—roses, calla lilies, carnations, and others I didn't recognize. The urge was so strong, I got up and walked up not knowing what I would do once I reached the altar. Instinctively I touched the statue the way I saw others had done, and at that point I also felt an electric current run through my body. At the same time, I felt an urge to go up to the podium where the woman who had been leading the rosary had been, but I was just too shy and didn't dare assume that I could go up. Although I "heard" the prayer that I was supposed to lead—the familiar, "*Dios te salve, María, llena eres de gracia . . .*" and the prayer my mother always used to close the Rosary, "*Por estos santos misertios de que hemos echo recuerdo, te pedimos o Maria. . . .*" But I was paralyzed and could not move. I was frozen with fear about what was happening to me as well as with an ecstatic and otherworldly feeling. It must have lasted a few seconds, but it seemed an eternity. Finally, I came back from whatever trance I was under, and crossed myself using the old prayer, "*Por la señal de la santa cruz, de nuestros enemigos líbranos señor, Dios nuestro, En el nombre del Padre, del hijo, y del espíritu santo, Amen.*" Small crosses on my forehead, mouth, and heart, and then the larger cross by touching my forehead, heart, left, and right shoulder and ending at the "amen" with a kiss to the cross I formed with my index finger and thumb. Shaken, I went back to the pew where I had been sitting and tried to make sense of what just happened, even as I felt bad not having gone up and publicly shared the prayers to Our Lady. To this day, I feel that I let her down. That she expected me to go up to that microphone and lead the prayers in her honor. My mother is now gone, but her prayers stay with me.

The other event at the *temazcal* at Alma de Mujer, at the Indigenous Women's Network retreat in Austin, was more private and more subtle. I am not sure it was the same energy, but it was certainly female and also just as powerful. As is customary, we were going around offering prayers, each one ending with "all our relations," so the next person could say her prayer. When it was my turn, I spoke aloud and thanked the spirits who had gathered with us; then I fell silent as I said my personal prayer. But when I had finished asking guidance and support for what was happening at that point in my life—I had just been named to an administrative position and I was unsure about my ability to undertake that task—I found I couldn't say the words, "all my relations." Everyone else assumed I was still in silent prayer. I was saying the words in my head, yet nothing would come out of my mouth. It went on and on, for far too long, and I knew everyone was anxious for me to continue. I could feel their silent urging. Their anxiety. Still, I couldn't move or speak. The heat was intense. The leader poured more water on the hot stones, I felt others shift, and the energy grew more intense. Still, I felt immobilized. Then it came to me—a sort of vision and a song. I can't sing, so I didn't know what to do. I didn't quite understand the words, but I knew they were either Latin or French. The female earth energy was coming up my spine as if in a deep yoga meditation. I felt that my body must be glowing. I remembered the stories in *A Separate Reality*, a book I had read decades earlier. Then, finally, as I kept repeating in my head, "all my relations," I regained my voice and softly said the words, "all my relations," so that we could continue. I remember that there was a woman there who kept crying and I sent her healing thoughts and good energy to help with whatever she was going through; I asked that female energy to help her. Most of us spoke little, and I wondered if they too were experiencing the same female power I felt when it was my turn.

LORETTA DIANE WALKER

Of the Beginning

In the beginning...—Genesis 1:1

I cannot find a metaphor for *the beginning*; it simply is.
Spilling from its bulging mystery, a throng of endings.
At the edge of each of those, there it is, grinning.
Its mouth fuller than a summer sky crowded with stars.

LORETTA DIANE WALKER

Sacrifice

Night is a single mother
who shyly disrobes in the sky's corner boudoir.
Behind its high doors, she unswaddles the stars,
sweeps them from the hem of her seal-black rebozo.

When she senses their light drifting down
the length of her wide ancient thighs, then scattering
across velvet heaven, she rocks.

Perhaps this is faith—
watching your hard labor fall,
un-netted, into the unknown.
Maybe this is prayer—
that spangled swallowtail,
newly released from a mason jar.

Watch each beating wing soaring toward the matins of sky,
breath caught, then released behind the sun's glaring eye.

ANGÉLIQUE JAMAIL

Epiphany

The first time the understanding hit
me that stars do not go away
in the daytime sky, that
their light is only blinded out
by the sun,

                    the sky dissolved from
blue to yellow to white,
                    the glass sphere of my
world shattered into a million glittering
paths,

                                        and later,
when all summer's heat focused into
the smallest, searing punctures
above the dusk-darkened trees,

a glowing crescent was already moving
across the sky, hanging in the balance.

URSULA PIKE

Thank You Very Much

UNCLE AL'S VISION

Your uncle is not the type of guy who has visions, so when he calls and tells you he had a vision of Elvis Presley dancing at a powwow, you think he is joking. Your uncle is always making jokes; a few of them are even funny. Turns out, this isn't a joke.

"Since when do you have visions?" you ask him.

"Since your auntie put me on that low-sugar diet," Uncle Al tells you. Al lost his job at the post office last year, and since then his stomach had gone from slightly pronounced to pumpkin shaped. Your auntie hid any food with sugar. Al hadn't lost any weight, but all that unsweetened coffee and zoodles gave him strange dreams.

"I want to dance in your powwow, as Elvis."

"It's not *my* powwow," you tell him. For the last five years, you have volunteered in the ticket booth at the Austin powwow.

"Well, you know what I mean," he says. "I want to dance."

"What about the inter-tribals? Anyone can dance in those."

"Yeah, but I want to be part of the Grand Entry," he said. You've seen him in his Elvis impersonator costume. Now you have a vision of him shaking his hips and curling his lip, as the jingle dancers give him side-eye and the tiny tots make a wide berth around him as they enter the arena floor.

"Exactly how Elvis-y is it?" He passes the phone to your auntie.

"Just wait until you see it," she tells you.

After he was laid off, your uncle entered a Partylandia contest trying to win a trip to Las Vegas. He hoped the casino lights and all-you-can-eat buffets would help him deal with his new reality. Instead of the trip, he won third place, a deluxe *Elvis in Vegas* costume. He stepped into the thin white jumpsuit, strapped the plastic belt around his belly, and fell in love. He didn't need a wig because his own hair, still thick and mostly black at sixty-three, was already styled appropriately and held in place by ninety-nine-cent hairspray. He was instantly transformed from an unemployed chubby guy to a manly entrepreneur. The day after he put on that suit, he answered an ad for an Elvis impersonator. He never made much money but enjoyed the hell out of it.

The next week Al and Carla drive down from Fort Worth so you can see for yourself.

*

The second year you attended the Austin powwow someone asked you to help them move garbage cans and, because you can't say no, you did. Turns out they thought you were someone else, but it didn't matter. You have been coming back every year. Now that you live in the middle of Texas, the powwow is the only time you are in a room with more than three Natives at the same time. You have no regalia, and the inter-tribals are the only time you dance. This powwow is held indoors and, while it's different from the outdoor powwows your mom took you to when you were little, it still has drums, dancers, and jewelry you can't afford.

The real obstacle to letting your uncle dance will be Doris, an Ojibwe woman who has been involved with the planning committee since the first powwow was held fifteen years ago. You like to think of yourself as a tough Indian woman, but Doris could intimidate a rock.

*

Uncle Al paid a lady from Oklahoma to turn his white Elvis jumpsuit into powwow regalia. Once you see that, you know he is serious. He is not going to drop this. The work must have cost him a couple of hundred dollars. It is unlike anything you have seen at a powwow before. Once he puts the suit on and slicks back his hair, you see the possibilities.

Around his neck is a red scarf secured in place by a silver pin. Running down the outside of both sleeves are little brown satin teepee appliqués. A six-inch beaded belt with large exploding diamond shapes has replaced the cheap gaudy belt of the original. Diamonds made of red and yellow beads line the border of each flared ankle. On his feet are white leather moccasins, partially covered with red and yellow beads that match the cuffs. Is that pride you feel? You aren't sure. This is a side of Al you've never seen.

Al's mother always swore that Elvis was an Indian. She thought he must have been at least part Sac and Fox Nation, like her. As Elvis aged, she grew more convinced of it. "Look at that paunch! Those bags under his eyes! You tell me he isn't Indian," she'd say to anyone who would listen. If only she could see Al now.

"What category are you going to dance in? Men's Traditional? Golden Age?" you ask.

"I don't care; I just want to be part of the Grand Entry." He fills out the form and gives you his registration fee in cash. You tell him, you'll do what you can. Uncle Al and Carla are the only family you have nearby; all three of you are economic refugees from Indian Country, looking for work and a place to live that you can afford. You owe it to them to at least present the idea to the powwow planning committee.

POWWOW PLANNING COMMITTEE

Two weeks before the powwow, the planning committee has their last meeting to finalize the details of the event. It is a damp Wednesday evening in October, and attendance is sparse. The smell of overcooked peas and carrots gives away the fact that the room doubles as a cafeteria for the senior center during the day. You have waited until this meeting to mention your uncle's plan. You hope they will be distracted by the other details of putting on the event and make a quick decision.

After running down the list of dances and how many contestants have registered, you say, "And there is one more, my Uncle Al wants to dance." You have introduced Al to many of these people at earlier powwows, but they probably do not remember him.

"Great, in what category?" asks Doris. She runs a tight ship, and there is no way to slip this past her.

"My uncle had a vision . . ." You begin with this because you know there will be people on the committee who will respond to this vision. Doris is not one of those people. You finish by telling them, "And he wants to dance in this suit in the Grand Entry."

"I don't think this is appropriate for our powwow," said Larry, the retired Yakima guy who recently started coming to the meetings. Doris raises an eyebrow, but she remains silent.

Jackson, a Blackfoot who runs a taco trailer says, "At least he is Indian, last year one of them PretenIndians almost won Men's Traditional." Everyone looks down, not wanting to linger on the issue of who is and isn't the authentic Native. In this room there are connections to tribes and Native communities that are as thin as a blade of grass, as thick as a piece of leather, and everything in between. People who grew up on their tribal homeland, others who discovered a Native birth mother in their adoption records, and some, like yourself, whose mother left the homeland to attend college and now only returns for funerals.

But the powwow has rules, regardless of the tribe of the dancer. The traditionalists argue with those committee members who believe nothing about the powwow should be rigidly defined. The Cherokee grad student reminds us that race and ethnicity are a social construct. He likes Al's idea.

Doris finally speaks. "He is going to be wearing a *costume*," Doris is addressing the whole room. "We will look like fools." The committee is silent for a long moment. The powwow chairman, a former Mississippi Choctaw Tribal Council member, tells us everyone thinks Elvis was an Indian because if you're born in Mississippi, you must either be black, an Indian, or a member of the KKK, and no one wants to think Elvis was a member of the KKK. Everyone exhales as they laugh, and the tension is released a little.

"Let's take a vote," you suggest. The powwow committee never votes on anything; most decisions are reached by consensus, but no one objects to your suggestion. Ten for, five against. The committee decides to let the executive board make the final decision at their meeting later that week. Doris gets a vote on that board.

*

As the days pass, you wonder what they will decide. If it weren't your uncle at the center of the question, you wonder what you would think. In college, you were part of a group of students who organized the first powwow on campus. One grass dancer came in his regalia as a favor to a Diné adviser. Everyone was happy to have that one dancer. Beggars can't be choosers. Now the college has a brand-new Native American Student Center and one of the biggest on-campus powwows in the state. But the pictures you see on the website tell you that there are still as many not wearing regalia as those who are. You could show up with your plain white shawl and dance.

The following week you receive an email from Doris. It is professional but barely contains her disdain. Using words like "authorize," "respect," and "non-traditional," you realize the executive board decided to allow Uncle Al to participate in one Grand Entry. The first one of the day, at 10 a.m., when the arena will be almost empty.

POWWOW

Finally, powwow day has arrived. You walk into the arena and are amazed at how it has been transformed from a dusty empty space into a vibrant warm showplace. Standing on the arena floor, you see the dancers lining up for the first Grand Entry of the day. You try to catch sight of your uncle, but he's nowhere. The emcee asks one of the drum groups to start things off, and from one corner of the arena you hear the thumping. You gasp and your heartbeat quickens.

The powwow is starting. You always try to be inside the building for these first sounds of the drums and singing because it is your favorite moment. You acknowledge what it means that these Native people, including yourself, can pull this off, to turn grants from the city's cultural office and twenty-five potluck committee meetings into an event. Then the moment passes, and you grab the clipboard to check in all the registered dancers.

Standing to the left of the entry gate for the dancers, you check each number bib to see if they are registered as they walk onto the floor. First the veterans enter with the flags, and then the head male and female dancers walk in. The women's hair is smooth and perfectly braided in a way that you've never been able to achieve. Then the rest enter in the registered categories, starting with Men's Traditional. You hear the Lady Jingle Dancers before you see them, each with rows of hundreds of jingles hanging from their ankle-length dresses. A shawl dancer sends a quick text before sliding her phone underneath her clothes. Even the older dancers are light on their feet, and the teenager dancers shuffle restlessly onto the arena floor.

Then you catch sight of your uncle. He is with the Golden Age dancers. You pat him on the shoulder as he passes by, showing your support. He is sweating already and only nods his head in your direction. As he walks out onto the arena floor, there are so many people in front of him and behind him that no one can see his outfit. The arena is only a quarter full, and many of the people in the stands probably have never been to a powwow.

As he passes by the drum, a few of the drummers turn their heads and notice him. You realize that it is his hair that gives him away. Most of the other male dancers are wearing a headpiece made of porcupine quills or eagle feathers. Uncle Al's well-sprayed pompadour of black hair sticks out. He continues dancing slowly to the beat. The drumming quickens and everyone speeds up. The Fancy Dancers become a blur of color. As Uncle Al passes Doris, she looks at the other dancers around him, her brow crinkled in worry. You hear a few of the dancers ask each other, "What is that guy wearing?" but they are quickly distracted by the colors and movements of the other dancers. One person says, "Is that Elvis? Wish I'd thought of that!"

Once all the dancers are on the floor, you turn around and notice the powwow chairman laughing as he looks at Uncle Al. You exhale, not realizing you were holding your breath. All the dancers make one last pass around the circle, and the drumming and chanting builds and builds and then with one last shout, stops. The crowd claps and the dancers disperse. There's coffee and donuts waiting for them in the hospitality area. Many of them have a long day of dancing and catching up with old friends ahead of them. You will spend the day running from one side of the arena to the other, trying to help wherever you can.

As he heads out the same gate he entered, you step toward your uncle so he will hear you. "Great job!" you say a little too loudly. You are proud and exhausted, glad that he danced and that it is over.

"Thank you, thank you very much," he says as he turns and leaves the building.

JOHN BLAIR

The Trail

There's no ending like a good
ending they say   or maybe
it's that there's no ending
that's a good ending or it's there's
no ending at all

      like that horse   tired
on a trail ride   some kid
kicking hard at her flanks for speed
or injustice   I just can't seem
to remember which or why

      while I ride regretful behind
in my place   the horse thinking
about stopping forever I know
      though probably thinking
nothing at all   the very air

and hour hard as heels   cold
and flogged with breath   my part
in this a gift   ill-conceived
      to a girl who loves horses
who dreams like Raskolnikov

of horses (the day gray and heavy
      the child seven years old
He ran beside the mare   ran
in front of her   saw her being whipped
across the eyes   right in the eyes!)

and then as if she has as an agent
of her truth   decided   the mare
begins to trot   stiff-foots it
off the trail past the hang-dog queue
of barn-mates and their burdens

    down a slippery slope of mud
and dead leaves to a creek edged
with scallops of ice   the kid
clutching at his pommel chanting *hey*
hey hey hey   terrified

at his own sudden powerlessness
    along for the ride   out in a quick
surge of moving water to the saddle-
high depths at the creek's middle
where the mare stops

and stands   and refuses to move
    kicking heels be damned   shouting
trail guide be double-damned
(if suffering is desire   what wouldn't
we do for more

    for just a little time to want
what we want   no matter
the consequences   small or large?)
    the trail-guide now yelling
at the kid to stay put   and saying

hey-now hey-now to his own mount
    circling it around   and the kid
being a kid throws his leg back over
the saddle   and slides into the cold
water and disappears for a moment

before rising   sputtering   up
    thrashing his way to the bank
and the mare abruptly   gloriously
self-possessed   surges from the creek
    back onto the trail

and away in the direction from which
we've all come   creek water
flying from the aspergillum of her tail
    and I can feel joy as though
it's handfuls of jewels flung

through the air as she gallops off
    shining   prodigal   momentary
as any freedom has to be   note before
the silence that defines it and makes it
a note   like a bell ringing

out endings that are no endings
at all   hoofbeats and plash of water
sounding the wild descant of *joy*
joy joy to shake to its ends the trail's
    long and untethered reaches.

ROBERT FLYNN

Guns and Hard Candy

My sister, brother, and I made our Santa Claus lists from catalogs—Sears Roebuck, Montgomery Ward, Bella Hess. We were a farm family in north West Texas, and when Santa didn't deliver our mail order presents in time for Christmas, our parents told us that Santa sometimes dropped by on New Year's Eve on his way back to the North Pole and maybe he would leave our Christmas wish then. And he did. But it was another whole week after we had been waiting months for Christmas.

Stores in our town didn't have Santas, but sometimes he was driven down Main Street standing in the back of a pickup and the elves at his feet threw unwrapped hard candy. I never really looked at Santa. I went for the hard stuff.

Santa did come to our two-room schoolhouse once. Our two teachers passed out bags of hard candy and Santa, who looked a lot like Dude Byars in women's makeup with a mess of cotton covering the rest of his face, said, "Ho ho ho," as though those were the only words Santa knew. The spectacle scared us so that Santa was never invited back.

We got another bag of hard candy at our church Christmas Eve celebration, and another bag of hard candy under our Christmas tree. Our dentist handed out hard candy with both hands. We racked up enough hard candy to rot our molars before our wisdom teeth arrived.

We didn't have a chimney. We lined up our boots in front of the radiant gas heater that kept the house toasty for up to five feet in front of it. When Mother opened the oven door to baste the turkey, we basked in the blast of heat. We put our hands on the outside of the oven to warm them, then we emptied our boots of an orange in each boot followed by hardshell nuts and hard candy to put our cold feet in the fire-roasted but sticky boots.

We knelt before the tree to discover what Santa had brought us. And also to keep our sockless feet from pressing against the overheated leather. My brother and I always got cap pistols, until we graduated to BB guns, then a .22, then a shotgun. In Texas guns outnumber armadillos, and Christmas blows in locked and loaded.

I spent one Christmas away from home in the Marines with seventy-one hours of liberty and no place to go. I hitchhiked to LA and spent one night in an all-night movie theater, one night in the bus station where I could sleep sitting up. If I stretched out I was awakened by a cop, who was respectful of my uniform, tapping on the sole of my shoes. I sat up and dozed until sunlight. I returned to the barrack where I could stretch out but had to get up at reveille, fall in outside for roll call, march to chow, and return to duty. It was the longest liberty I ever had.

I spent one Christmas in Vietnam and handed out hard candy and toys to kids who had never tasted candy, seen picture puzzles or sidewalks on which to skate, sent by people back in the world who wanted to help. The Marines had removed war toys—guns, tanks, helicopters, war planes with which the children were familiar—and taught them how to throw footballs and frisbees, skip rope alone or with others, hopscotch; and of course there were baby dolls, white babies, blonde babies, Barbie babies.

My wife, Jean, gave me a hunting rifle one Christmas and an automatic shotgun another Christmas. I always think of guns at Christmas.

When I was little I loved stuffed animals more than guns, and I had asked Santa for a stuffed bear in a military uniform. America was at war. There was no bear of no kind under the tree. What had I done that was so bad? My thumb had been crushed when I was six months old, and the nail was attached only to the first half of the nail bed. I could point my thumb at a girl and bend half the nail back to make her scream, but that wasn't mean. That was using my potentials, as Dad always told us.

I found a dead hawk that someone had shot and took it to Dad. He cut off one claw, tied a string to a tendon and I could pull the string and the claw would close in some girl's hair or maybe the back of her neck, but that wasn't bad. The other boys thought it was funny. One of the older boys gave me a nickel for it. He asked to see it and when I handed it to him to look at he walked away with it. I followed him asking for it back, my voice a little louder each time so that the teachers would notice, and he gave me a nickel.

I still had another claw, but I would have to tell Dad what happened to the first one.

And who told Santa? I had always been faithful to Santa and Santa had been faithful to me. I had heard older boys at school laughing about—No.

"Mom, Bob didn't get a stuffed animal," my sister said. I wasn't really crying, but my cheeks were wet and cold. Bettye was the oldest, and she protected me from my brother who was older, bigger, and didn't like stuffed animals unless they were mine.

"Did Santa bring you a teddy bear?" Mother asked, while I waited for the dreaded another-whole-week speech.

"No, Ma'am," I said and sniffed.

"Did you look everywhere?" she asked.

Why didn't Mother say that Santa would bring it on his way back to the North Pole? I had been good and Santa—why couldn't he stop by on New Year's Eve?

"Jim, have you seen Bob's teddy bear?" Mother asked.

"No ma'am."

My heart failed me. Santa Claus failed me. I was afraid to speak for fear I would cry.

"Maybe Santa dropped it outside," Mother said. What kind of Santa was that? Spilling presents all over the world and breaking kids' hearts?

Mother opened the door and the porch was covered with snow. There were boot prints in the snow. Then I saw the stuffed bear. It wasn't in uniform but that didn't matter. I picked it up to hug but it was cold and wet. Santa had dropped my bear in the snow and had ruined it. I knew I was going to cry, and I was too big.

Mother said, "I'll put it in the oven, and when it's dry you can play with it."

I was still in my flannel drop-seat longhandles, and my boots were wet and cold, but I walked around the corner of the house to follow the tracks. The tracks went to the garage and the barn. Dad must have opened the barn doors so the reindeer could get inside where it was warmer and the toys wouldn't get wet. I didn't know why the tracks went to the garage. I could think about that later when it no longer mattered.

I went inside to stand by the stove to shiver and get warm and watch my bear dry. Anybody could drop a bear in the snow. It wasn't Santa's fault. I knew that. Probably one of the deer had knocked it out of Santa's bag and Santa hadn't noticed. Reindeer were like that.

Wait 'til I told the kids at school. I had seen Santa's boot prints in the snow. Dad had let the reindeer into the barn. I had almost seen Santa. And he wasn't scary like he was when he came to school. He was a little scary but he loved everyone. How could I have ever doubted Santa?

Mother handed me the bear. It was almost too hot to hold and the oven had singed a bald spot on it. Santa almost ruined my present but I pressed it to my heart. I had a teddy bear. It wasn't factory perfect with shiny buttons on its uniform, but I loved it all the more for its imperfections.

Santa stopped by on New Year's Eve and left me a bag of hard candy and a heavy glass pistol filled with tiny pills of hard candy. I broke it almost before I ate all the candy inside it.

My favorite Christmas was one that Jean and I and Deirdre and Brigid had celebrated alone. Our special Christmas. Christmas trees had not arrived, no houses were decorated, no Santas had appeared in stores. It was our special Christmas because I was leaving for Vietnam. Brigid, who counted the long days until her twelfth birthday, had won a ribbon at her school's bicycle contest and the opportunity to compete in the city-wide contest. Brigid wanted a racing bicycle with gears for Christmas. Deirdre, who was almost fourteen, wanted an Appaloosa filly. She and Brigid each had a horse, but Deirdre wanted a filly she could train and later breed.

I don't remember what Jean or I received. It didn't matter. We would make our girls' dream come true.

I woke up to our traditional breakfast tacos. Jean and the girls had been up for an hour, Jean preparing breakfast, the girls almost beside themselves trying to be quiet so as not to wake me. There was neither a bicycle nor a filly under the tree. After the first round of tacos, I put on my Santa cap and passed out presents. We each opened our presents, expressing thanks and admiring what the others had received. Yet, something seemed to be missing. We asked Brigid to go outside and see if Santa spilled a present on the way inside. Sure enough, a careless reindeer had knocked a racing bicycle with gears out of Santa's sleigh.

Santa was bringing Deirdre's filly from Pleasanton, and they had not arrived. We told Deirdre her Christmas package was late but would be delivered. It was our Christmas, but the mail still ran. Brigid asked if she could ride her bicycle until Deirdre's present arrived. We whispered to her that Deirdre was getting her Christmas wish and let her take her bike for a spin. She returned and asked us to watch her run through the gears.

Deirdre waited outside for her package to arrive. Brigid rode her bicycle on short jaunts, ready to race home when Deirdre's gift arrived. Jean and I waited inside, watching for a truck and horse trailer. When the truck stopped and began backing the trailer down the driveway, Brigid raced for home. Jean and I went outside and Deirdre watched, afraid to believe she was getting her Christmas wish. Then the rancher opened the tailgate and introduced us to Teresa Babe or Teresa B, as Deirdre called her, a registered Appaloosa with a Joker B bloodline. Deirdre waited years for Teresa B's promised spots to appear. They never did, but it didn't matter.

Maybe there are no perfect Christmases free of broken dreams, old sorrows, fearful futures, ancient grievances, dark shadows of Christmases past. But this was ours. We sang our hymns, prayed our prayers. There were other Christmases, with much of the world celebrating the same day, with grandparents, aunts and uncles, cousins, and some little girl crying because she didn't get the bicycle that she didn't know she wanted until Brigid got one. But this was our special Christmas.

No need for Santa on his way back to the North Pole.

Our special Christmas was the last Christmas that the four of us were together. Shortly after I returned from Vietnam Brigid died, still short of her twelfth birthday.

I had been faithful and Santa failed me. There's no way to describe the hollowness of our family, the void, the silence, the extra plate, cup, spoon that no one wanted to see and no one wanted to remove. Laughter had vanished and might never reappear; photographs appeared documenting a missing person. The little dog that Brigid had rescued waited for her at the end of our road every day, although the bus didn't stop anymore.

The death of every child is violent, regardless of the cause, blowing a huge hole in dreams of future birthdays; Christmases; Easters and hunts for plastic eggs until candy inside the eggs was replaced with hard cash; Thanksgivings with family, friends, food, and football; Halloweens with scary masks and funny tricks; graduations, weddings, anniversaries, new births, reunions, trips to Mexico. The kind of violence no automatic weapons, extended clips or bump stocks can stop, no Pentagon budget can prevent.

We each were in our own private hell, missing a piece of ourselves, each of us knowing that two other people needed us to help them carry their unbearable burden when we were driven into the earth by our own unbearable load. I wanted to run someplace where I felt no one else's pain so that I could endure my own. Jean held us together as best she could. Jean and I talked of a suicide pact, but it couldn't be murder/suicide. We had to go together, but we couldn't both desert Deirdre. Which of us was the stronger to stay behind and help Deirdre with her grief and the confusion of teenage years?

Teresa B. was a companion when Deirdre needed to be alone but not by herself so that Deirdre could talk and cry. Deirdre's friend, Pam, called us Mom and Dad, and brought laughter into the house.

What had we done that was so bad? Nothing. We were ordinary parents, giving our children what we believed they needed—love, time, vacations, vaccinations, braces, regular checkups with their doctors, education, Sunday school, piano lessons for Deirdre, guitar lessons for Brigid, riding lessons for both, although they believed they knew everything they needed to know. Some things spilled. Some things were singed or got wet. Most of all, we wanted to give them a safe home and a safe life that every parent wants to give and no parent can give. Not even God.

I endure Christmas with its joy as fake as the snow in store windows, as false as Rudolph's red nose, as artificial as the lighted Christmas trees.

Santa will return on New Year's Eve, but it's the longest week of the year.

ACKNOWLEDGMENTS

"Pagans" from *The Lives of Rocks* by Rick Bass. Copyright © 2006 by Rick Bass. Reprinted by permission of Mariner Books, an imprint of HarperCollins Publishers LLC. All rights reserved.

Blair-Lavallais, Yvette. "Wading in the Water of the Trinity River: A Womanist Perspective." *Visible Magazine*, May 13, 2019. https://visiblemagazine.com/wading-in-the-waters-of-the-trinity-river-a-womanist-perspective/.

Bond, Bruce. "The Border." *Image*, no. 94 (2017): 49-54.

Bradford, Robin. "Memos from Afar." *Texas Highways*, March/April 2020. https://texashighways.com/travel-news/find-wisdom-and-comfort-in-the-voices-of-these-6-texas-poets/.

Crook, Noel. "Smith Canyon." International Poetry Contest, *Atlanta Review*, 2008.

Crook, Noel. "Smith Canyon." *Salt Moon*, Southern Illinois University Press, 2015.

Cuba, Nan. "Way-Seeking." *Voices de la Luna* 9, no. 4 (August 2017): 27-28.

Dollar, Heath. "A Frontier's Passing." In *Waylon County: Texas Stories*, 48-51. Sleeping Panther Press, 2017.

Egerton, Owen. "The Martyrs of Mountain Peak." Puerto del Sol, 2005.

Egerton, Owen. "The Martyrs of Mountain Peak." In *How Best to Avoid Dying: Stories*. Soft Skull Press, 2014.

Faizullah, Tarfia. "Kafir 1." *Indiana Review* 37, no. 2 (2015).

Faizullah, Tarfia. "Kafir 2." *Indiana Review* 37, no. 2 (2015).

Flynn, Robert. "Guns and Hard Candy." *Voices de la Luna* 10, no. 2 (2018).

Fry, John. "credo." In *with the dogstar as my witness*. Orison Books, 2018.

Geis, D. G. "A Stockyard Liturgy." In *A Journal of Poems and Prose on Poetry* 7, 56. Poetry City, USA, 2017.

Guez, Julia. "The New Cartography." In *In an Invisible Glass Case Which Is Also a Frame*. Four Way Books, 2019.

Guez, Julia. "Still Life When All Our Symptoms Seem to Have Symptoms of Their Own." In *The Certain Body*. Four Way Books, 2022.

Haley, Albert. "Five Images of Jarrell, Texas, May 27, 1997." In *New Texas '99*, edited by Donna Walker-Nixon and James Ward Lee, 146-50. University of Mary-Hardin Baylor, 1999.

Hoheisel, Peter. "Old Lady Hunting Treasure." In *Reunion: The Dallas Review* 8. University of Texas, Dallas, 2018.

Jamail, Angélique. "Epiphany." *Poetry Super Highway*, 2001. https://www.poetrysuperhighway.com/psh/psh-poets-of-the-week-617/.

Jamail, Angélique. "Epiphany." *Falcon Wings*, 2002.

Kimzey, Blake. "And Finally the Tragedy." *Tin House*, October 18, 2013. https://tinhouse.com/and-finally-the-tragedy/.

Kimzey, Blake. "And Finally the Tragedy." *Families Among Us*, Black Lawrence Press, 2014. Print.

LaVilla-Havelin, Jim. "West News from the Little Bend of South View." *Voices de la Luna* 10, no. 1 (2017).

López, Diana. "El Cuarto de los Milagros." In *BorderSenses*, 2012.

Mojtabai, A. G. "Trew Reade: A Reporter's Story." In *Shine on Me: A Novel*, 22-30. Northwestern University Press, 2016.

Musgrove, Laurence. "Bluebonnet Sutra." In *The Bluebonnet Sutras*, 89. Lamar University Literary Press, 2019.

Nye, Naomi Shihab. "Grandfather's Heaven." In *Words Under the Words*. Far Corner Books, 1994.

Nye, Naomi Shihab. "Shoulders." In *Words Under the Words*. Far Corner Books, 1994.

Nye, Naomi Shihab. "The Road Between San Antonio and Comstock, Texas." *Texas Highways*, March/April 2020. https://texashighways.com/travel-news/find-wisdom-and-comfort-in-the-voices-of-these-6-texas-poets/.

Nye, Naomi Shihab. "Texas, Out Driving." In *Voices in the Air: Poems for Listeners*. Greenwillow, 2018.

Patterson, Leslie Jill. "On Forgiving." In *Her Texas: Story, Image, Poem and Song*, edited by Donna Walker-Nixon, Cassy Burleson, Rachel Crawford, and Ashley Palmer. Wings Press, 2015.

Pike, Ursula. "Thank You Very Much." *The Rio Review: The Literary Journal of Austin Community College* (2013): 95-101.

Prufer, Kevin. "In This Way." In *Voices Amidst the Virus*. Lily Poetry Press, 2021.

Quintanilla, Octavio. "God's Hands." *Windward Review* 15 (2017).

Quintanilla, Octavio. "Grace, 1982." *Arcadia Literary Journal* 10, no.1 (2016).

Quintanilla, Octavio. "Psalm 2." *Huizache*, no. 4 (2014).

Quintanilla, Octavio. "[Through plaster walls I hear the wailing]." *Texas Highways*, March/April, 2020. https://texashighways.com/travel-news/find-wisdom-and-comfort-in-the-voices-of-these-6-texas-poets/.

Quintanilla, Octavio. "[Through plaster walls I hear the wailing.]" Slough Press, 2014.

Sanders, Mark. "The Ghosts on Farm Road." In *Landscapes, with Horses*, Stephen F. Austin University Press, 2018.

Sanders, Mark. "The Ghosts on Farm Road." Rpt. *In a Good Time*, Wayne State College Press, 2019.

Sen, Chaitali. "When I Heard the Learn'd Astronomer." *Ecotone* 13, no. 2 (2018): 34-49. Project MUSE.

Specht, Mary Helen. "The Pilot." *Southwestern American Literature* 38, no. 2 (2013).

Taylor, Charles. "Heart of the Heart." In *At The Heart*. Inkbrush Press, 2011.

Van Reet, Brian. "The Window." *Gulf Coast* 24, no. 1 (2012).
Van Reet, Brian. "The Window." *New Border Voices: An Anthology*, edited by Shuler, Garza-Johnson, and Johnson, Texas A&M University Press, 2014.
Walker, Loretta Diane. "Sacrifice." *Langdon Review of the Arts in Texas* 15, (2018-19).
Weathers, Steve. "Witnesses." *Langdon Review of the Arts in Texas* 3, (2006-07): 102-14.
Wilbanks, Jessica. "Made in Nigeria." In *When I Spoke in Tongues: A Story of Faith and Its Loss*. Beacon Press, 2018.
Wilson, Steve. "Call It a Kind of Grace." In *Lose to Find*. Finishing Line Press, 2018.
Wiman, Chris. "Tender Interior" In *My Bright Abyss*. Farrar, Straus and Giroux, 2013.

CONTRIBUTORS

RACHEL ASSELTA is currently a senior at Baylor University, studying English literature. As a senior, she currently works as a student grader for Dr. Elizabeth Dell, who offered her the opportunity to assist in editing this anthology. She primarily assisted with citations and late-stage proofreading.

RICK BASS was born in Fort Worth, Texas, the son of a geologist, and he studied petroleum geology at Utah State University. He grew up in Houston and started writing short stories on his lunch breaks while working as a petroleum geologist in Jackson, Mississippi. In 1987, he moved with his wife, the artist Elizabeth Hughes Bass, to the remote Yaak Valley, where he works to protect his adopted home from roads and logging. Rick serves on the board of both the Yaak Valley Forest Council and Round River Conservation Studies. In 2011 Rick moved from the Yaak area of Montana to Missoula, Montana. He continues to give readings, write, and teach around the country and world. He lives in Montana with his family.

JOHN BLAIR has published six books, the most recent of which is *Playful Song Called Beautiful* (University of Iowa Press, 2016), which won the Iowa Poetry Prize. His poetry often explores the intersection of a central Texas landscape and a particularly fluid and changeful sort of faith that borrows from both Eastern and Western traditions. He is a University Distinguished Professor at Texas State University, where he directs the undergraduate creative writing program.

YVETTE R. BLAIR-LAVALLAIS is a womanist theologian and one of the cofounders of The Gathering, a Dallas-based worshipping community led by three womanist preachers. She holds degrees from the University of North Texas and Perkins School of Theology at Southern Methodist University. She is a writer, blogger, manuscript editor, and the author of the 2017 book *Being Ruth: Pressing Through Life's Struggles with Fearless Faith*. Connect with her at yvetteblair.com, @damselfly_faith, and on IG at preachergirl716.

BRUCE BOND is the author of twenty-one books including, most recently, *Black-out Starlight: New and Selected Poems 1997-2015; Dear Reader*; and *Rise and Fall of the Lesser Sun Gods*. His work explores the difficulty that the idea of the divine poses to individuals in their capacity for empathy, reverie, transformation, and a tolerance of difference and doubt. Both personal and cultural in scope, his poems seek neither to defend nor attack institutional religions, but rather to situate them relative to inner life, to the temptation to identify with absolutes figures in our most defining conflicts, creativities, and acts of sacrifice and conscience. Presently he is a Regents Professor of English at the University of North Texas.

ROBIN BRADFORD is a Dobie Paisano Fellow and O. Henry Award winner. Her poems have appeared in the *Texas Observer*, *Friends Journal*, *Mudfish Review*, and *Texas Poetry Calendar*. Her 2016 poetry chapbook is titled *Confidence*. Originally from Oklahoma, Robin has lived in Austin, Texas, for more than thirty years, working as a nonprofit fundraiser. She began practicing Zen Buddhism after witnessing the suffering of Hurricane Katrina evacuees. She leads meditation and writing retreats, undertakes racial justice work, and is a knitter and swimmer. She donated more than one hundred protective masks she sewed on her grandmother's 1899 treadle machine.

GREG BROWNDERVILLE's third book, a poetry collection entitled *A Horse with Holes in It*, was released in 2016 by LSU Press on Dave Smith's Southern Messenger Poets series. His first collection of poems, *Gust*, made the Poetry Foundation's Best-Seller List and was included among "Top Picks" by *Library Journal*. *Deep Down in the Delta*, a collection of folkloristic poems, features paintings by outsider artist Billy Moore. Collaborating with composer Jacob Cooper, Brownderville wrote the words to "Jar" (Silver Threads, Nonesuch Records, 2014) and *Ripple the Sky*, which premiered with the Los Angeles Philharmonic in 2016. An associate professor of English and the director of Creative Writing at SMU, Brownderville edits the *Southwest Review*.

J. SCOTT BROWNLEE is a poet-of-place from rural Texas. His poems appear widely, and he is the author of three prize-winning chapbooks. His first full-length collection, *Requiem for Used Ignition Cap*, was a finalist for the National Poetry Series and selected by C. Dale Young as the winner of the 2015 Orison Poetry Prize. It also won the 2016 Bob Bush Memorial Award for Best First Book of Poetry from the Texas Institute of Letters. He currently lives in Austin and teaches for Brooklyn Poets as a core faculty member.

NORMA ELIA CANTÚ is the Norine R. and T. Frank Murchison Distinguished Professor of the Humanities at Trinity University. Her recent works include *Transcendental Train Yard: A Collaborative Suite of Serigraphs; Canícula: Snapshots of a Girlhood en la Frontera, Updated Edition* (UNM Press); and the coedited anthology *Entre Guadalupe y Malinche: Tejanas in Literature and Art.*

RACHEL CRAWFORD is a teacher, writer, and editor with roots in central and West Texas. Her poetry and short stories appear in a wide range of literary journals and are shaped by a fascination with the ways the landscapes and cityscapes of border zones—particularly the border between Texas and Mexico—influence the inner lives of the people within them. Currently a doctoral student in arts and humanities with a concentration in creative writing, she attends and teaches writing at the University of Texas at Dallas.

NOEL CROOK's debut collection, *Salt Moon*, was selected for the 2013 Crab Orchard Series in Poetry First Book Award and published by Southern Illinois University Press. *Salt Moon* was given the 2015 Julie Suk Award, received an honorable mention from *Forward Review's* INDIEFAB competition, and was a finalist for the Texas Institute of Letters Bob Bush Award, the Brockman-Campbell Book Award, and the Texas Writers' League Award for a book of poetry. Crook's poems have appeared in *Best New Poets*, *Crazyhorse*, *New Letters*, *Shenandoah*, and other journals.

NAN CUBA is the author of *Body and Bread*, winner of the PEN Southwest Award in Fiction and TIL's Steven Turner Award; it was one of "Ten Titles to Pick Up Now" in *O, Oprah's Magazine* and was a "Summer Books" choice from *Huffington Post*. Other work has appeared in *Antioch Review*, *Harvard Review*, *Columbia*, and *Chicago Tribune's Printer's Row*. As an investigative journalist, she reported on the causes of extraordinary violence in *LIFE*, *Third Coast*, and *D Magazine*. *Texas Monthly* included Cuba in its "Ten to Watch." She has received a Dobie Paisano Fellowship and an artist residency at Fundación Valparaiso in Spain. The founder of Gemini Ink, a nonprofit literary center, she is writer-in-residence at the MA/MFA Program in Literature, Creative Writing, and Social Justice at Our Lady of the Lake University in San Antonio. Her website is http://nancuba.com.

ROBIN DAVIDSON is a poet, translator, and professor of English for the University of Houston-Downtown. She is author of three poetry collections: *Kneeling in the Dojo*, *City that Ripens on the Tree of the World*, and *Luminous Other*, as well as co-translator with Ewa Elżbieta Nowakowska of two volumes of poems from the Polish of Ewa Lipska—*The New Century* (Northwestern UP) and the forthcoming *Dear Ms. Schubert* (Tavern Books). She is also editor of the anthology *Houston's Favorite Poems*, a collection modeled on Robert Pinsky's national Favorite Poem Project that showcases more than two hundred Houstonians' best-loved poems. The recipient of Fulbright and NEA awards, Davidson served as 2015-2017 Houston Poet Laureate and has twice been a finalist for Texas State Poet Laureate.

WILLIAM VIRGIL DAVIS's most recent book of poetry is *Dismantlements of Silence: Poems Selected and New* (2015). He has published five other books of poetry: *The Bones Poems*; *Landscape and Journey*, which won the New Criterion Poetry Prize and the Helen C. Smith Memorial Award for Poetry; *Winter Light*; *The Dark Hours*, which won the Calliope Press Chapbook Prize; and *One Way to Reconstruct the Scene*, which won the Yale Series of Younger Poets Prize. His poems have appeared in *Agenda*, *Atlantic Monthly*, *Gettysburg Review*, *Georgia Review*, *Harvard Review*, *Hopkins Review*, *Hudson Review*, *Literary Imagination*, *Malahat Review*, the *Nation*, *New Criterion*, *TriQuarterly*, and *Yale Review*, among many others.

M. M. DE VOE has won many writing awards, including first prize in Literal Latte's Flash Fiction competition. She writes in every genre, from urban fantasy to literary fiction, often addressing themes of identity. She was born in Texas to Roman Catholic Lithuanians, discovered paganism in Germany, was taught by nuns in Baltimore, ran away with a group of jugglers, got an MFA from Columbia University, and now lives in Manhattan with a husband, two kids, and an urban rabbit. She is the founder of Pen Parentis, a literary nonprofit for parents. Find her on Twitter @mmdevoe.

HEATH DOLLAR is the author of *Waylon County: Texas Stories* and *Old Country Fiddle*. He has won the *Texas Observer* Short Story Contest and the Gary Wilson Short Fiction Award, been named a finalist for the Kay Cattarulla Award for Best Short Story by the Texas Institute of Letters, and twice been recognized as a semifinalist for the American Short(er) Fiction Prize. Dollar, a Fort Worth native and former Yellowstone National Park employee, also once served as the lyricist and frontman for a European rock band signed with a Prague record label. He can be found online at heathdollar.com.

Award-winning novelist and filmmaker **Owen Egerton** is the author of several of books, including *The Book of Harold the Illegitimate Son of God*, *How Best to Avoid Dying*, and *Hollow*, which was named one of NPR's Best Books of 2017. He is the writer/director of a number of films, including the psychological thriller *Mercy Black* and the horror comedy *Blood Fest*, and is one of the talents behind the Alamo Drafthouse long-running comedy show *Master Pancake*. He lives in Austin, Texas, with his wife, poet Jodi Egerton, and their two children.

Chris Ellery is the author of five poetry collections, most recently *Canticles of the Body* and *Elder Tree*. A member of the Texas Institute of Letters, he has received the X.J. Kennedy Award for Creative Nonfiction, the Dora and Alexander Raynes Prize for Poetry, and the Betsy Colquitt Award.

Kendall Elliott recently received her bachelor of arts in English from Baylor University. During the last semester of her undergraduate education, she had the privilege of assisting Dr. Elizabeth Dell on this anthology. Her primary roles were corresponding with the authors whose work was selected and ensuring that the editors had the necessary permissions to move forward with publication. She also helped proofread.

Jill Alexander Essbaum was born in Bay City, Texas. Her most recent collections are *Harlot* (No Tell Motel, 2007) and *Necropolis* (neoNuma Arts, 2008). She currently teaches at the University of California Riverside Palm Desert Graduate Center in the Masters of Creative Writing Graduate Program. Essbaum's debut novel, *Hausfrau*, was published March 2015 (Random House), and her most recent work is *Would-Land* (Cooper Dillon, 2020).

Tarfia Faizullah is the author of two poetry collections, *Registers of Illuminated Villages* (Graywolf, 2018) and *Seam* (SIU, 2014). Her poems appear widely in the United States and abroad and have been translated into multiple languages.

Robert Flynn is the author of a stage adaptation of Faulkner's novel *As I Lay Dying*, an ABC-TV documentary, nine novels, three story collections, two memoirs, a collection of essays, and two nonfiction books. His latest book is *Holy Literary License*. His honors include past president of Texas Institute of Letters (TIL); Fellow TIL; and member of the Texas Literary Hall of Fame. His awards include the following: Special Jury Award—Theater of Nations, Paris; Best 20 Books of the Year list of the *New York Times*; Two Wrangler Awards from the

National Cowboy Hall of Fame; Two Spur Awards from the Western Writers of America; best novel of the year from TIL; and a lifetime achievement award from TIL. Flynn is "a native Texan and a non-evangelical Baptist."

Originally from South Texas, **JOHN FRY** is a poet whose work inhabits the intersections of Christianity and homosexuality. He is the author of *with the dogstar as my witness* (Orison Books, 2018), which was a finalist for the Orison Poetry Prize; the Dorset Prize; and the Nightboat Poetry Prize. His poems have appeared or are forthcoming in *Poetry International*, *West Branch*, *Colorado Review*, *Blackbird*, *Waxwing*, and the anthologies *Imaniman: Poets Writing in the Anzaldúan Borderlands* and *New Border Voices*. A graduate of Texas State University's MFA program and a poetry editor for *Newfound Journal*, he is currently a PhD candidate at UT-Austin. He lives in the Texas Hill Country.

Although **ROBIN GARA** grew up in Ohio, she often feels that her mother's down-to-earth, no-nonsense attitude would have been well suited to a Texas landscape. She has lived in San Antonio for thirty-two years. Her experiences in both Texas and Ohio have shaped who she is today. As a child, she used to wish her mother would have entertained her desire to have beautiful, elaborate answers to her spiritual questions. Now she is thankful she did not, allowing her to find her own way.

D. G. GEIS (d. 2018) was the author of *Fire Sale* (Tupelo Press/Leapfolio) and *Mockumentary* (Main Street Rag). Among other places, his poetry appeared in the *Irish Times*, *Fjords*, *Skylight 47* (Ireland), *A New Ulster Review* (Northern Ireland), *Crannog Magazine* (Ireland), *The Moth* (Ireland), *Into the Void* (Ireland), *Poetry Scotland (Open Mouse)*, *The Naugatuck River Review*, *Solstice*, *Cloudbank*, *Press 53*, *Soul-Lit*, the *Kentucky Review*, *Ink and Letters*, *Psaltery and Lyre*, *Cleaver*, and the *New Guard*. He was the winner of the 2017 Firman Houghton Prize. He was a former Anglican priest (and Native Texan) who lived in Lakehills, Texas.

LIAUNDRA GRACE is a native Texan who believes poetry is the gateway for those who have yet to find a connection to written words. Grace received her MFA in Creative Writing from Columbia University and is a Cave Canem Fellow. For Grace, Covid-19 has been a reflective period as she continues to explore religion through the lens of a preacher's daughter while experiencing frontline worries as sister to a nurse who provides care during this pandemic. Currently, Grace is working on her first collection of poems. She resides in Katy, Texas, with her husband and two children.

JULIA GUEZ is the author of *In an Invisible Glass Case Which Is Also a Frame* (Four Way Books). Her poetry, prose, and translations have previously appeared in *Poetry*, *Guernica*, the *Guardian*, *Kenyon Review*, *PEN Poetry Series*, and the *Brooklyn Rail*. Guez has been awarded the Discovery / *Boston Review* Poetry Prize, a Fulbright Fellowship, and the John Frederick Nims Memorial Prize for Translation. She teaches creative writing at Rutgers and works at Teach For America New York. Born and raised in Houston, Guez now lives in Brooklyn and online at www.juliaguez.net.

AL HALEY is the author of *Home Ground: Stories of Two Families and the Land* and the novel, *Exotic*, which received the John Irving First Novel Prize. He is a previous winner of the Rattle Poetry Prize. He left Alaska and arrived in Texas in 1993 to enter the University of Houston's creative writing program, and he has stayed in the Lone Star State to serve as writer in residence at Abilene Christian University. He'd like to state that if those focused on evangelism are "evangelicals," then it might be convenient to have a name for those like himself who are more than mildly obsessed with theodicy.

PETER HOHEISEL has published poems in national publications such as the *Nation*, and many regional ones, a few of which are the *Langdon Review*, *Grasslands Review*, *Nebo*, and *Iconoclast*. As well as teaching creative writing, literature, and composition at Lon Morris College in Jacksonville, Texas, he was also chair of the Department of Religion and Philosophy at that institution. Before he moved to Texas, he was awarded numerous grants to teach poetry in schools through the Michigan Council for the Arts and in Tyler, Texas, under a grant from the Texas Commission for the Arts.

ANGÈLIQUE JAMAIL's writing has appeared in over two dozen anthologies and journals, including *New Reader Magazine*, *Waxwing*, *The Milk of Female Kindness—An Anthology of Honest Motherhood*, Femmeliterate, and *The Enchantment of the Ordinary*. She is the author of the magic realism novelette *Finis.* and the poetry collection *The Sharp Edges of Water* (both Odeon Press). She was raised in a landscape of magical Catholic thinking and finds now that its mysticism is its most enduring legacy in her life and work. Find her online at Sappho's Torque (www.SapphosTorque.com) and on social media.

A native Texan, **Blake Kimzey** founded and directs Writing Workshops Dallas and Writing Workshops Paris. Named one of *D Magazine*'s Artists to Learn From, he is a graduate of the MFA Program at UC-Irvine and sits on the Board of the Elizabeth George Foundation. His is the author of *Families Among Us*, and his short fiction has been broadcast on NPR, performed on stage in Los Angeles, and published by *Tin House*, *McSweeney's*, *VICE*, *Longform*, *D Magazine*, and selected by Robert Olen Butler for inclusion in *The Best Small Fictions*. Blake has been awarded fellowships to attend the Squaw Valley Community of Writers and the Vermont Studio Center and has taught creative writing at UC-Irvine and the University of Texas at Dallas. He lives in Dallas with his wife, artist Danielle Kimzey, and their three children.

Ulf Kirchdorfer was born in Sweden and grew up in Texas, where he attended Trinity University and Texas Christian University (TCU). A bad market for English professors when he graduated steered him to Georgia, where he and his wife live, dreaming of a return to greener or even drier pastures. His work explores the intersection of spirituality, formal religion, and the time and space too many people spend detached from nature in their working lives. An avid photographer and birder, he spends as much time as he can outdoors.

Jim LaVilla-Havelin's poetry is grounded in a sense of place, close observation, and sympathy with his environment. *West: Poems of a Place*, his 2017 volume of poems published by Wings Press, chronicles his move over thirteen years ago from San Antonio to the small town of Lytle, Texas—from an urban lifestyle to time spent in the country. Educator, retired arts administrator, critic, poetry editor at the *San Antonio Express-News*, and coordinator of National Poetry Month in San Antonio, LaVilla-Havelin finds inspiration, joy, and healing in the each of his worlds and in stimulating creativity in others.

Rich Levy is a poet and, since 1995, executive director of Inprint, a literary nonprofit organization in Houston, Texas. His collections include *Why Me?* and the letterpress chapbook *One or Two Lights*. He holds an MFA from the Iowa Writers Workshop and is a member of the Texas Institute of Letters. Born in Brooklyn, raised in Chicago, a Texan for more than thirty years, he is the son of loving secular Jews who endowed him with a sense of wonder and bafflement and a deep commitment to the world beyond the world.

DIANA LÒPEZ is the author of several novels, including *Confetti Girl*, *Lucky Luna*, and a novel adaptation of the Disney/Pixar film *Coco*. An advocate for literacy and for the promotion of Latinx children's literature, López frequently speaks at conferences and book festivals. You can learn more about her by visiting her website, Author Diana López. She has lived her entire life in Texas, in a triangle of cities—Corpus Christi, San Antonio, and Victoria. She grew up in a devout Catholic home, taking day trips with her family to the border to visit the Basilica of Our Lady of San Juan del Valle. This shrine with its miracle room remains a very important part of her personal landscape: she states, "Every time I light a candle, I feel connected to all the petitions and prayers of thanks that people leave there."

MONICA MACANSANTOS was a James A. Michener Fellow in Writing at the University of Texas at Austin, where she earned her MFA in fiction and poetry; she also holds a PhD in creative writing from the Victoria University of Wellington. Her fiction, nonfiction, and poetry have appeared in *failbetter.com*, *Women's Studies Quarterly*, *The Masters Review Anthology*, *Day One*, *TAYO Literary Magazine*, *Aotearotica*, *Takahe*, and *Asian Cha*, among other places. Her essay, "Becoming A Writer: The Silences We Write Against," was a Notable Essay in *The Best American Essays 2016*. Her novella, *Leaving Auckland* (serialized in *failbetter*), was a Top 25 Finalist in the Summer 2016 *Glimmer Train* Fiction Open. She is currently Branches Nonfiction Editor of *Rambutan Literary* and is working on her first novel.

GARY T. MCDONALD, award-winning playwright and filmmaker, is a fifth-generation Texan now living in California. His latest film is *The Fourth Noble Truth*. Though a practicing Buddhist, he has made a lifelong study of the New Testament. These two strands entwined in his first novel *The Gospel of Thomas (The Younger)*—a Buddhist reboot of the Jesus cult's first century origins. Learn more about Gary at www.garytmcdonald.com.

When not thinking of awesome lessons for his writing students at the University of Texas Rio Grande Valley, CHARLES MCGREGOR habitually dreams of putting his memories on the page in divergent ways. Many of the themes in his poetry deal with exploring his agnosticism in a clear-eyed, non-polemic way. He misses church, the community it provides, and the intimacy with others it demands, yet he cannot deny his incapacity to feel something spiritual. As a doubter, he hopes to find some capacity to develop spiritual gifts.

A. G. MOJTABAI (sometimes listed as "Grace" or "Ann" Mojtabai) has published novels, short stories, and nonfiction. She has taught at the University of Tulsa, Harvard, and New York University. Among her awards are a Guggenheim fellowship, the Richard and Hinda Rosenthal Award from the American Institute of Arts and Letters, the Award in Literature from the American Academy of Arts and Letters, the Lillian Smith Award for the best book about the American South, and a fellowship from the Radcliffe Institute for Advanced Study. She has two children, three grandchildren, and lives in Amarillo, Texas.

Author of the poetry collection *Local Bird*, LAURENCE MUSGROVE is professor of English at Angelo State University where he teaches creative writing, literature, comics, and meditation. His poems have appeared in *Buddhist Poetry Review*, *Elephant Journal*, *Southern Indiana Review*, *Concho River Review*, *descant*, *Inside Higher Ed*, *Southwestern American Literature*, *Ink Brick*, and *New Texas*. He is also coeditor with Terry Dalrymple of the anthology *Texas Weather*, a collection of poetry, fiction, and nonfiction on the power and beauty of weather in the Lone Star State.

NAOMI SHIHAB NYE has lived in San Antonio since her teens, moving to Texas from Jerusalem, her Palestinian father's home, after being born and growing up first in St. Louis, her mother's home. Both parents were devoted to ecumenical thinking. She graduated from Trinity University with majors in religion and English and began working as a writer-in-the-schools through the Texas Commission on the Arts, a wandering life that continues till now. A visiting writer for many years at the Michener Center for Writers, UT-Austin, she is now a visiting writer at Texas State University in San Marcos. She and her husband, documentarian Michael Nye, live in old downtown San Antonio. She has published around thirty-five books of poetry, essays, and children's stories and is poetry editor of the *Texas Observer*.

JOE O'CONNELL is the author of *Evacuation Plan: A Novel from the Hospice* and an award-winning short story writer. He is the director/producer of the documentary films *Rondo and Bob* and *Danger God*. A former newspaper reporter, O'Connell is currently an associate professor of English at Austin Community College, where he directs the Balcones Fiction Prize.

ROBERT OKAJI is a half-Japanese poet splitting time between Austin and rural Medina County, Texas. His interests lie in the liminal, in silence and the spaces between, and he has recently taken up the *shakuhachi*, the traditional Japanese bamboo flute, as a means of better acquainting himself with these. The author of five chapbook collections, three micro-chapbooks, and a mini digital chapbook, he is a regular contributor on *Vox Populi*, and his work has appeared or is forthcoming in *Crannóg*, *Oxidant|Engine*, *Panoply*, *Wildness*, *MockingHeart Review*, *Eclectica*, and elsewhere. Visit his blog, *O at the Edges*, at http://robertokaji.com/.

LESLIE JILL PATTERSON's prose is forthcoming or has recently appeared in *Texas Monthly*, *Grist*, *Gulf Coast*, *Baltimore Review*, *Literature: A Pocket Anthology* (7th edition), and *Bring the Noise: The Best Pop Culture Essays from Barrelhouse*. Her recent awards include the 2012 Embrey Human Rights Fellowship; the 2013 Everett Southwest Literary Award; the 2014 Time and Place Prize in Brittany, France; and a 2014 Soros Justice Fellowship, funded by the Open Society Foundations in New York. In 1999, she founded *Iron Horse Literary Review*. Today, she has a growing interest in social justice literature and works as the case storyteller for attorneys representing indigent men and women charged with capital murder and facing the death penalty in the state of Texas. Most recently, she received a Pushcart Prize.

URSULA PIKE is the author of *An Indian among los Indígenas: A Native Travel Memoir* (2021) from Heyday Books. Ursula lives in Austin, Texas, and writes about identity, Native American issues, economics, travel, and powwows. She has an MFA in creative nonfiction from the Institute of American Indian Arts and a master's degree in economics from Western Illinois University. Ursula is a member of the Karuk Tribe. Her work has appeared in *LitHub*, *Yellow Medicine Review*, *Ligeia Magazine*, *World Literature Today*, and *O'Dark 30*. Visit ursulapike.com for more information.

KEVIN PRUFER's newest books are *How He Loved Them* (recipient of the Julie Suk Award and named to the long list for the 2019 Pulitzer Prize) and *Churches* (listed as one of the *New York Times Book Review*'s "Ten Best Poetry Books of 2014"). He teaches at the University of Houston's Creative Writing Program.

Although OCTAVIO QUINTANILLA's work ranges in style and theme, one of the themes he often explores in his work is that of spirituality. Some of these themes can be found in his first collection of poetry, *If I Go Missing* (Slough Press, 2014). He served as the 2018-2020 Poet Laureate of San Antonio. His poetry, fiction, translations, and photography have appeared, or are forthcoming, in the journals

Salamander, *RHINO*, *Alaska Quarterly Review*, *Pilgrimage*, *Green Mountains Review*, *Southwestern American Literature*, and elsewhere. His Frontextos (visual poems) have been published in *Poetry Northwest*, *Borderlands: Texas Poetry Review*, *Midway Journal*, *Gold Wake Live*, among many others. Find him on Twitter @OctQuintanilla; his website: octavioquintanilla.com.

Perhaps because she spent much of her childhood on a cattle ranch in the Sierra Nevada foothills, CAROL COFFEE REPOSA turns to the natural world for both inspiration and insight. Cityscapes also compel her attention, though, particularly those of her San Antonio bailiwick, and she sees in both urban and rural life affirmation of Ralph Waldo Emerson's observation, "Though we travel the world over to find the beautiful, we must carry it with us or we find it not." Author of four books of poetry and a four-time Pushcart Prize nominee, Reposa is a member of the Texas Institute of Letters and the 2018 Texas Poet Laureate.

MARK SANDERS has been a resident of Texas for eighteen years: during the 1990s in the Houston metro and for the past ten years in Nacogdoches. He has long been an advocate of regional literature and, most specifically, poetry. A native of Nebraska, he received the Mildred Bennett Award from the Nebraska Center for the Book in 2007 for fostering Nebraska's literary heritage. Sanders's poetry often examines the spiritual connection between people and their physical world, where he is certain God resides and notices and watches, which is among the holiest of lessons we might learn.

CHAITALI SEN is the author of the novel *The Pathless Sky*, published by Europa Editions in 2015. Her short stories, essays, and reviews have appeared in *Ecotone*, *New England Review*, *New Ohio Review*, *Colorado Review*, *Los Angeles Review of Books*, *Catapult*, *LitHub*, and other publications. She lives with her family in Austin, Texas.

MARY HELEN SPECHT's debut novel, *Migratory Animals*, was both a *New York Times Book Review* and an *Austin American-Statesman*'s Editor's Choice, an IndieNext Pick, and an Apple iBook selection. *Migratory Animals* also won the Texas Institute of Letters Best First Fiction Award and the Writers' League of Texas Best Book of Fiction. A previous Fulbright Scholar to Nigeria and Dobie-Paisano Writing Fellow, Specht is currently an associate professor of creative writing at St. Edward's University. *Texas Monthly* has named her one of "Ten Writers to Watch."

Charles "Chuck" Taylor Jr., a Texas Yankee raised in Texas, Minnesota, Illinois, and North Carolina, won the 1988 Austin Book Award for *What Do You Want, Blood?* His latest, *Being Beat*, was published by Albuquerque's Hercules Press in 2018. He has worked in a Poets-in-the-Schools program, been a CETA poet, operated a bookstore, owned a small press, worked in Japan, was Creative Writing Coordinator at Texas A&M, and taught at UT Austin, El Paso, and Tyler. Retired in 2015 to the Texas Hill Country, he has been married three times and has three children, three stepchildren, seven grandchildren, and one great-grandchild.

Brian Van Reet is the author of *Spoils*, a novel that won the Balcones Fiction Prize and was longlisted or a finalist for other awards, including the Andrew Carnegie Medal for Excellence. *Spoils* was named one of the best books of 2017 by *British GQ*, the *Guardian*, *Military Times*, and the *Wall Street Journal*, which called it "the finest Iraq War novel yet written by an American." A US Army veteran, Van Reet is the recipient of a Bronze Star for valor. He has received a James A. Michener Fellowship and has twice won the Texas Institute of Letters short story award.

Loretta Diane Walker, a Best of the Net nominee and a multiple Pushcart Nominee, won the 2016 Phyllis Wheatley Book Award for poetry for her collection *In This House* (Bluelight Press). Named "Statesman in the Arts" by the Heritage Council of Odessa, Walker was honored to be the featured poet in February 2017 for *Red River Review*. Her work has appeared in numerous literary journals and anthologies. Much of her work concerns the sky, which she has been obsessed with since childhood. For Walker, it is a symbol of revelation, destination, wisdom, comfort, and a bond she shares with her mother. Loretta Walker teaches music in Odessa, Texas. She received a BME from Texas Tech University and earned a MA from the University of Texas of the Permian Basin.

Reared in the Deep South, the product of an intensely scriptural upbringing, **Steve Weathers** has devoted much of his writing life to an exploration of the darker sides of the Christian experience. An imaginative, impressionistic depiction of actual facts, "Witnesses" constitutes yet another attempt to air and clarify his conflicted feelings about fundamentalist approaches to faith. Steve's fiction and essays have appeared in a number of literary journals and Christian magazines. He has served over three decades in higher education at Abilene Christian University in West Texas.

JESSICA WILBANKS is the author of *When I Spoke in Tongues*, a memoir about faith and its loss (Beacon Press, 2018). She has received a Pushcart Prize as well as creative nonfiction awards from *Ninth Letter*, *Sycamore Review*, *Redivider*, and *Ruminate* magazine. Her work has appeared in *The Guardian*, *Salon*, *Houston Chronicle*, *Sojourners*, *The Rumpus*, *Longreads*, and *LitHub*, and has received Notable Mentions from *Best American Essays* and *Best American Nonrequired Reading*. For more information, visit http://jessicawilbanks.com.

Recent poems by STEVE WILSON are out or forthcoming in the journals *Beloit Poetry Journal*, *Borderlands*, *Bluestem*, *Cimarron Review*, *Commonweal*, *Poem*, *Georgetown Review*, *North American Review*, *America*, and the *Christian Science Monitor*, among many others, as well as in a number of anthologies, including *O Taste and See: Food Poems* (Bottom Dog Press); *Visiting Frost: Poems Inspired by Robert Frost* (University of Iowa); *Stories from Where We Live: The Gulf Coast* (Milkweed Editions); *Like Thunder: Poets Respond to Violence in America* (University of Iowa); *What Have You Lost?* (Greenwillow); and *American Diaspora: Poetry of Displacement* (University of Iowa), among others. His books include *Allegory Dance* and *The Singapore Express* and *The Lost Seventh*.

CHRISTIAN WIMAN's recent books are *He Held Radical Light: The Art of Faith, the Faith of Art* and *Hammer Is the Prayer: Selected Poems*. He grew up in West Texas and now teaches at Yale Divinity School.

ABOUT THE EDITORS

ELIZABETH JOAN DELL, an émigré from Virginia, calls central Texas home. Fiction editor and coeditor of this anthology, she is a senior lecturer in the English Department at Baylor University, where she teaches literature and creative writing and serves as Literature Program Director. She is coeditor with Joe B. Fulton of *American Literary Cultures: A Reader* (Baylor University Press, 2020).

DONNA WALKER-NIXON (1953–2021), a native Texan, attended a two-room school outside of Stephenville, an experience that led her to teach and write. She went on to build a thirty-year career teaching English literature, composition, and creative writing at the University of Mary Hardin-Baylor and Baylor University. She founded *Windhover: A Journal of Christian Literature* (1996) and *The Langdon Review of the Arts in Texas* (2003). She was lead editor of *Her Texas* (Wings Press, 2015). On a personal level, she survived a subdural hematoma, which made her more passionate about writing and its purpose in our lives.